Collect for Club Women

Keep us O Lord from pettiness; let us be large in
thought , in word and deed

Let us be done with fault finding and leave off self
seeking

May we put away all pretence and meet each other
face to face, without self pity and without prejudice

May we never be hasty in judgment and always
generous

Let us take time for all things: make us grow calm,
serene, gentle

Teach us to put into action our better impulses
straight forward and unafraid

Grant that we may realize that it is the little things
that create differences; that in the big things of life
we are one

And may we strive to touch and know the great
human heart common to us all, and O Lord God let
us not forget to be kind

Mary Stewart

Their Dreams, Never Ending
© Laura N. Pottie, 2000
Printed in Canada.

Canadian Cataloguing in Publication Data
Pottie, Laura, 1971-
Their dreams, never ending
Includes bibliographical references
ISBN 0-9687209-0-0

1. Women's Institutes -- Prince Edward Island -- History.
I.   Prince Edward Island Women's Institute
II. Their Dreams, Never Ending

HQ1909.P8P67 2000   305.4 ' O6 ' 0718   C00-950089-8

Federated Women's Institute of Prince Edward Island
P.O. Box 2000, Farm Centre
420 University Avenue
Charlottetown, PEI
C1A 7N8

Printing: Province of Prince Edward Island, Document Publishing Centre.
Cover design: Graphic Communications, Charlottetown, PEI.
Cover Printing: Williams & Crue, Summerside, PEI.
Cover photo: PEIWI 75th Anniversary wall-hanging competition winning quilt, designed and quilted by the Oyster Bed Bridge branch, 1988.

This book received funding from the Federated Women's Institute of Prince Edward Island, the Prince Edward Island Department of Agriculture, the Millennium Bureau of Canada, and Human Resources Development Canada. The views expressed herein are those of the author's only, and do not necessarily reflect the views of the Government of Canada or any of its agencies.

2000
Canada

President's Message

The Women's Institutes of Prince Edward Island have worked "For Home and Country" for nearly 100 years.

The Women's Institute is the strength of our communities. Therefore, it is important that we carry on with the accomplishments of past years as we move into the new century.

In this book, you will find the record of what Women's Institutes of Prince Edward Island have provided. This is the history of our Island.

We all know that history never stands still. We preserve it with the hope that our history will become a background for those in the future who will carry out the aims and objectives of the Women's Institute.

Betty Millar

President
Prince Edward Island Women's Institutes

Author's Acknowledgements

This history is largely the result of the PEIWI's support, encouragement, and generous funding. I did not write this book alone, and so there are a number of people to thank.

First and foremost, I must thank the PEIWI provincial board for having confidence in the project, and ensuring that we made it to the press! The PEIWI History Committee, with Kaye Crabbe, Joyce MacKenzie, Lois Thompson, Betty Watts, Betty Millar, Joan Dawson, and Doreen MacInnis, worked diligently over this last year, and their help was invaluable in ensuring that all the facts were correct, and that my portrayal of the Women's Institute did justice to the story. PEIWI provincial President-Elect Reta MacDonald also went that extra mile, and helped to see that all of the "i"s were dotted and the "t"s crossed! Karen Craig and Dorothy McGee of the PEIWI Charlottetown office were also essential to this project, with logistical support, encouragement, advice, and an oft-needed sense of humour. I sincerely thank the WI members who welcomed me into their homes and graciously agreed to be interviewed for this project – their stories form the backbone of this book, and to them I am truly grateful. I must also thank all of the branch members who took the time to respond to the request for updates of their histories. Encapsulating fifty years or more of activity into a page or two is no easy task, and I am in awe of your work. Finally, thanks go out to the many members who provided photographs; their time and generosity was well appreciated.

A number of people outside of the Women's Institute supported this project. Andy Robb, Chair of the History Department at the University of Prince Edward Island, has been there since the beginning with guidance and helpful comments. Joan Sinclair generously volunteered her editing skills for Part One, and believe me those edits were needed!

Finally, I would be remiss if I did not also thank my family at this time. They put up with me through all of the late nights, unfolded laundry, and endless hours in front of the computer, and they tore me away for Sunday dinners when I might otherwise have forgotten about food completely! James, Dad, Elaine, Will, Jim, and Eathan, I couldn't have done it without you.

While I cannot take all of the credit, the ultimate responsibility for final edits and layout of this book rested with me, and so I must take the blame for any errors of style, grammar, design or omission.

Table of Contents

Part One:

Chapter One: A Dream is Realized 1

Chapter Two: The WI in Action 20

The local community 20

The province 26

The nation 35

The world 37

The stamp of accomplishment 40

Chapter Three: Membership has its Benefits 41

Fellowship 41

Learning 44

Choices 50

A place to call their own 56

The more you put into it... 58

Chapter Four: Their Recipe for Success 59

The kitchen 59

The cooks 65

The ingredients 67

The proof is in the pudding 73

Reflections 74

Past Presidents 75

Part Two: Branch Histories 81

Notes 269

A note on sources 270

Chapter One:
A Dream is Realized

In April of 1911, in York, Prince Edward Island, seventeen women met at "the Hall". They gathered in a circle while their husbands sat nearby, probably hoping that they might get some lunch for the trouble of taking their wives out that night. As the story goes, someone's husband had come home from a Farmers' Institute meeting in Ontario with news about women getting together and forming Women's Institutes. It probably seemed a good idea at the time, but they could never have known just how good an idea it was.

Try to imagine those seventeen women sitting in the Hall, with the wood stove blazing nearby, and what they might have discussed. They might have talked about the Model T that one of them had seen on the road last Wednesday in Charlottetown, and about how glad they were that those noise-makers were still not allowed around their area. Someone might have mentioned the fracas at the last Sons of Temperance meeting down the road. But to be sure, at least one of them made the suggestion that they follow in the footsteps of their sisters in other provinces, and organize themselves for the improvement of their home lives and their communities.

After all, why not? Hadn't their husbands and fathers been attending Farmers' Institute meetings for more than forty years? Since 1870 Prince Edward Island's farming men had, through the Farmers' Institute, organized educational programs, traded and discussed new agricultural ideas, and arranged commercial sales. These York women had a few ideas of their own. Since the women of PEI

The Charter Members of Alpha York Women's Institute, April 1911.
Photo courtesy of PEIWI archives.

could not yet hold political office, or even vote, their only practical means to implementing their ideas was to do it themselves. So that is what they did.

The Women's Institute organization in Canada began under the leadership of Adelaide Hunter Hoodless, a Hamilton, Ontario woman whose youngest son died in 1889 after drinking impure milk. Her son was only eighteen months old when he died, and Mrs. Hoodless' grief only worsened when she learned that she could have prevented his death, if only she had known how. Adelaide Hoodless made it her mission to encourage rural women to raise their standards of sanitation, nutrition, and care of the family by educating them to be better homemakers. Hoodless worked tirelessly, telling her story to all who would listen. She was a key player in founding the National Council of Women in 1893, in introducing courses in domestic science and cooking at the recently organized YWCA, of which she was President, and in forming the

Victorian Order of Nurses.

In 1897 a young farmer named Erland Lee, who happened to be the Secretary of the Farmers' Institute in his area, heard Mrs. Hoodless speak at the Ontario Agricultural College. Mr. Lee was impressed with what he heard, and invited Mrs. Hoodless to speak at a Farmers' Institute meeting. As a result of this invitation, the first Women's Institute was organized on February 19, 1897, in Squire's Hall, Stoney Creek, Ontario. There were one hundred women at the first meeting, and one man – Mr. Lee. The constitution of this fledgling organization read as follows:

> *The object of this Institute shall be to promote that knowledge of household science, which shall lead to the improvement in household architecture, with special attention to home sanitation, to a better understanding of economics and hygienic value of foods and fuels, and to a more scientific care of children with a view to raising the general standard of health of our people.*[1]

Adelaide Hoodless began with the goal of teaching women to become better mothers and homemakers, and in the process of achieving that objective, she taught Canadian women so much more, as we will see in the following pages. Now we return to the Island story.

It took the Prince Edward Island Department of Agriculture about a year to notice what the women of York were up to, but the Department then took some initiative to assist the women of PEI in organizing themselves. As far as government endorsement was concerned, the Women's Institute could not have arrived in PEI at a better time. The Prince Edward Island Department of Agriculture was ready to make some real inroads into improving agriculture and education after having their federal grant for agriculture increased first by the Federal Aid

Act, and again by the Agricultural Instruction Act. There was new money at the Department, and having already established themselves in eight of Canada's provinces and to a smaller extent in PEI, the Women's Institute was a worthy recipient.

Thus, in March of 1913, the PEI Department of Agriculture secured the services of Mrs. A. E. Dunbrack of New Brunswick to address meetings in Summerside and Charlottetown regarding the benefits and means of establishing a Women's Institute in Prince Edward Island. These meetings resulted in the organization of the first two government-sponsored Women's Institute branches in PEI – one in Marshfield and the other in Cornwall. One month later, the Department hired Katherine James of Charlottetown to serve as the "Supervisor of Women's Institutes". Miss James and Mrs. Dunbrack traveled throughout the Island with great success – for by the end of that year their efforts had resulted in twenty-one branches being organized, with a membership of over four hundred women.

Change rarely comes without some sort of resistance, and the organization of women in PEI was no exception to this rule. While Premier John Mathieson's Tory government was happy to see Women's Institutes begun on the Island, not all Islanders shared that view, and particularly a few worried husbands. Joe Devereux grew up on PEI at the turn of the century, and tells this story:

> *As might have been expected, the Women's Institute was not greeted by anything resembling universal approval. Something very similar to the blind, unreasoning hostility that had obstructed the suffragette movement in Britain surfaced in several localities throughout the Island. In [one area], there were demands that the Institute ladies be forbidden the*

use of the district schoolhouse as a meeting place. These demands were threshed out and rejected in a stormy special-school meeting, during which several participants had to be forcibly restrained from coming to blows. As one ratepayer remarked at the close of the meeting, "Seems like everythin' that damn Mathieson does starts people to fightin'.[2]

Not only was there initial resistance on the part of a few husbands, but some women of the opposite political persuasion were initially reticent about the new "Institutes". Party politics was a lifestyle for most on PEI , and divisions along party lines ran deep. It took some convincing before Liberal

Marshfield Women's Institute, 1920. Back Row, from left: Mrs. Duncan Darrach, Miss Cairns, Mrs. L.H.D. Foster, Jane Heartz Wilson, Petha Darrach, Mrs. Franklin Mill, Erna Boswall, Blanche Boswall, Mrs. Chas Robertson, Charlotte Munn O'Neill, Mrs. John Milton. Middle Row: Mrs. Claude Mill, Mrs. Peter Stewart, Mrs. Edgar Hearth. Front Row: Bessie Crosby VanDusen, Eva Stewart Burhoe, Hilda Dennis.

women were willing to join an organization funded by a Conservative government, but within a short time they did, and Adelaide Hoodless' goal of a non-partisan, non-religious women's organization began to take shape in PEI.

Women's Institutes in PEI had the benefit of nearly fifteen years of organization in other parts of Canada to draw upon – not to mention their own initiative and intelligence – when organizing their branches, and this served them well. Within a year of the first official branch incorporation, Prince Edward Island's first Women's Institute Annual Convention was held in June of 1914. The topics at the first convention ranged from the practical to the en-

Adelaide Hunter Hoodless, founder of Women's Institutes, and Emily Murphy, first President of the Federated Women's Institutes of Canada, as recently immortalized by Canada Post .
Courtesy of PEIWI archives.

tertaining, and encompassed ideas such as working with the school inspectors to improve the school conditions and implementing medical "inspections" of the children, to presentations on dressmaking and gardening.

These early women took their motto, "For Home and Country," to heart. Within two years of their existence on PEI the Department of Agriculture considered the Women's Institute an integral part of the province's plan for agricultural instruction. Rightfully so, since by that time the Women's Institute had managed to get very busy. The main thrust of the first two years of organization in PEI was providing for the schools, organizing "Household Science" short courses, and establishing school gardens. It was only a short time, however, before their mandate expanded greatly by necessity.

Just one year after official organization, World War I began. At this time, what was to become a long relationship with the Red Cross began, in the form of the war effort. "Institute" women, as they were known, quickly began to do their part for the war effort – sending shirts, knitted socks, caps, bandages, care packages, and money through the Red Cross. As an indication of the magnitude of their work, Hazel Stearns, Supervisor of Women's In-

PEI delegates to the first FWIC open National Convention in Ottawa, Ontario, 1957, being entertained by an Island Senator and Members of Parliament. Front row, from left: Mrs. Elsie Laird, Kensington, editor of the Federated News, Mrs. Sally MacKinnon, Uigg, Convener of Public Health, Mrs. Florence Matheson, Mrs. Loretta Doyle, Mrs. Jean Wilkie, Mrs. Jean Mutch, Mrs. Hilda Ramsay. Back row: Senator Orville Phillips, Mrs. R.L. Burge, MP Heath MacQuarrie, Mrs. Louise MacMillan, MP Angus MacLean, Mrs. Stuart MacGregor, MP John A. MacDonald.
Photo courtesy of Louise MacMillan

stitutes in 1919, reported that the PEIWI had sent over twelve thousand "knitted garments" to soldiers over the course of World War I.

Institute women across Canada began to realize that there was much to be gained by coordination of their efforts. Mary MacIsaac, originally from Charlottetown but by this time serving as a home economist and superintendent of Women's Institutes in Alberta, provided the original impetus behind nationalizing the organization. Delegates held a preliminary organizational meeting in Ottawa in February of 1918, but decided to wait until the First World War was over to pursue the idea. In 1919 the Federated Women's Institutes of Canada (FWIC) was founded. The first President of the FWIC was none other than Emily Murphy of Alberta, known to us now from the CRB Heritage Minutes as the first female magistrate in what was then still the Dominion of Canada.[3] The PEI Women's Institute waited a year to join, and Mrs. John MacGuigan of Hope River was the first delegate from the Island to attend an FWIC convention in 1920. Now Institute women in PEI were not only in contact with each other, they were in contact with other women from coast to coast, long before most Islanders had a telephone, never mind a long-distance calling plan!

While the first few years of Institutes in PEI saw significant initial growth to the membership, in the 1920s and 1930s that growth became exponential. By 1929, there were 196 Women's Institute branches on PEI, with a membership of approximately 4000 - ten times what it had been only a few years earlier. This growth happened for a number of reasons. When teachers on the Island discovered that Women's Institutes were willing and able to help, they realized that it was in their interest to promote the organization. A number of branches formed when the local teacher approached women in the district and requested their help. It is likely that the end of the war had much to do with the growth of the Women's Institute as well. A number of early branches either disbanded for war-work or at least concentrated their energies on that from 1914-1918, and so the end of the war meant that women could return to focusing on their communities and their families. In those areas where Women's Institutes had not already organized, the war also hindered any significant growth. In addition, the Institute's increasingly positive reputation was an impetus for expansion. After having demonstrated the organization's strength and abilities, the idea of Women's Institute likely became more appealing to a majority of rural Island women.

As their numbers grew, so did their interests. The Women's Institute's original mandate was to further rural women's education in homemaking, but more members meant that the PEIWI could effectively look at larger issues and expand the scope of its mandate. W.J. Reid, Director of Agricultural Services at the provincial government, noticed this expansion of interests for the WI. In his report to the federal government of 1922, he noted that "the original object in establishing Women's Institutes was for the giving of instruction relating to domestic economy and its various branches, but they have since developed into a valuable medium for rural organization and social upbuilding."[4]

Other organizations learned to tap into Women's Institute resources when they wanted to get something done. The Red Cross was one of the first of such organizations. Prior to the 1920s, the Red Cross had mainly concerned itself with war work. In 1920, however, the national and provincial Red Cross expanded its operations to include disease prevention, disaster relief, and public health issues. On PEI, Women's Institutes were part of that plan. Judge F.L. Haszard was the President of the PEI Red Cross at that time. In his President's Report of 1920-21, he remarked that "cooperation with the Red Cross of all societies..., and above all Women's Institutes, could do much toward the removal from the Public Schools, and other public places, conditions which are detrimental to public health and should not exist."[5] Women's Institutes had worked closely with the Red Cross during World War I, and would continue that cooperation for many years to come.

While Women's Institutes in PEI did much work for the one-room schools during the war, after World War I the tradition of significant involvement in school affairs really took hold. The schools in PEI at that time needed the help. Before the Institute became involved, many of them were run-down, drafty, and short on supplies. Women's Institutes contributed everything from blackboards to flags, from cod liver oil to hot lunches for the children. By 1928, a majority of Institute branches on PEI had established a committee to regularly inspect the schools and assess their needs, and several branches assigned representatives to serve on the school boards.

"Institute women" of the 1920s were not satisfied with providing just for their schools and their soldiers, however. They began traditions of community activity, many of which continue as strong today. Community beautification, immunizations, a handicraft exchange, a self-published newsletter – Institute members undertook each and every one of these innovations. They took the expertise that they gained as teachers, farmwomen, and homemakers, and used that knowledge to organize conventions, concerts, sales, campaigns, and fundraisers, and, as we shall see, to successfully lobby the provincial government on more than one occasion. They gained the cooperation of their husbands and the respect of their neighbours by working tirelessly to make their island a better community, and their lives more enlightened. They educated themselves, and then applied their knowledge and shared it with others.

Their tireless work resulted in more than one success story for the PEIWI, not the least of which was the establishment of a provincial Sanatorium for Tuberculosis patients. Institute women in the 1930s brought music teachers to the schools, 4H Clubs to their communities, and the Carnegie library system to the province. These accomplishments will be discussed in greater detail in later chapters, but at this point it is clear that the Women's Institute in PEI took its job seriously.

Meanwhile, the Federated Women's Institutes of Canada (FWIC) were among those represented at a conference in London, England in 1929, called with the goal of forming an international women's organization. This meeting laid the groundwork for a second conference in Vienna in 1930, where the delegates formed a committee to help women's organizations worldwide to communicate in an organized way. Three years later, in 1933, that committee met in Stockholm and decided to form a permanent international women's alliance. They formulated and adopted a constitution at that meeting, and took the name Associated Country Women of the World (ACWW). Headquartered in London, the ACWW would prove itself able to facilitate major international efforts in many fields such as disaster relief, the status of women and rural women's health and education, and would be the first, and for a number of years the only women's organization to achieve consultation status with the United Nations. Rural women in Prince Edward Island had become members of an organization that enjoyed local, provincial, national, and now global recognition.

World War II again required the focused efforts of all Canadians, and Women's Institutes in PEI again responded to the call for assistance. The effort was much the same as during the First World War, but because of the growth in the Institutes' membership, the magnitude

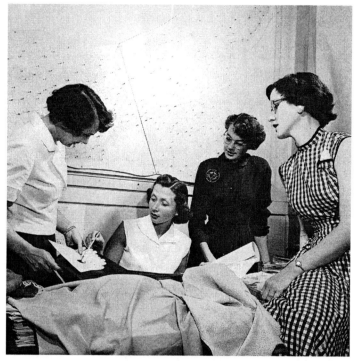

Instructors and WI members plan the next stop for the Handicraft Van, 1953.
Photo courtesy of the National Film Board of Canada

of results increased greatly. Institute members knitted literally tens of thousands of articles for soldiers and war-weary families in England, donated many thousands of dollars to the Red Cross, and sent many care packages to prisoners-of war. The cumulative total of donations to the Red Cross over the course of the two world wars was over

$25,000.

The most remarkable aspect of this effort was that Institute women seemed to accomplish these tasks without missing a beat. They still held their district and provincial conventions and household science courses, canvassed for

Women's Institute members look on as the Handicraft Van arrives in Emerald, PEI, 1963.
Photo courtesy of the National Film Board of Canada

new branches and members, undertook research projects, supported the Provincial Sanatorium, provided for the schools, published a cookbook - the list goes on and on.

Even that inventory falls short of the total picture however, because Institute women always participated in the
farm work, raised children, and took great care of their
homes. Most of these families were still without electricity, and the notion of modern conveniences had yet to
take hold on PEI. Institute members who remember those
days are unaware of their superwoman status; they were
simply doing the work that was in front of them.

World War II was over for what must have been five
minutes before Institute members were discussing new
ideas for their Island. Helen Herring of the Borden
branch, a lifetime WI stalwart and a fixture in the minds
of many Islanders as "Mrs. Institute", recalled a Provincial Board meeting where someone (and she won't name
names) said, "I'm so sick of war, I think we should turn
our attention to the cultural side of things." Turn it they
did. The late forties saw the PEIWI successfully initiate
province-wide music and drama festivals, an expansion to
the Provincial Sanatorium, the first women's radio program in Eastern Canada, and leadership training courses
for Institute members and the branch executives.

Membership continued to grow as the provincial executive reported new branches year after year, reaching a
total of 290 branches in 1948 with a membership of approximately 5000 rural women. Bearing in mind that
there were only about 11,000 rural homes on the Island at
that point, it is clear that the Women's Institute had
firmly entrenched itself as a pivotal element of rural life
in PEI – in the lives of both women and their families.

The early years of the PEIWI were all about outward
growth, both in terms of membership and in their areas of
interest. In the post-war period, however, the Institute
saw itself growing in an inward direction, as what were
previously relatively new programs and ideas began to be

Dave Ford, MLA, and Priscilla Borden, President of York Point WI, cut the ribbon at the newly renovated York Point Community Centre, formerly the one-room schoolhouse, May 28, 1978.

Photo courtesy of York Point WI

refined and improved upon as experience and expertise grew. For example, the Women's Institute had always encouraged the art of handcrafts, and had given many short courses on various methods of crafting. In 1953 the PEIWI convinced the government to purchase a van for their use. Institute women equipped and staffed the van with all manner of handcraft supplies and expertise, and traveled throughout the Island, bringing handicraft courses to the communities so that women would not have to travel to Charlottetown for the information. The Handicraft Van provided courses in such crafts as sewing, weaving, textile painting, copper tooling, and leather craft. The Handicraft Van remained in use for the next fourteen years, until the Community Schools program began, thereby eliminating the need for traveling instructors.

The University of Prince Edward Island's Montgomery Hall Residence is another standing example of the increased potency of the post-war WI. In 1946, Mrs. William MacKinnon of the Uigg branch brought attention to the fact that young ladies from rural PEI were attending Prince of Wales College, but they did not have appropriate housing in which to safely and comfortably complete their studies.

The following year the WI began petitioning the government for a residence for girls. The government responded by procuring a site for the residence in 1949, but six years later construction still had not yet begun. In 1955 the Women's Institute decided they were tired of waiting. They sent a representative to the Legislature, and as the story goes this WI representative politely informed the Premier that the Women's Institute intended to have a residence for girls built, and they would continue presenting themselves in the House until they got it. The WI had to make good on that threat, presenting fourteen times on this same topic over the next few years, but their persistence paid off and in 1963 the Prince Edward Island Women's Institute cut the ribbon to open Montgomery Hall Residence for Girls.

Meanwhile, the face of rural PEI was changing significantly. Women were spending more and more time in paid work outside the home, and rural life for many women no longer involved helping out on the family farm. By 1973 almost half of Women's Institute members on the Island lived in rural non-farming households. The one-room schools were closing. Women were entering the paid workforce in larger numbers, and staying there after marriage. As Prince Edward Island entered the latter part of the twentieth century, life for women was becoming more complicated, and they had less time for voluntary organizations. Many members expressed concerns about the future of the Women's Institute.

As Prince Edward Island modernized, however, so did the Women's Institute. With a dedicated membership still numbering in the thousands, the WI had its feet firmly planted in the red Island soil. The 1960s and 1970s saw the PEIWI begin to take a more proactive stance in promoting rural life and rural issues on a broader scale. In doing this, Institute women reiterated that as country women, they had something to contribute not only to the lives of those in their communities, but to all Islanders, rural and urban alike.

Women's Institute members traveled around the world, studying agricultural and social practices, and reported their findings both to their membership and to the rest of the Island. They undertook research projects and held public seminars on such wide-ranging topics as alternative energy uses, youth and law-related issues, environmentalism, and defensive driving. In 1976 the PEIWI hosted the Federated Women's Institutes of Canada's National Convention – right in the middle of an airline employee strike and as the story goes, the hottest June ever. In 1981, they assisted in establishing and supporting Prince Edward Island's first shelter for battered women. Instead of supporting the one-room schools, the PEIWI moved to supporting local Community Centres and consolidated schools. Never straying from their original goal of educating and assisting women and families, the Women's Institute continued to adapt that goal to the demands of the times.

By the 1980s, however, there was no mistaking that Women's Institutes across Canada were losing members. When nation-wide membership reached about half of what it had been thirty years earlier, the PEIWI realized

Joyce MacKenzie, past PEIWI President, plants an Adelaide Hoodless rose at Government House in Charlottetown, 1986. With her are then Governor General Lloyd MacPhail and Mrs. Helen MacPhail, and Mrs. Geneva King.

Photo courtesy of PEIWI archives

that it needed to remain relevant to Island women in order to survive. The provincial board of directors conducted a membership survey in 1985 to assess the status of the Women's Institute on the Island, and the results were mixed. Member responses regarding the WI's public image ranged from "a very strong organization and always willing and able to help", to "a bunch of old gossipers!" Still, many members reported that the Women's Institute remained relevant to them and their communities, that the educational programs were still interesting, and in many areas the Institute was still the only organization attending to community development.

The PEIWI was still hard at work, and its membership continued a high level of activity both provincially and in their local communities. PEIWI members and executive were still receiving appointments to important committees and research projects, members were still recognized as important contributors to the Island, and new ideas for WI projects were still being developed. And yet, morale seemed to be low. Many lifetime members worried that there would not be a younger generation to replace them and to continue the work that they had begun.

True to their usual form, the PEIWI has responded to these concerns. Many branches now report successful membership drives in their communities, simply by reaching out to new and existing residents, paying them a visit and inviting them to a meeting or two. It seems the old ways work the best sometimes, and there is no substitute for simple personal contact. As will be discussed in later chapters, the PEIWI has developed the unique ability to adapt itself to the interests of any member, and the needs of any community, and that ability to adapt will keep it alive for generations to come.

So onward and forward the PEIWI goes, always staying ever so slightly ahead of their time, and always looking for new ways to contribute. One of the interesting things about the PEI Women's Institute in the last twenty years is the way that members have seamlessly blended their traditional concerns and interests with those of today. A WI member might on one day represent the organization at a public hearing on New Reproductive Technologies, and the next day she might represent that same organization in welcoming a new Canadian citizen to the country, a tradition that the PEIWI began in the 1920s. She might attend workshops on traditional quilting, and then attend a National Farmwomen's Conference and learn how to lobby for equal rights for farm women. She is a woman who is interested in, and willing to strive, "For Home and Country".

Chapter Two:
The WI In Action

The chronology of the Women's Institute in PEI very much speaks for itself, but the accomplishments of these women have not occurred in a vacuum. The Women's Institute operates within communities – locally, provincially, nationally, and indeed globally. Each member has contributed to each one of these communities, and she has seen the results of her involvement as it influenced her life and the lives of others. This chapter examines these four communities of the WI, and looks at the ways that Prince Edward Island has both benefited itself as a province, and has entered the "global village" as a result of the efforts of the Federated Women's Institute of Prince Edward Island.

The Local Community

It would be easy to take the influence of the Women's Institute in PEI communities for granted. One could drive down the country roads, enjoy the beautiful scenery, and never know that the WI played a large role in ensuring both the existence of that rural community and the betterment of it. Nevertheless, the unmistakable signs of both their past and present involvement are there, and if we take an imaginary drive down one of these country roads, we will see the results of their endeavors.

One of the first things that both Islanders and visitors alike notice about rural communities in PEI is how well kept and attractive the homes and gardens are. The Women's Institute always recognized the benefits of an attractive community – their very first "Household Sci-

Working hard: Kelvin Grove WI erects a welcome sign at the entrance to their community, 1991. In the photo, from left to right: Mary Webster Houston, Sandra Caseley, Roger Caseley, Susanne Skinner.
Photo courtesy of Mary Picketts, Kelvin Grove Women's Institute

ence Short Course" in 1915 contained a lecture on landscape gardening methods. The responsibility for encouraging and recording developments in this regard fell to the Convener of Agriculture. Early records indicate that tree planting, rubbish collecting, and maintaining and improving gardens and cemeteries in the community were always a priority for the Institute branches. By the mid 1940s, the WI encouraged Islanders to beautify their communities by supporting and promoting the Rural Beautification contest, which continues to this day. As one member who joined over sixty years ago noted,

> *This fellow would fix his place up, then the next would see that, and the incentive was there. There were good prizes. Prior to that, there were a lot of places that were being let go and getting run down, and I think that we saw that if we made the island attractive then the tourists would come.*

If our drive through rural PEI was in mid-May, we

would see the continuation of that effort to keep Island communities attractive. For over twenty-five years, Women's Institutes have been organizing successful annual Roadside Cleanup Days. This initiative began in 1973 when the PEI Environmental Commission asked the Women's Institute to spearhead a highway cleanup for the spring. The provincial board embraced the idea, and through their marketing and networking, enlisted the support of over six thousand individuals on May 12 that year.

Clyde River School, 1910
Photo courtesy of Clyde River WI

The Women's Institute initially intended the Roadside Cleanup as a one-time affair that would take care of the messes of the past, and encourage people to refrain from littering in the future. The event itself was a great success; so much so that it landed Prince Edward Island on Canada's national news that night. Unfortunately, however, by the time the next spring arrived, another clean up was necessary. The provincial board agreed to support the Roadside Cleanup for another year, but lobbied the Department of Highways to enforce the provincial littering laws. Their lobbying on this matter would prove to be one of the very few instances where the provincial government did not take heed, and the Roadside Cleanup became an annual event. Roadside Cleanup day has not been without impact, however. Each spring thousands of Islanders pick up literally tons of garbage from ditches and roadsides.

As we continued on our drive, we would stumble upon one of the many Community Centers that dot the Prince Edward Island landscape. These buildings exist in no

Clyde River School today— now the Riverview Community Centre. Residents celebrate Canada Day.
Photo courtesy of Clyde River WI

small part due to the early and continued efforts by the Women's Institute.

Chapter One of this book noted that the PEIWI gave great support to the schools, but the magnitude of this involvement deserves further detail. Institute members at the branch level provided all manner of supplies for the one-room schools in Prince Edward Island. It is impossible to chronicle every contribution made by Institute branches to the schools, but as a sampling, they purchased blackboards, maps, desks, lamps, dictionaries, and pencil sharpeners. They provided lunches, cod liver oil, and made immunizations available. WI branches donated prizes for good students, gave funds to hire music teachers and buy instruments, and held ice-cream days during the summers to raise money for all of this.

Their support did not end there. The Women's Institutes over the years contributed endless funds for building and property maintenance – they replaced floors, painted

The Save our History photo albums, 1973
Photo courtesy of PEIWI archives

indoors and out, erected fences, and installed indoor plumbing. They paid janitors and labourers, erected playground equipment, and had sport facilities installed. In short, Institute branches worked ceaselessly to ensure that the children in their communities received the best possible care and education that they could provide.

In the late 1960s and early 1970s, the era of one-room

schools on Prince Edward Island came to an end. Popular opinion at the time was divided as to whether or not consolidated schools were a benefit or a loss to Island students, as one by one the old schoolhouses closed. At that time many branches rallied to ensure that these historic buildings were not lost to progress. Either independently or in cooperation with the local Community Councils, Institute branches purchased a number of the old schoolhouses and converted them into Community Centers. In other areas of PEI, Community Centers already existed – often because the Women's Institute branches had built these facilities and maintained them.

Recognizing the historical value of the old schoolhouses and churches in PEI, the Provincial Executive mounted the "Save Our History" project in 1971. Branch members contributed pictures and slides of almost every school and church on Prince Edward Island, with Helen Herring, Leone Ross and Beatrice Reeves heading the committee that collected the photos. Mrs. Herring filled numerous albums and compiled a narrated slideshow. The PEIWI made this material available to the branches, and the Save Our History project became so successful that the PEI Heritage Foundation exhibited the material at its headquarters in Beaconsfield for a month in 1973.

If we stopped our drive and ventured inside one of these Community Centers for a brief rest, we might chance upon one of the many activities organized by Women's Institute branches for community members. Institute members are so much more than caterers, but any Islander who has been to an Institute fundraising supper knows that the treats in store are well worth the price of admission.

The Women's Institute brings community members together for more than suppers, however. They hold showers for babies and newlyweds, variety concerts, bake sales, and demonstrations. They have card parties, meet-your-neighbour nights, and Christmas celebrations, just to name a few. Youth groups, church groups, Community Schools, and Community Councils use the Community Centers. They are the sites of heated debates and friendly exchanges. All over Prince Edward Island, these Community Centers remain the focal point of the rural community, and continue to bring Islanders together.

In striking up a conversation with anyone present at a Community Center, we would be informed of the other contributions that WI branches make to their communities. All branches support provincial initiatives and donate to various worthy causes, but in their own communities they assist in disaster relief, visit the sick and those unable to travel, and welcome new residents. They contribute to community skating rinks, baseball diamonds, swimming lessons, and countless other facilities and activities for rural Islanders. They sit as WI representatives on community organizations and committees, boards and task forces, thus ensuring that the perspective of the rural family is not forgotten in decision-making. Many branches have also published their own community histories, ensuring that their stories and those of their neighbours are read by generations to come.

The province

One of the benefits of the Women's Institute having the branches represented by a board of directors is that the opportunity exists for coordinated effort on a provincial level. This has translated into major undertakings and successes over the years. If an individual member, a branch, or any member of the PEIWI executive identifies an issue that qualifies as affecting the entire province, that issue is taken up by the organization as a whole. When the membership of the PEIWI takes on a problem, the "rural woman-power" of thousands of women in Prince Edward Island is brought to bear on the issue at hand.

One early story that demonstrates this strength began in the 1920s. At that time, Tuberculosis was a major issue for Prince Edward Island and much of the world. There were hundreds of known cases of the disease in PEI, and as many or more undiagnosed instances. Tuberculosis is a treatable illness, but was a real threat on PEI due to a lack of early diagnosis and intervention; the death toll was beginning to rise. Prince Edward Island had no official sanatorium, and those in Nova Scotia and New Brunswick were already overcrowded and because of the distance, too expensive for most Islanders. A number of doctors traveled throughout the Island in those years, speaking to all who would listen about the dangers of Tuberculosis and the need for a sanatorium in the province.

One such doctor, Dr. P.A. Creelman, then Chief Health Officer for PEI and Traveling Tuberculosis Diagnostician, spoke to almost every Institute branch on the Island in the early 1920s about the dangers of apathy towards Tuberculosis. The provincial executive of the Institute took up the cause, and began a major fundraising and awareness campaign. The branches participated fully, circulating countless petitions and raising thousands of dollars. Meanwhile, Mrs. William Mutch of Rocky Point WI led delegation after delegation to the provincial government in the hopes of convincing them to construct a sanatorium.

By 1928 the situation in Prince Edward Island seemed to have reached a crisis point. In March of that year, the Women's Institute joined forces with the Charlottetown

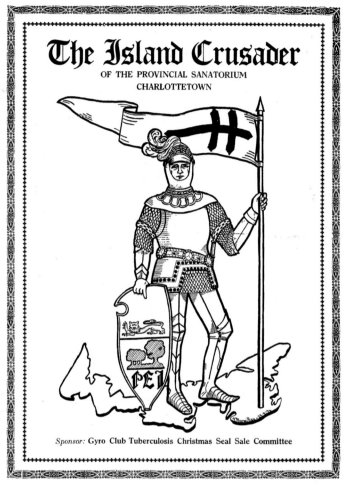

"The Island Crusader", written and published during the 1930s by patients at the Provincial Sanatorium. This monthly newsletter, supported by the TB League, carried news and information about Tuberculosis and Island patients.

Board of Trade, the Catholic Women's League, and the Rotary Club, and together they presented a resolution to the Legislature in Charlottetown. Their efforts paid off; two years later, in 1930, the new Provincial Sanatorium opened its doors.

According to W.J.P MacMillan, PEI's first Minister of

Health, "The building of a Provincial Sanatorium seemed a tremendous and doubtful proposition... but it was a fortunate move when the sympathy and active support of the Women's Institutes of this province was obtained."[1] Mrs. Mutch served as the only female member on the Board of Directors of "The San", and by that time she was also President of the PEIWI.

The Women's Institute's commitment to fighting Tuberculosis did not end when the construction finished. With the Sanatorium holding only sixty beds, and located in Charlottetown – in the middle of a province where cars were still very much out of the ordinary – it was evident that the battle against Tuberculosis would require ongoing attention. In 1935 the Women's Institute joined forces with the Gyro Club of Charlottetown and a committee from Summerside to form the Tuberculosis League. This organization hired a nurse, Miss Olive Ings, who traveled the Island attending to Tubercular patients in their homes, and bringing "contacts" – or families who had been exposed to the illness – to the Sanatorium for x-rays and examinations. The Women's Institute also continued to petition the government for more beds for the Sanatorium, and in 1938 thirty more beds were added.

The story does not end there, since Tuberculosis remained a problem for Prince Edward Island well into the 1940s. In 1942 an Institute member from the Parkdale branch died while waiting for a bed to become available at the Sanatorium. The petitions to the government began anew, and three years later the government opened a new wing at the facility. The Parkdale WI initiated "Flower Day", when all patients convalescing received a bouquet of flowers and a hand-written message donated by Women's Institute members. For many patients, this was the only correspondence they received all year.

It became clear that only a massive preventative effort would bring this illness under control on Prince Edward Island. In 1945 the Tuberculosis League purchased a mobile x-ray unit and began intensive screening clinics throughout the province. In advance of the arrival of the mobile clinic in a community, Women's Institute members would canvass door to door, encouraging people to attend the clinics and providing them with information about the illness. As testament to the mobile unit's success, 52,000 Islanders had received Tuberculosis tests before the mobile screening clinic was more than five years old. By the late 1950s, Prince Edward Island had gone from having one of the highest rates of Tubercular death in the country to having one of the lowest. It took more than twenty years to bring Tuberculosis under control on Prince Edward Island, and without the efforts of the Women's Institute members, it would have taken much longer. The old Sanatorium still stands in Charlottetown, now known as the Dr. Eric M. Found Health Centre.

Another example of the impact of the Women's Institute's years of efforts and the organizational abilities of their provincial executive members is their success in promoting traditional handcrafts. Recognizing the value of traditional arts from the very beginning, the Prince Edward Island Women's Institute incorporated instruction in handcrafts into their earliest courses.

By 1924 demand for WI crafts was such that the Provincial Board initiated the Handcraft Exchange as a means to raise funds for Island concerns, by selling items donated by Institute members. Beginning with a corner in their provincial office to display hooked rugs, the Handcraft Exchange soon moved of necessity to a larger location at 52 Lower Queen Street, Charlottetown. Within a few years the Prince Edward Island Tourist Bureau had realized the potential of the Women's Institute members' efforts, and began displaying Institute wares for sale in their offices in 1931. The last mention of the Handcraft Exchange in the WI archives dates from 1933, but the their interest in promoting the arts did not end there.

The Women's Institute also presented displays at the Provincial Exhibition beginning in the early 1920s. These first booths primarily displayed gardening and preserving methods. In 1934 the WI began sponsoring the Provincial Handcraft and Arts Exhibition as a component to what is now known as Old Home Week. Beginning with a small display of member's contributions and instructional materials, the WI booth at the Exhibition quickly developed into an arts competition open to all Islanders, and became a means to encourage Islanders to learn and maintain the traditional arts.

The popularity of the Women's Institute booth grew to the point that when the old Exhibition building was destroyed by fire in April of 1945, the Women's Institute was granted a new building of their own. The number of entries grew each year, as did the categories for submission. What began as a competition mainly of quilts and knitted goods evolved into a major display featuring hundreds of artisans, gardeners, and amateur chefs who submit their wares each August during Old Home Week. The effect of the Women's Institute display is almost staggering, with everything from homemade pickles to floral arrangements, from oil paintings to intricately crafted lacework, and, of course, some of the best quilts to be found anywhere.

The effort that Institute members voluntarily give to this exhibition each year is an accomplishment in itself. Each entry must be received, catalogued, and judged. The prize-winning entries and other notables must be attractively displayed, and winners must be put into contact with prize donors. The WI does more than show crafts at this event; each day a skilled craftsperson gives a demonstration of his or her trade. The entire exhibit is organized, mounted, supervised, and cared for by Women's Institute volunteers – a mammoth task when one considers the size and breadth of their display.

The number and variety of submissions indicates the success of the Women's Institute in promoting these arts. By showing the traditional with the modern and the amateur with the professional, the message is clear that the Women's Institute considers handcrafts and arts an occu-

A quilt-in-progress at the PEI Provincial Exhibition, circa 1980.

Photo courtesy of PEIWI archives

pation for all. Their message has reached its objective, as one can almost picture the thousands of hours spent by so many Islanders during the year in preparation for this annual event. The inclusion of young persons' categories in many of the competitions, and the excellent quality of participation in these, indicates that the traditional arts of Prince Edward Island are being passed on to new generations, thus ensuring their survival.

It is evident that the health of Islanders is, and always has been, a major concern for the Women's Institute. The final contribution that the Institute has made to the province of PEI, that this chapter will discuss, is found in the story of one of their contributions to the Queen Elizabeth Hospital. This account serves as only one of many examples of WI involvement in Prince Edward Island's well being, since both at the branch and at the provincial level donations are constantly given in support of the health care system. For example, in 1989 the PEIWI donated over twenty thousand dollars to the Queen Elizabeth Hospital's Cat Scan fund.

In 1964 the PEIWI presented 28 hooked chair seats to the dining room of Government House. These chair seats have since been removed and framed in order to preserve them as part of Prince Edward Island's artistic heritage. They are currently on display at Confederation Centre in Charlottetown. Here Kaye Crabbe and Betty Millar admire the handiwork of their fellow WI members.
Photo courtesy of PEIWI archives.

Through the years, Institutes have also educated their members and their communities about all manner of health issues, from the benefits of exercise to the debate over generic prescription drugs. The fundraising drive for the new stereotactic mammography machine at the Queen

Elizabeth Hospital however, serves as an excellent modern example of the ability of the Provincial Board to enlist the support of the members, and thereby achieve goals that benefit all Islanders.

Breast cancer has been a growing concern for women and their families for many years. Like Tuberculosis, breast cancer is a treatable illness, but successful recovery hinges on early detection. In 1996 the Women's Institute saw the need in Prince Edward Island for improved diagnostic tools. The provincial Institute board had received requests from the Queen Elizabeth Hospital for assistance in acquiring a Stereotactic Mammography Unit. As it happened, the provincial President at the time was a nurse.

The President championed the cause to the provincial board, and received their full support. The only question that remained was where the Women's Institute was going to find the money to purchase the unit – a mere $250,000. The Women's Institute was no stranger to successful fundraising, but that amount represented a sum larger than any other single effort that WI had undertaken to date.

Undaunted, the WI enlisted the support of the membership at large, and the provincial board held a Founder's Day luncheon for two years. Individuals, organizations, groups, businesses, and casual day supporters participated in helping the WI to reach their goal. PEI corporations came on board and helped immensely. For instance, one company held a celebrity auction, raising thousands of dollars at this event. It seemed that all of PEI wanted to participate and help. Twenty busy months later, the grand fundraising total reached over $260,000 – a truly phenomenal sum, and more than enough for their purpose. The new stereotactic mammography machine operates at the Queen Elizabeth Hospital today, a standing testament

Joan Dawson, then President of the PEIWI, presents a cheque for over $250,000 to the Honourable Marion Reid, for the purchase of a Stereotactic Mammography Unit at the Queen Elizabeth Hospital, 1997.

Photo courtesy of PEIWI archives.

to the dedication of the Women's Institute and its members, and a great support to Prince Edward Island's arsenal against breast cancer.

The Nation

The Federated Women's Institutes of Canada has taken on many of the same issues as the provincial organizations, but approaches them with a broader outlook. Focusing on projects related to public health, child welfare, agricultural issues, home economics, education, and the encouragement of the arts, to name just a few, the FWIC conducts research on a national scale, and thus provides the provincial Women's Institutes with assistance in developing their own agendas.

As the representative of the provincial Women's Institutes, the FWIC is able to represent all members in projects that pertain to Canadian national interests. For instance, the FWIC has taken responsibility for maintaining the former home of Adelaide Hoodless, founder of the Women's Institutes. They now maintain the site as a historic landmark, and all provincial Women's Institutes contribute to its upkeep.

By publishing its own regular newsletter, *The Feder-*

ated News, the FWIC assists branches to communicate with each other and share knowledge and ideas. The PEIWI has made its own contributions to the national agenda, including the agricultural producer-to-consumer link promotion of the 1980s. Developed as a means to promote understanding between farming and non-farming Canadians, the PEIWI undertook initiatives such as

The Buy... PEI traveling display, showcasing Island products and their manufacturers.
Photo courtesy of PEIWI archives

"From Farm to Table", a series of food demonstrations using Island products, and "Farmer-A-Day" interviews on radio and in the newspaper. The PEIWI continues the producer-to-consumer link approach today with the "Buy... PEI" program. Buy... PEI helps Islanders to support local growers and food processors by identifying those brands that are Island made.

The PEIWI took these marketing approaches to the national FWIC convention in Ottawa in 1981, and their ideas met with wide approval. The FWIC set this new focus for agricultural promotion as a national agenda, and provincial branches worked together to help promote agriculture by educating the consumer. This technique of promoting agriculture through publicity has been a great success, as Canadians have accumulated significant knowledge about agricultural issues, and these issues now receive frequent media attention.

The world

The PEIWI first made itself known internationally during the First World War. Many branches prepared care packages, which they then forwarded to soldiers and prisoners-of-war, much to the recipients' delight. One such beneficiary was R. Cadgen, of the 1st Canadian Mounted Rifles, 7th Battalion, a prisoner-of-war in Camp III, Gefangenenlager 3. Mr. Cadgen wrote four postcards of thanks for the packages sent to him by the Bonshaw WI. On the nine lines of writing that each postcard allowed, Mr. Cadgen said that his parcels were "worth their weight in gold."

One can almost imagine the joy Mr. Cadgen felt when he received a parcel on Christmas Eve, as "that's [our] main point of amusement here you know." In his last postcard, Mr. Cadgen told Mrs. Beaton of Bonshaw that there was enough in the parcel that he could "afford to give the Russians a bit". While these Russian co-prisoners of his were enjoying their home-made goodies, there was a Bolshevik revolution going on in their home country, and they surely thanked the Bonshaw Women's Institute as they wondered what they would be going home to.

During the Second World War, the PEIWI again received reports of the mark they were making on the international scene. Early in the war the PEIWI had donated an ambulance to the Red Cross. Major Charles M. Williams of Charlottetown happened to take a drive in that very ambulance while on duty overseas. Major Williams wrote a letter to the PEIWI saying that as he was getting into the ambulance, he noticed a plate affixed to the side of the vehicle. The plate stated "This ambulance was donated by the Women's Institutes of PEI, in September of 1940."

By the time the Second World War ended, the Associated Country Women of the World had gathered steam. Mrs. Raymond Sayre, the second president of the ACWW, described the organization as "a bridge of understanding, a window to the world." To expand this definition, the ACWW is not only a window, but also a door which members may walk through, in order to help each other.

The ACWW is a way for women's organizations around the world to combine their efforts and reach out to marginalised women, wherever they may be. With more than nine million members, the ACWW is the largest women's organization in operation, and as such has the ability to reach places where others cannot. Since the ACWW is essentially a worldwide conglomerate of national women's organizations, it is able to coordinate the wealth of one nation and direct it to another nation in need. For example, the ACWW is very active in Mali, one of the poorest countries in the world today. Mali has an illiteracy rate of 75 percent, a seemingly insurmountable difficulty. The ACWW is currently one of the few international organizations that has not essentially given up on poverty-stricken Mali, and continues to try to alleviate the situation there. One of their projects in Mali is funded by

Former provincial President Doreen MacInnis shares the WI experience with women in Lesotho, Africa as part of the "Landrover for Lesotho" program sponsored by the FWIC and the Canadian International Development Agency, 1981.
Photo Courtesy of PEIWI archives.

the National Lottery Charities Board in the United Kingdom, and is implemented by ACD (Action Couverture et Developpement), the ACWW partner non-governmental organization in Mali. This program has established literacy centres and market gardens, provided medical supplies, and gives training to traditional birth attendants, community workers, and literacy teachers, among other things.

The ACWW also reaches out to women who are politically marginalized. For example, the Countrywomen's Association of Germany was admitted back into the organization after World War Two, helping women there to begin to rebuild their society after the horror and shame that they felt when the Nazi horrors came to light. One PEIWI member listened to an address given by one of these German women at an ACWW conference, and was deeply moved by what she heard. The German woman thanked the ACWW for their magnanimity, saying, "We will never forget ACWW. You offered and restored our dignity when we desperately needed it." Today, women in many countries, such as China, are still outsiders to the modern world and the ACWW welcomes them as much as their political situations permit.

The PEIWI, as a member society of the ACWW, has made use of the information available through their conventions and newsletter, *The Countrywoman*, to participate in many ACWW projects. The PEIWI is particularly active in assisting women and families in developing countries with items such as sewing machines, and funds for wells, vehicles, and food. In 1996 PEIWI members knitted over three thousand squares, which they then sent to Zambia where women were able to use the materials to make toys, blankets, and socks.

One of the PEIWI's ongoing efforts in support of ACWW programs is their contribution to Pennies for Friendship. Branches regularly donate to this continuous fundraising effort in support of ACWW.

The stamp of accomplishment

In a survey once taken in a small Ontario town, a woman was asked if she knew anything about the Women's Institute. The woman replied, "Oh yes, that's the place where they put wayward women!" Well, times have changed since that survey, and the Women's Institute has become known to all as a force to be welcomed and respected.

It began as an organization whose chief aim was to raise the physical, intellectual, and cultural conditions in the home, and to raise the standards of homemaking. The Women's Institute has become that and so much more. WI members have enriched the lives of their neighbours, their province, their country, and the lives of women around the globe. One Prince Edward Island School Inspector in the early 1930s said, "Show me a Women's Institute, and you show me a better school." At this point, it is probably safe to say, "Show me a Women's Institute, and you show me a better world."

Chapter Three:
Membership Has its Benefits

A Women's Institute branch meeting or convention can be a powerful event indeed. There is the unmistakable feeling that one is in the presence of very remarkable women. Rich and poor, young and old, life-scarred and wide-eyed, all sit together and share their time. They listen to strangers and to each other, and with the inimitable grace that only comes from knowing who they are and where they belong, they share their time, their knowledge, and their strength.

Each and every branch, initiative, and success story is the result of the efforts of individual women working as part of a team. For members, the Women's Institute is both a place to give and to receive. This chapter tells the story of the individual Institute woman.

There were various reasons that so many women joined the Women's Institute in its early years. Their lives were not ones of leisure, since every one of them held a full plate of duties to fill their days. Nevertheless, join they did, and the time they dedicated was nothing short of phenomenal. Aside from their obvious interest in improving their communities, the Women's Institute filled many of the needs of rural women in PEI, and to a great extent still does.

Fellowship

Ask an Institute member what one of the greatest benefits that she receives as a member is, and she will invariably place the sociability high on her list. This was especially important for women in the early years, since loneliness and rural living went hand in hand. Until not so very long ago, when women married they stopped working outside of their homes and moved onto their husbands' property. When the

nearest neighbour was a mile away, the opportunities for social nights were slim. For many women, the Institute was a
way to meet and know their neighbours. The monthly Institute meeting allowed these women an opportunity to discuss
business, and to enjoy each other's company.

This sense of fellowship among the women continues.
Many members report that the friendships they have made in
the Women's Institute last them a lifetime. They not only
meet and get to know the women of their communities, they
also establish friendships with women across the country

"The giggles" on Institute night, circa 1975
Photo courtesy of Delma Horne

and around the globe. By attending national and international conferences, many members have had the opportunity
to know women worldwide. In addition, Women's Institutes
often practice what they call "twinning", which involves two
branches maintaining close contact with each other. Through
twinning, members and branches exchange ideas and knowledge, form friendships, and visits between the branch members serve to reinforce the relationships established.

Because Prince Edward Island is so small, for many years the divisions within rural society ran deep. Political affiliations and religious convictions have long separated PEI society. Several women's clubs co-existed with the Women's Institute, such as the I.O.D.E, the Catholic Women's League, and others, and many Institute members were and are simultaneously active in more than one of these. Yet the Women's Institute for many years represented the only non-partisan, non-sectarian organization available to women. This meant that women of all persuasions met and worked together at a time when they could easily have remained strangers to each other. As one lifelong Institute member noted,

> *I used to say, that's the only way I'd get to know the women from the other churches. Some of them were Roman Catholic, some Church of Scotland. Here on the island, in some districts, it was very much separated between Catholic and Protestant, and I grew up that way and didn't know any different.*

Rural isolation in Prince Edward Island is no longer so great, but the need for organized contact among neighbours remains. Whereas one used to feel isolated due to distances or lack of transportation, today's rural lifestyle often involves commutes to work in towns or cities, long-distance travel to bring children to various sporting or social clubs, and very little time left for social activities for women. Neighbours may live much closer to each other, but because they now do so much outside of their communities, they may be strangers nonetheless. Institutes continue to bridge these gaps in rural society, not only by holding various social events but by members visiting individual community women and inviting them to attend Institute meetings.

Learning

Some women arrive at their first WI meeting with barely a high school education. Others bring university degrees. All spend a significant amount of time learning. This is why the Women's Institute has long been known as the "university for rural women".

The branch meetings and conventions are designed so that at each meeting, members share and receive knowledge. All branch meetings begin with roll call, which is not simply answered with a "yes" or "here". Each roll call is answered with a different tidbit of information. Sometimes these are humourous, with topics such as their favourite expression about women. Other roll calls are practical, requiring members to bring recipes or donate articles for fundraisers. Many topics are informational, asking members for a health hint or a handcraft demonstration, for example. Thus, at the beginning of Institute branch meetings, the sharing begins.

Branch meeting and convention protocol also dictates learning. Branches will often invite guest speakers on various topics, again ranging from the entertaining to the educational. The provincial WI office maintains a substantial library of "program kits", each of which contains pre-prepared learning materials available to the branches. The Institute has been compiling these program kits for over fifty years, and consequently the range of topics is very comprehensive. Branches can and do access materials on everything from farm safety to legislative procedure, from cancer prevention to Robert's Rules of Order.

At the district and provincial conventions, Institute branches bring forth resolutions from the branches, and presentations on the resolutions usually follow. Experts, involved parties, and members are invited to provide their perspective on the issues at hand, and opposing views are encouraged. In addition, many conventions include a panel dis-

WI members, young and young-at-heart, share their experiences.

Photo courtesy of PEIWI Archives

cussion on a current issue. The Institute invites experts and interested parties to participate in these panel discussions. In this way, the Women's Institute provides members with solid information on a wide range of issues affecting their communities and the province as a whole.

WI members not only learn from outside experts, however, they also learn from each other. By involving themselves with women from generations both older and younger than themselves, members share a wealth of wisdom, ideas, and knowledge. Many members report that one of their more valuable experiences as part of the Women's Institute has been the opportunity to work with so many remarkable and accomplished women. Seeing the achievements of their peers, drawing on the wisdom of their cohorts who often become mentors, and witnessing the growth in other members has inspired them to become more accomplished women themselves.

This mentoring experience was particularly valuable in the early days, since women had few role models to provide encouragement in their interests in public life. Women still need positive role models today, but with the erosion of the extended family relationship they have fewer sources of example, and the media's portrayal of the modern woman is fickle and often irrelevant. By involving themselves with the Women's Institute, however, young women learn from those who have been mothers, homemakers, career women and wives (often simultaneously!). They learn that they have choices, and that they can achieve without sacrificing their values or their family interests.

Public speaking is a large part of the WI learning experience. Catherine Callbeck, then Premier of Prince Edward Island, speaks to the PEIWI Annual Convention in 1995.

Photo courtesy of PEIWI archives.

The structure of the Women's Institute is also a source of education for women. Each level of the organization – branch, district, and provincial – appoints members to serve as conveners for the various standing committees that the Institute maintains. Some convenerships have changed over the years (for instance, there is no longer a standing committee to deal with the League of Nations!), but many remain in their original form. The Women's Institute currently has standing committees on agriculture, citizenship and legislation, cultural activities, home economics and health, international affairs, Canadian industries and safety, and the environment. Given the number of convenerships available, and the two-year term for the position, there is opportunity for all interested members to participate in this role.

The conveners' role is to select the members for her committee, research the relationship of her particular issue to her community, and assess the resources that the Women's Institute possesses to deal with the topic. She then informs the members of her findings. The convener also proposes what she determines is a practical plan of action that the Women's Institute can take to improve the issues she has identified.

To fulfill her role as convener, the Institute member must learn to coordinate the efforts of various numbers of individuals. She must learn to communicate with industry and government officials in order to gather information and communicate the intentions of the WI. She learns to assess findings and search for practical solutions. She also learns to prepare and present reports to her branch or her board of directors.

Some women arrive with these skills already in hand. For others, however, their experience as an Institute convener is their first exposure to some of these tasks. Through the guidance of the women who went before, they learn skills that help them to succeed not only in their positions as WI members, but also in their other life endeavours. This represents the duality of the Women's Institute experience; in the process of gathering information and sharing it with others, the Women's Institute member may discover herself, and the talents she never knew she had.

This duality is also well represented by the example of the *Institute News*, the PEIWI's quarterly news publication. The first of its kind in the Maritimes, the *Institute News* was the brainchild of Evelyn Harrison Windsor, who proposed the idea to the Provincial Board of Directors in 1927. Miss Windsor saw the publication as a way to unite the branches, and dedicated much of her time to its development. Unfortunately, Miss Windsor died of a sudden illness before the PEIWI published the first issue in March of 1928, but the *Institute News* continues today.

The *Institute News* brings stories of common interest and Institute concern to the members, keeps them informed of current events, and serves as a communication tool between the PEIWI Board of Directors and the membership. Various members and conveners write the articles, and although they may not be experienced journalists, they create interesting articles. They share their knowledge, and in the process learn to communicate.

These learning experiences have always been a part of Women's Institute membership. As early as 1931, when Institute membership was still in its first generation, a Mrs. Donald of Seaview WI made the following comments about WI membership.

> *Never before in the history of the world have women been taking the prominent places in every phase of work as they do today. Never before have they shown the ability to take such positions, and never before have they measured up to the standards to which they have aspired as they are doing in the present time, all because women are fitting themselves through just such organizations as our Women's Institutes to take up more burdensome tasks, particularly of community welfare, that are yearly being assigned to them. These were almost unheard of a generation or two ago, and yet do we get the most from this privilege.*[1]

In learning these skills, WI members gain not only ability, but also confidence. Women, some of whom never dreamed that they could, have found themselves in positions of public responsibility – perhaps president of their branch, or even of the provincial organization. For many, overcoming their shyness and insecurities were personal triumphs, and their pleasure in participation speaks volumes about the distance they have traveled as members of the WI. For example, one current member started out as an extremely timid woman, who would always dress in muted colours so as not to stand out in a crowd. She was literally terrified when she had to speak publicly as part of her role in the Institute, but forced

Then PEI Premier Alex Campbell presents the Premier's Award for Distinguished Citizenship to Helen Herring, Louise Marchbank, Florence Matheson, and Leone Ross in 1973.

herself to overcome this fear. Today she is an outspoken member, a former provincial president, and speaks at various Island functions about the Women's Institute in PEI. She now wears bright red sweaters to these occasions, a symbol of her courage gained.

How do we know that the Women's Institute creates successful women? We know this because of the number of WI women who have gone on to receive honorary degrees, the Order of Canada, Woman of the Year awards, appointments to community councils and provincial committees. Indeed, the first female Speaker of the House in the Prince Edward Island legislature was a WI member. Moreover, these are only the public accomplishments – many members' accomplishments are more private, but equally significant in their own lives. Call it either a direct or an indirect result of membership, but Institute women learn leadership, presentation, coordination and above all, determination.

Choices

The Prince Edward Island Women's Institute does not now, nor has it ever called itself a feminist organization. As one member put it, "We weren't exactly out there burning our bras!" On the other hand, the PEIWI recognized from its earliest days that women have rights along with their responsibilities, and has never shied away from working to improve the status of women in society. The PEIWI has given much towards the progress of women's rights on Prince Edward Island, and they continue these efforts today.

As mentioned, the Women's Institute began on PEI before women here even had the right to vote. The Prince Edward Island legislature began debating this issue in 1918, but for three years did not enact any legislation granting women the franchise. Meanwhile, Women's Institutes were beginning to realize their potential. They began petitioning the government for equality in the franchise, and in 1922, they were successful.

Once women had the vote, the next question was what were they going to do with it? We have already discussed some of the various occasions when the Women's Institute marched into the legislature. Did the PEIWI, however, actually promote women's participation in the political process? They certainly did, with their trademark cautious progressivism. Agnes MacGuigan, Convener of Legislation in 1934, summed up the PEIWI views this way:

> *More or less uncertainty exists in the minds of Institute members regarding women in politics. Canadian women, for all their pride in their patriotism have never been much given to showing it in political activity. But at the present time when economics*

are so closely linked in all its aspects, there is some pretty stiff economic thinking to be done before we get out of the present muddle the world is in, and it is up to the women to do their share of the thinking. That woman's true and permanent place is the home, and that her duties as homemaker are so remote from political problems as to make her less apt than man to acquire political knowledge or to take too active a part in politics will always be true of the wives, mothers and daughters whose time is devoted to domestic occupations. But hundreds of our daughters have gone for longer or shorter periods into professional, industrial, or commercial occupations. The conditions surrounding and affecting them are not always satisfactory. For the majority, neither the remuneration, the hours of labor, nor the sanitation and safety are up to the required standards. Most of the measures necessary to remove these abuses will have to come through legislation. They can only come through law and order.[2]

In other words, while the primary place for women was in the home, the WI acknowledged the needs of the women who chose to enter and/or stay in the workforce, and would support those needs. They kept that promise. In 1938 the PEIWI was successful in obtaining a grant from the federal Department of Labour to train young unemployed women in such topics as first aid and health.

The Second World War consumed any excess energies the Women's Institute had, but once the war was over they were able to concentrate again on their membership and their community. The Women's Institute executive began providing leadership training courses to its members in 1947 under the direction of Helen Herring, then provincial President of the PEIWI. Mrs. Herring, having entered the position of

The first PEIWI Leadership Training class, held in the Legislative Assembly of PEI, 1947. In the front row, past Presidents Mrs. George Martin, Mrs. Edith Gates, Mrs. Harrison MacFarlane, Mrs. Currie, Mrs. Gordon Ives, Mrs. Marion Stewart, Mrs. Allison MacNeill, Mrs. Lulu Yeo Birch, Mrs. Walter Leard, Mrs. Helen Herring, Mrs. Harold Laird.

Photo courtesy of PEIWI archives.

president feeling somewhat untrained for the job, made it her mission to assist future members of the WI executives. They held their first leadership course in the provincial legislature, and included instruction in parliamentary procedure, briefs and presentations, and writing motions and resolutions. As a result of these training courses, the Women's Institute became, in Mrs. Herring's words, "A group of women that could take their place on PEI or anywhere, and do it well."

To appreciate this, we must view this encouragement to women and their accomplishments in its proper context. While women's rights enjoyed a brief and limited heyday in the early part of the twentieth century because of the suffragette movement, there was little room for women in public life, especially married women. This situation remained the same until the 1960s, when women began agitating for change. We cannot forget that what may seem today like normal career choices simply did not exist for women before that time. For the Prince Edward Island Women's Institute to have been training women in political procedure and providing them with the opportunity to interact with governments, business people, and various other organizations in a professional and efficient manner was nothing short of radical for its time. As one member put it, "I wasn't just happy scrubbing the floor you know, and the Women's Institute was the place to be."

Photo courtesy of PEIWI archives.

Helen Herring presents the scholarship that bears her name to Heather Walker. The Dr. Helen Herring Scholarship fund established in 1977, replaced the Jubilee Endowment Scholarship in Home Economics, established in 1949, and the Law Scholarship, given from 1975-1977.

As women became increasingly interested in combining their home and public lives, the PEIWI was at the forefront of the women's movement in this province. While never undermining the value of motherhood and "good homemaking", the Institute was called upon many times to advise governments on issues relating to women, and the WI never failed to produce. In 1965 for example, when a Member of the Legislative Assembly asked the Women's Institute to state its views on the topic of women serving on juries, the PEIWI polled its members. While the results were not unanimous, the majority was in favour of this new role for women. The WI presented their views to the House, and in 1966 the government responded with an amendment to the legislation regarding jury selection. On November 16, 1966, four women served on a jury at the Supreme Court of Prince Edward Island in Summerside. Three of these four women were Women's Institute members, and one of them served as forewoman.

The PEI Women's Institute's continuing concern for the condition of women is further demonstrated by the time that they have dedicated to this issue since the early 1960s. The PEIWI was represented in the provincial branch of the Council of Women – the first federation of organizations designed to bring together various associations – with the purpose of combining efforts and perspectives in examining women's issues. The Prince Edward Island branch of the Council of Women formed in 1968, and a PEIWI past president served as its first president.

When the Royal Commission on the Status of Women arrived in PEI in the early 1970s and spent two years studying the issue here, the Women's Institute was there. When the University Planning Committee met in the late 1960s to draft plans for the new University of Prince Edward Island, the Women's Institute took part, requesting the presence of "at least one Island woman, knowledgeable and keenly interested in the field of higher education" on the new university's Board of Governors. When the provincial government established the Prince Edward Island Advisory Council on the Status of Women, the Women's Institute got involved, and another past president served as its first chairperson.

When the provincial government established a committee in 1975 to study setting up a family court on the Island, and there were no women on that committee, the Women's Institute wanted to know why. The government responded that no women in the province were qualified to advise the com-

WOMEN AND THE LAW

sponsored by

P.E.I. WOMEN'S INSTITUTES

The P.E.I. Women's Institutes are sponsoring four seminars where competent resource people will discuss women's rights and the P.E.I. laws regarding property, inheritance and the family.

Attendance at each seminar must be limited but 25 seats will be allocated on a first come basis, for individuals, male or female, who pre-register before March 24. Those who cannot be accommodated will have their registration refunded.

Seminars will be held as follows:

April 5–Park Royal United Church, Parkdale,
9:45 a.m. - 4:00 p.m.

April 9–Hillcrest United Church Hall, Montague
9:45 a.m. - 4:00 p.m.

April 12–Legion Home, Summerside,
9:45 a.m. - 4:00 p.m.

April 15–Park Royal United Church, Parkdale
1:45 p.m. - 9:00 p.m.

*The "Women and the Law" seminars, as advertised in **The Guardian**, 1975.*

Clipping courtesy of PEIWI archives.

mittee. Within a year the Women's Institute had established an annual scholarship for women entering law school. That same year, Women's Institutes held seminars across the Island, advising women of the legal system in Prince Edward Island and how it related to women's issues.

These few items just mentioned merely scratch the surface of PEIWI involvement in furthering the status of women on the Island. Even beyond the WI's formal involvement in status of women issues, membership empowers women by encouraging them to learn and attain their personal best at all times. The WI continues to encourage women today. We must also bear in mind that the efforts made in this regard are concurrent with all of the other WI activities. Again, how any one organization can successfully participate in so many activities boggles the mind, but Chapter Four will attempt to address this issue.

Aside from the fact that the PEIWI is an often forgotten player in the struggle for women's rights on the Island, there is another interesting aspect to the WI's relationship to women's rights. This organization started from a position that it has taken the rest of us many years to reach. The PEIWI never, even for a second, devalued women's responsibilities as mothers and wives. The WI continued their courses in home economics, and still provide scholarships to students studying this field at the University of Prince Edward Island (In 1999, for the first time, the home economics scholarship was presented to a male student!). The Women's Institute has always taken the position that parenting and home life are vital aspects of the survival of families and of communities, yet it has never asserted that these were the limits of women's capabilities. There was never an occasion when any Women's Institute member was looked down upon by the organization for choosing to place child rearing as her top priority. Neither was there ever a moment when an Institute member felt that she should not expand her horizons as far as she wished to take them. That is one of the unique features of the Prince Edward Island Women's Institute that sets it apart – women are allowed choices.

A place to call their own

In the early years, women joined the PEIWI because it was the "in" thing to do. If you were a teacher, you needed the WI to help you do your job. If you were a homemaker, the WI was a place to learn and share. By the time the second generation of PEIWI women arrived, the Institute had become a fixture in the minds of most rural Islanders.

Little girls would sneak to the stairway long after they were supposed to be sleeping, and listen in awe as their mothers and aunts and grandmothers and neighbours talked about what seemed the most important of things. Husbands gladly drove their wives to the Institute meetings, and played cards while they waited for the women to conduct their business. Children knew that "Institute night" was mother's evening, and come what may, she was off to her meeting. Newcomers to rural communities would seek out the local Institute branch immediately upon arrival, bringing with them news from their former branch and possibly a recipe or two. Joining the Women's Institute was something that many young Island girls could not wait to do. Some, in fact, did not wait, and joined before the official eligible age of sixteen. As one member put it,

Women's Institute was something that I just assumed that I would join. You washed on Monday, scrubbed on Saturday and had beans for Sunday; it was just a tradition!

For Institute women, their involvement became a way to create a place for themselves in their communities. By giving to their communities, they took ownership of them, and shaped them into neighborhoods that they wanted to live in. Their successes and contributions provided a sense of accomplishment and belonging, and the knowledge that they had made some small (or often not-so-small!) difference in their own world.

By bringing their experiences with them, good and bad, Institute members created a place for themselves within the organization. Members are able to give in ways that help them realize their dreams and cope with their losses. A member who has experienced a family loss due to alcohol can share that; the Institute can be her vehicle to educate others about the dangers of drinking and driving. Another member who has an idea to improve her town can promote that to the branch or the district, and the strength of the Institute can provide the legitimacy that new ideas need for others to consider them. An individual with a thought or an idea is just that – a thoughtful individual among many. An Institute member with the same thought or idea is part of a powerful, interested, and sharing organization that can develop that idea, and give it the potential to become a reality.

The more you put into it...

As any Institute member will point out, membership in the PEIWI is as beneficial and as enriching as the individual member makes it for herself. Over the years, literally thousands of Island women have given the Women's Institute all the energy they had available. The Women's Institute has given back.

Chapter Four:
Their Recipe for Success

Upon listing a few of the accomplishments of the PEI Women's Institute over the years, it becomes obvious that the PEIWI is a dynamic, cohesive organization. The question for this chapter is, what quality or qualities of the PEIWI has allowed it to remain dynamic for so many years? What is the Prince Edward Island Women's Institute's "recipe for success"? The analogy could be a dangerous one, since to even hint at characterizing the PEIWI as merely cooks is to ignore the myriad other things that they have accomplished. In addition, as all cooks know, a good dish is rarely captured in its totality by a mere recipe. Still, all success stories have their basis either in sheer luck or in a strong foundation. The longevity of the PEIWI's success excludes the luck explanation, and so we turn to the latter: a strong foundation.

The kitchen

As a well-organized kitchen is a primary requirement to good cooking, so a well-organized Women's Institute has been a key element in its success. The PEIWI has always had the tools and the people to bring ideas forward and see them to completion. But the structure of the organization is a part of the formula that made it possible, and that structure remains essentially the same today as it was in the beginning. They always had a good thing going. By combining solid systematization with flexibility, the PEIWI has been able to turn ideas into reality.

The PEIWI has five levels of organization – branches, district areas, the provincial executive, the Federated Women's Institutes of Canada, and the Associated Country Women of the World. Branches generally meet

Reta MacDonald, Betty Millar, and Margie Stewart, all members of the PEIWI board of directors, hard at work for WI members, circa 1997.

Photo courtesy of PEIWI archives

monthly, districts annually, and the PEIWI holds a provincial convention in Charlottetown every second year. Provincial conventions and county conventions take place on alternate years, a recent development that streamlined the coordination process. The FWIC and the ACWW also hold conventions every three years. Each level communicates with the other through a system of delegates – branches send delegates to the district and provincial conventions, and the provincial executive sends delegates to the national and international conventions. Some branch members also attend these. As mentioned in Chapter Three, each branch, district, and province also elect conveners to oversee the standing committees that the Institute maintains. These conveners communicate with their counterparts at other levels of the organization and the members, and thus further the direct lines of communication within the local, provincial, and national agendas.

One of the more revealing elements of the Women's Institute structure is its configuration of authority. All levels of the organization elect executive officers and a president, and it is the president's job to preside over her sector. Those elected to executive positions, either at the branch or at international level, act with authority. But because the Women's Institute is an entirely volunteer operation, one does not sense from members in executive positions that they see themselves as removed from "mere membership". A provincial president is still a member of her branch, and still participates in her branch's activities. More often than not, the WI executive members exude an attitude of assisting from above rather than controlling. Thus, the Women's Institute maintains an executive that promotes cohesiveness and coordination, but retains equality among its members.

The length of executive service serves this same purpose. Executives at the provincial level serve for only two years at a time, with a maximum of two terms in a position. This turnover of provincial officers gives greater opportunity to those who wish to advance within the WI. As one member put it,

> *If from time to time each Institute has someone who can be on the Provincial Board, it just sort of brings that idea of Women's Institute closer to you. Everybody can't be on every year, but from time to time, or if someone in your area is on it, and comes and talks to you, you don't lose that continuity. You take that back to your branch as well. It helps break down that idea that a Provincial Board is hierarchy, and shows that it can be anybody that can be on the Provincial Board, and that each person is accepted as an individual. You don't have to be a teacher and you don't have to*

be a nurse or a doctor's wife... you're equal what-
ever you are. Whether you're a farmer's wife, or if
you have a great amount of education or a less
amount. It breaks down those barriers.

Branch meetings themselves are another example of
the Women's Institute's structured flexibility. Over the
years, the PEIWI has refined the art of productive and enjoyable meetings and conventions. Branches receive direction in all aspects of meetings and protocols, including
program planning, guest speakers, preparing resolutions,
electing branch executives, and providing leadership
within their communities. The skeleton structure of a WI
meeting is almost identical today to meetings of earlier
years, a testament to the insight of the founding members.

Institute meetings are not, however, subject to rigid
formalities. A PEIWI branch operates as an independent
entity within a larger body. The basic meeting format is
available, but there is no authority figure looming over-
head to chide a branch for adopting its own meeting format. The system is in place – the recitation of the Mary
Stewart Collect, roll call, reading and approving the minutes, statements by conveners and branch officers, hearing speakers, discussing resolutions, social time, and so
on. But the branches operate semi-autonomously, and so
are free to meet in essentially whatever manner they
choose. The information on standardized meeting protocol is available to them, and they may use it at their dis-
cretion. The program kits are available from the provincial office, but the branches may use them or create their
own programs as they desire.

This freedom for the branches has been one of the
PEIWI's greatest strengths. Instead of operating in an at-
mosphere where direction and agendas filter from the top
down, the PEIWI's agendas travel both ways. All mem-

Meadowbank WI celebrates their 60th anniversary, June 1999. Seated from left: Anna Hamming, Lulu Clow, Flossie Hyde, Florence Murray, Eileen Drake. Standing from left: Cheryl Jewell, Elaine Jewell, Miriam MacLean, Donna Cantwell, Dolphie MacFadyen, Laurie Smythe, Esther Hovingh, Lorna Tierney, Jane Wilting, Alice Vanderzwaag, Ferne MacPhail, Lavina Luymes, Helen MacPhail.

Photo courtesy of Eileen Drake, Meadowbank WI.

bers of the Institute have the opportunity to be full participants in all aspects of their organization. No member need feel that they are blindly following an executive that is removed from the reality of the front lines. Certainly some projects begin with an idea from the national or the provincial executive, but most come from the branch level and work their way up from there. The Prince Edward Island Music Festivals provide a perfect example of this.

In 1945, Mrs. Preston Beck and Mrs. Nadine Archibald of the Central Royalty Women's Institute decided that Prince Edward Island was ready for a Music Festival. After all, Institute branches across the Island had been sponsoring music teachers in the schools for almost ten years. Mrs. Beck and Mrs. Archibald saw that a competition could provide students with an incentive to raise their standards. The Central Royalty branch took up the idea, and presented a resolution on it to the provincial convention that year. The resolution passed, but no concrete results or direction came from that convention.

Mrs. Beck and Mrs. Archibald were determined, however, and so they took matters into their own hands. They contacted the secretaries of the nine branches in their district area and Louise Haszard of the provincial office, and invited them to a meeting. Together these women established a committee to organize the first Prince Edward Island Music Festival for May of 1946. At that point, the committee had no budget, no publicity, and no experience in organizing such a venture!

With a $200 grant from the Department of Education, a mammoth cake sale, and $5 each from the nine branches in the district, the PEI Music Festival was underway. The WIs hired a music teacher to draw up a syllabus for the first competition and travel to district schools during the weeks before the festival, instructing students and encouraging them to participate. The first Festival boasted no less than 126 entries, a great success for such a new endeavour. So much interest was generated that the Prince Edward Island Music Festival Association immediately came into being, and the entire province participated in the Music Festival in its second year. Apart from an honorary presidency position, the early executive of the PEI Music Festival Association was entirely comprised of Institute members. The Music Festivals continue today, and have inspired generations of young Islanders to pursue their talents and their dreams. All this began with the idea of two individual Women's Institute members.

The cooks

A recipe is only as good as those who use it. The PEIWI has been blessed with the cream of the crop it seems, since its membership through the years has featured women of determination, intelligence, and above all, tact. They took the tools given them by the organization, and created works to be proud of.

As part of the dynamic of an almost wholly voluntary organization, respect for fellow members runs throughout the Women's Institute; this comes through in all conversations with "Institute women". In over eighty years of organization, it is impossible to believe that there would be no conflicts, and in fact, there have been a couple. Some resolutions passed at the federal level were too controversial for some members, and occasionally personality conflicts emerged. All records and accounts, however, point to one thing – that Institute women always show respect for each other, including those with conflicting views. While the resolutions generally stand, and the majority rules, all opinions are counted as worthy.

The dedication and determination of Institute women is one of the organization's major strengths. When the PEIWI decides that something needs to be done, it is done, and without any unnecessary fanfare. As one member put it,

> They're just down do earth, and when something needs to be done they just get down and do it. For instance, we were talking about the government. It takes them so long to talk about something, and forever to finalize it. The Women's Institute wanted to clean up the roadside, they go out and they pick up all that stuff, and if you

wanted to know how many pieces had been picked up it would be counted and done and that would be all there was to it, and you'd go on and do something else. I think over the years that's been something that's helped.

The more Institute women accomplished, the more they realized they could do. The irony is that the Women's Institute was never intended to be a service organization. Their main focus has always been leadership and personal development for rural women. But in the process of learning, women became aware, and awareness is the first step to action.

It is evident that Institute women are nothing if not determined. They faced challenges from the very beginning, and yet they persevered. For example, when the Harrington WI first organized in 1913, such was the resistance from the community that the women were barred from using the school or the church for their meetings. Undaunted, the Harrington WI held their meetings on the side of the road! While that sort of resistance did not last, the WI faced another barrier – apathy and inertia. As one former provincial President noted,

They don't want change. We'd be wanting to do something and, "Oh, that won't work, you'll never do that." We'd say, "Oh yes, we'll have to try it. We'll just go by faith." And we'd take on a project and it would go over. But some of the older people would just shake their heads, they wouldn't want to be any part of it. But then when they saw it turn out well it would be, "Oh yeah, that turned out great, you did a good job."

While rejecting radicalism as detrimental to the overall organization and its credibility, PEIWI women have never been afraid to blaze new trails, and they do not give up easily on their goals.

The ingredients

A cake is a cake, but a really special cake has one or two unique ingredients that set it apart from the rest. The Prince Edward Island Women's Institute has these unique ingredients. Specifically, these are cooperation, flexibility, and great public relations!

Chapter One touched on the fact that the Women's Institute cooperated with the Red Cross in order to work for better health conditions for young Islanders. Throughout the 1920s and 1930s, Institute members canvassed for new Red Cross members and for funds to support the two organizations. When the Red Cross recommended dental clinics, the PEIWI facilitated their implementation. When the Red Cross called for immunizations, the Women's Institute made the necessary arrangements. In 1920 the Red Cross initiated the Public Health Nursing pilot project. This project continued for the next eleven years, until the PEI government established the Department of Health. Women's Institutes were highly involved in this initiative — they supported the nurses, facilitated school inoculations and organized Junior Red Cross clubs for the children, for instance.

The Red Cross was the first organization that the PEIWI collaborated with, but it was not the last. Today, the PEIWI is represented on everything from community councils to government round tables. Branches support hospital funds, community fire departments, seniors' homes and sporting organizations, just to name a few. In addition, Island WI women are often members of anywhere from one to nine other organizations, with the average being two.

The PEIWI and its members' willingness to collaborate

with other organizations is one of the ingredients that has kept the organization relevant and active for so many years. By maintaining contact with those on the "front lines" of issues, the WI is able to stay abreast of the questions that affect members and their communities.

Then PEIWI President Kaye Crabbe presents Lois Thompson with the "Friend of the WI" award in 1991. Mrs. Thompson worked in the provincial office for almost 40 years, and is an active WI member.

Photo courtesy of PEIWI archives.

This is one aspect of the organization that the PEIWI is now considering refining. At one time, the Women's Institute branch was simultaneously the home and school association, the department of health, and the continuing education center. Many of the functions that the Women's Institute used to be the primary provider of have now been taken over by single-issue organizations. The Women's Institutes still play a crucial role in these aspects of family and community life, but they are no longer the only organization concerned with those issues.

One of the major difficulties that new and/or potential members report is the concern that they cannot belong to too many organizations at the same time, and must choose where they will spend their energies. The Women's Institute helps women to avoid this dilemma by formally representing itself in more of these latter-day organizations. For example, a WI branch or district could designate one member to sit on the local School Board. That member would represent the concerns of her branch (or district, as the case may be), and report on school issues to the mem-

Roadside Cleanup day, 1998, with Sherbrooke WI, the Sherbrooke 4H, and the Sherbrooke Council - cooperation!

Photo courtesy of Sherbrooke WI.

bership. Likewise, other branch members might take a similar place on other committees. Thus the branch as a whole would have access to a broad range of information and input, without each member having to personally participate in each – a mammoth task given today's schedules!

This system already exists in a fashion by virtue of the convenerships. While the convener of agriculture, for example, might be the only member in the branch actively researching a particular issue, all members benefit from the information she gathers. In addition, the provincial executive has already incorporated this idea, since the PEIWI is represented in various organizations. Expanding the WI's areas of influence in this way will meet the needs of more women, and hopefully increase its membership.

The second ingredient that has contributed to the longevity of the PEIWI, and will likely continue to do so, is the flexibility of the organization. A mandate as broad as "for home and country" can be interpreted to mean many different things. This is not to say that the WI lacks focus – one could hardly have read this far and make that mistake! What it does mean is that the Women's Institute's mandate has no end. Helping women to educate themselves, assisting families, and helping communities worldwide are goals that are ongoing, and that can take on many different forms.

The PEIWI has demonstrated its ability to adapt their goals to the changing times. For example, many mistakenly associated the Women's Institute solely with the one-room schools. When the schools consolidated, the Women's Institute demonstrated its flexibility by turning the old schools into community centres. When the fight against Tuberculosis on the Island ended, Institute members turned their attention to cancer. When women entered the workforce in larger numbers, the PEIWI informed them of their rights, and showed them how to create healthy packed lunches while they were at it!

This adaptability is complimented by a firm knowledge of where the Institute comes from. Branches write their community histories, make projects of reading old minute books, and cherish their early records. They maintain their communities' historic monuments, and they remember those members who are no longer able to attend meetings with visits and cards. This symbiotic relationship between the past, the present, and the future is one that will serve to cement the Prince Edward Island Women's Institute in years to come. The more modern we get, the more we cling to our histories for a foundation and a sense of belonging. By embracing the new with the old, the

Betty Millar and Edna Watts present prizes to the young winners of the "Be Island Proud: Keep it Clean" contest, 1998. By involving the community in their activities, the Women's Institute stays in touch with all Islanders.

Photo courtesy of Thelma Johnson.

Women's Institute can stay relevant and grounded.

Institute women have never been fond of self-congratulation, yet neither do they hide their accomplishments. By recognizing each other, they encourage members to achieve to their full potential, and honour those members who stand as examples for us all. Members receive recognition within the organization in the form of "Life Memberships", for example, presented to those with twenty years or more of active WI membership. In addition, the Women's Institute formally honours women who have made extraordinary contributions to the organization. In 1973 the PEIWI began their annual "Woman of the Year" award, given in cooperation with the Summerside Lobster Carnival. In 1985, they instituted the Adelaide Hoodless Award of Honour, also given to a woman in the community who demonstrates exceptional leadership skills.

The PEIWI communicates not only with its members, but with the rest of the Island. From the very beginning the PEIWI published its meeting minutes in detail in local newspapers. This was a very effective form of communication in early years, since most rural Islanders were isolated. While Island newspapers no longer carry all of the WI's meeting minutes, their relationship continues. Island newspapers regularly publish the details of the PEIWI's conventions, and upcoming events are faithfully publicized.

In 1948, Helen Herring took the PEIWI's publicity to a new level. She began hosting a radio program on CFCY in Charlottetown, the first program of its kind in the Maritimes. Mrs. Herring had fifteen minutes per week, all free public service time. She interviewed experts, reported Institute and community news, and linked Institute members across the Island with her live radio show. Twenty years later, Mrs. Herring (by then well known as "Mrs. Institute") brought the Women's Institute to Prince Edward Island television, with the "Today at Home" program. For ten years, she interviewed visitors to Prince Edward Island in her TV "living room", and shared recipes. Mrs. Herring ended her broadcasting career in the mid-1980s, at the same time ending the PEIWI's television career, but her radio legacy is carried on today by the Provincial Board's Radio personality.

Keeping the community closely apprised of Women's Institutes activities and accomplishments has resulted in a very good public image for the organization. Most Islanders know the Women's Institute to be exactly what it is — a dynamic and very busy group of women! By remaining on the public's mind, the PEIWI can remain a source of knowledge and guidance to other organizations. Many organizations and government departments regularly contact the PEIWI in order to receive input into various issues. By taking on these tasks, the PEIWI continues its mandate of educating its members and in the process, making the Island a better place to be.

The proof is in the pudding

The Prince Edward Island Women's Institutes do not have a monopoly on organizational success, but they certainly seem to have a lock on the skills that are necessary to stay alive. As the rural landscape changes, the Island economy changes with it, and so do the lifestyles of Prince Edward Island's rural women. The PEIWI has the recipe to adapt with these changes, and has put this recipe to use time and time again.

Reflections

The PEIWI has stood the test of time, yet some wonder whether there really is a future for the WI, given the speed at which our province and our world is changing. But these changes seem to be what Women's Institute members thrive on. Their ability to quickly adapt to the needs of rural women, their families, and their communities can only serve to strengthen the organization in the future.

The Women's Institute will continue to thrive in PEI. The main issue that caused the drop in membership in the first place, namely that many rural women have little time outside of their daily commitments, may change as the "baby boomers" retire. There are many "country commuters" living in rural PEI, and those that retire will likely be looking for ways to further enrich their lives and their communities. In addition, technological advances and improvements in education mean that young people are more and more aware of the world around them, and as this book already noted, awareness is the first step to action. The Women's Institute provides a perfect vehicle for the concerns of either of these demographics, since as we have seen the organization is essentially what its members wish to make it. There is no prerequisite political or religious affiliation, no familial or ancestral ties necessary, and all women are welcome.

As we move forward into our new millennium, the Institute is moving with us, and is keeping an eye on our "Fair Isle". What will their next big move be? We'll have to watch and find out. Better yet, the opportunity is there to become a part of this formidable and welcoming group of women, and make the Prince Edward Island Women's Institute organization one that is even more a reflection of the power of all Island women to grow and to effect change.

PEIWI Provincial Presidents

1913-1921   No Presidents or Executive (oversight of PEIWI in this period performed by Supervisors and Assistant Supervisors hired by the Department of Agriculture)

1922-23	Mrs. T.G. Ives, Montague
1923-24	Mrs. Henderson
1924-25	Mrs. George MacDonald, Cornwall
1925-27	Mrs. Lester Brehaut, Murray River
1927-29	Mrs. Lulu Birch, Northam
1929-31	Mrs. Imogene Mutch, Rocky Point
1931-33	Mrs. S.J. Rose, East Baltic
1933-35	Mrs. Harrison MacFarlane, Fernwood
1935-37	Mrs. Annie MacMillan, Fairview
1937-39	Mrs. Lester Mellish, Montague
1939-41	Mrs. Walter Leard, Fernwood
1941-43	Mrs. Fred Gates, West Royalty
1943-45	Mrs. George Martin, New Perth
1945-47	Mrs. Helen Herring, Borden
1947-49	Mrs. Alan Stewart, Bonshaw
1949-51	Mrs. Malcolm MacLeod, Lorne Valley
1951-53	Mrs. Harold Laird, Kelvin Grove
1953-55	Mrs. Michael Doyle, North Rustico
1955-57	Mrs. Murdock McGowan, Kilmuir
1957-59	Mrs. Jean Wilkie, Alberton
1959-61	Mrs. Florence Matheson, Oyster Bed Bridge
1961-63	Mrs. Lois Dewar, New Perth
1963-65	Mrs. Hilda Ramsay, Indian River
1965-67	Mrs. Roma Campbell, Spring Brook
1967-69	Mrs. Inez Dixon, East Baltic
1969-71	Mrs. Louise Marchbank, Traveller's Rest
1971-73	Mrs. Leone Ross, Parkdale
1973-75	Mrs. Beatrice Reeves, Cross Roads
1975-77	Mrs. Mary MacLean, Central Lot 16

1977-79	Mrs. Louise MacMillan, Alberry Plains
1979-81	Mrs. Hazel Graham, Murray River
1981-83	Mrs. Doreen MacInnis, Covehead Road
1983-85	Mrs. Mary Palmer, Kensington
1985-87	Mrs. Joyce MacKenzie
1987-89	Mrs. Geneva King, Fortune Cove
1989-91	Mrs. Kaye Crabbe, Charlottetown
1991-93	Mrs. Betty Watts, Clyde River
1993-95	Mrs. Helen Nicholson, Brackley, Fairview—New Dominion
1995-97	Mrs. Joan Dawson, Augustine Cove
1997-99	Mrs. Betty Millar, Wilmot
1999-2001	Mrs. Elizabeth MacDougall elected but resigned for family reasons, Betty Millar agreed to continue for this term.

Federated Women's Institutes of Canada

| 1964-67 | Mrs. Florence Matheson, FWIC President |
| 1985-88 | Mrs. Bea Reeves, FWIC President |

Associated Country Women of the World

| 1989 | Geneva King, World United Nations Committee |

Past Presidents' Photos*

Mrs. T.G. Ives

Mrs. Imogene
Mutch

Mrs. Harrison
MacFarlane

Mrs. Annie
MacMillan

Mrs. Walter
Leard

Mrs. Edith Gates

Mrs. Helen
Herring

Mrs. Malcolm
MacLeod

Mrs. Harold
Laird

* Regrettably, photos were not available for all past Presidents of the
PEIWI.

Mrs. Michael
Doyle

Mrs. Murdock
McGowan

Mrs. Jean
Wilkie

Mrs. Florence
Matheson

Mrs. Lois
Dewar

Mrs. Hilda
Ramsay

Mrs. Roma
Campbell

Mrs. Inez
Dixon

Mrs. Louise
Marchbank

Mrs. Leone
Ross

Mrs. Beatrice
Reeves

Mrs. Mary
MacLean

Mrs. Louise
MacMillan

Mrs. Hazel
Graham

Mrs. Doreen
MacInnis

Mrs. Joyce
MacKenzie

Mrs. Geneva
King

Mrs. Kaye
Crabbe

Mrs. Betty
Watts

Mrs. Helen
Nicholson

Mrs. Joan
Dawson

Mrs. Betty
Millar

Branch Histories

What follows are the individual histories for most branches of the PEIWI, past and present. Many of these were submitted within the last few years by branch members themselves. They permitted me to edit, but I have tried to keep these in as close to their original form as is possible. Where no branch history was submitted, I attempted to include the branch nonetheless. Here you will also find recorded dates and first officers of branches for which we know little else, since they have long since disbanded and records of their activities are slim.

This is by far the longer section of this book, and while it may not be practical to sit and read branch histories one after another, taking a few minutes to read a few at a time gives a sense of the magnitude of the Women's Institute in PEI, and the fact that this organization is still very strong. The writing that the WI members did for this section is more often than not engaging and inspiring - these are words to read when one needs to be reminded that people care about their communities, and they do make a difference.

Abram's Village

Abram's Village WI first organized in 1967. In the early 1970s members helped in 4-H clubs and took part in an area festival. We also helped in community projects.

Seven of Abrams Villages' members received Life Membership awards, and they hosted the Area 5A Convention in 1996. This branch disbanded in 1997.

Alaska

Miss Mary Robin organized Alaska WI on September 15, 1951. The officers at that time were Mrs. James Buote, President; Mrs. Robert Sharp, Vice-President; Helen McCabe, Secretary-Treasurer.

Alaska WI operated for thirty years, until low membership numbers resulted in their disbanding in 1981. While active, however, Alaska WI concentrated their efforts on their community school, while contributing to other worthy causes.

Alberton

The Alberton branch organized on November 3, 1927. The original officers were Mrs. H.J. Larkin, President; Mrs. Herbert Clark, Secretary; Mrs. A. L. Purdy, Treasurer.

Some years before the Alberton Institute was organized, a number of women formed the Prince County Hospital Aid organization. It was at a meeting of this group that a motion was made to organize a branch of the Women's Institute. They saw that in this way they could continue to work for the Hospital and at the same time, work for the benefit of the community.

As one of their first projects, Alberton WI purchased and renovated a Community Hall. They also continued to provide upkeep for the Alberton Room in the Prince County Hospital. When the Western Hospital opened, Alberton Institute furnished a room and provided bassinets for the nursery.

Over the years, Alberton WI collaborated closely with the Red Cross. They sponsored swimming and first aid classes, blood donor clinics, and donated sickroom supplies and a "loan cupboard". The women of Alberton also supported their local school and many charitable causes.

In 1956 the Institute honored its first President, Mrs. H.J. Larkin, by presenting her with a Life Membership.

The first Cancer Clinic held on Prince Edward Island took place at Western Hospital on October 26, 1978. Members of Alberton Women's Institute assisted by promoting interest and by providing refreshments. Because of the success of this clinic, they held a second clinic in April 1979.

Alberton WI disbanded in 1992. At that time, they were down to three members, and felt that they were unable to carry on the work themselves.

Alexandra

Alexandra WI first organized in May of 1939 by Supervisor Haszard. The first officers were Mrs. Gay Judson, President; Mrs. Ernest MacCabe, Secretary; Mrs. Lester Beaton, Treasurer. Their date of disbanding is unknown.

Albany Village

Albany Village WI organized in 1927, with Gladys Pineau serving as first President. They worked in their community for a number of years before disbanding.

Alberry Plains

Alberry Plains WI first organized in December of 1936. The membership at that time was nineteen, and we have yet to surpass that number!

These enthusiastic early women worked together for their school, their community, and for the Red Cross war effort. When the community built a new school in 1950, Alberry Plains WI supplied many articles, including books, furniture, an organ, a music teacher, and other necessities.

Our Institute has always been closely involved with the 4H Clubs in our community. Many members serve as project leaders, and we are always proud of our youth's achievements.

Our Institute began holding Cancer Education clinics in the late 1970s. We participate in various fundraising initiatives such as bake sales, blind auctions, collections at meetings, and fruitcake lotteries. Our fundraising assists many organizations, too numerous to mention!

We are very fortunate to experience such closeness and friendship as we have worked over the years, and we hope for the same kinds of blessings in the years that lie ahead.

Albion

Albion WI organized in October of 1938. Mrs. W.D. Fraser served as its first President. This branch operated for more than thirty years, before disbanding in 1974.

Albion Cross

This WI branch organized on October 28, 1932. Mrs. A.D. Matheson was its first President. The date the Albion Cross WI disbanded is unknown.

Alliston

Ena Beck

Lives of great men all remind us
We can make our lives sublime
And departing leave behind us
Footprints on the sands of time

These lines came to mind as I was reading over minutes while researching this project. The earliest minutes I have are dated May 1930. Mrs. James Beck held the meeting at her home, and there were twelve members present. Mrs. Beck was also the Secretary.

In the early years our WI's role centered around the local school. They purchased things like chalk, a globe, maps, window blinds, and many other things – the teacher was very grateful! To make money for these projects, members organized and produced concerts, suppers, ice cream festivals and dances, crokonole parties, and the list goes on. In the days when polio and TB Clinics were held in the local school, the WI served tea and cookies to the staff. All the work was volunteered and the men helped.

As time progressed and the schools consolidated, Institute work became broader. We were responsible for starting the milk program in Southern Kings Consolidated School in 1975. We donated a trophy to be presented to the most deserving pupil in the Grade eight graduating classes each year. When the Northumberland Fisheries Festival started, we co-sponsored a beauty pageant candidate. Helping a group trying to get soft drinks sold in returnable bottles, helping in roadside clean-up, and having road signs put up were among our community efforts.

Through the years we supported various worthwhile projects as our budget allowed. Among these, the Red Cross swimming classes and 4-H come to mind.

Our work is not always for others. Speakers on subjects as varied as flower arranging, leather craft, quilting, seatbelt legislation, abortion, and alcohol and drug abuse, have enriched our lives and stimulated our thinking.

We now have ten members on our roll, four of whom are Life Members. Although our interests have changed some over the last forty years or so, we still focus on our homes and our community.

Alma

Miss Maylea Boswell organized the Alma WI on January 18, 1949. The first officers were Mrs. Archie Barbour, President; Mrs. Isaac Dunbar, Vice-President; and Mrs. Jack Clark, Secretary-Treasurer.

The Alma WI participated in community efforts and assisted with the upkeep of the school. They enjoyed over forty years of fellowship before disbanding in 1985.

Alpha-York

The Alpha-York WI has been very active in our community. We promote the beautification of our community by sponsoring the PEI Rural Beautification Competition On-Going Award Category each year since 1981, when York became one of ten communities to receive a plaque in this category. We will receive a tab each year until 2000, if our community upholds the standards of the Rural Beautification Society. In 1988, York received the Shaw award, given in appreciation of continued beautification efforts. In both 1989 and 1995 we received first prize in Community Improvement.

In 1979, members of the Alpha-York WI submitted the name of our President, Dorothy Lewis, for the Woman of the Year Award. We were thrilled when she won this honour. In later years other members of Alpha-York WI also won this award – Irene Jewell, 1980; Patricia Watts, 1982; Dorothy Vessey 1985; and Jean Lewis, 1988.

In 1982 we purchased the property of the former York School. A committee consisting of WI members and members of the community cares for the property, now known as the York Community Center. In 1989 the community renovated the Center extensively, and expanded it so that it now provides a 225-seat auditorium, a stage, kitchen and other facilities. On July 1, 1989 residents took ownership of the building and unveiled a plaque to acknowledge the efforts of the WI. The Duke and Duchess of York officially opened the new Center. We have free access to the Centre for meetings and fundraising events.

In 1986 our WI was instrumental in organizing the first Canada Day Celebration in York. This event has become more popular each year. We continue to support this project financially, and members take on active roles in the planning.

In 1995 Alpha-York WI had a memorial window restored and installed in the newly built York United Church. Our WI had placed this memorial window in 1928, in remembrance of those who served in World War I.

In April of 1996 members of Alpha-York WI, together with our spouses and special guests, met at the Community Centre to celebrate the 85th Anniversary of the first Women's Institute on PEI, which began in York on April 10, 1911. The York United Church Choir catered dinner and provided entertainment.

We now have twenty active members and eight inactive Life Members on the roll of Alpha-York WI. Members continue to work diligently for the betterment of "Home and Country". We give financial support to such organizations as Queen's County Music Festival, Upper Room Angels, and the Salvation Army Red Shield Appeal. Members canvass the community for worthy appeals, and we provide support to special projects of the PEIWI and the FWIC.

Anglo Rustico

Miss Schurman organized the Anglo-Rustico WI organized on December 30, 1927. The first officers were Mrs. Edison Rollings, President; Mrs. Fred Toombs, Vice-President; Mrs. J.L. LePage, Secretary; Miss Ella Clark, Treasurer.

This branch focussed mainly on their local school, but also sponsored a 4H Garment Club in their community, and contributed to other local endeavours before disbanding in 1973.

Annadale

Annadale WI was organized in November of 1927. Margaret Preston served as its first President. Annadale was still active in the late 1960s, but subsequently disbanded.

Argyle Shore

Miss Boswell and Miss Robbins organized Argyle Shore WI on February 23, 1950 at the home of Mrs. John D. (Pauline) MacPhail. The first President was Edith MacPhail and the Secretary-Treasurer was Pauline MacPhail.

Over the years our Institute has been very active and very involved. Our WI has provided help to various charity organizations, and to people in our own community and other provinces who have needed assistance due to circumstances such as fire, accident, or sickness. We make quilts for victims of fires and floods, and prepare meals and boxes of food for needy families.

In the 1950s we were instrumental in lobbying Maritime Electric to provide our community with electricity.

During the days before consolidation, our branch used the funds we raised to support our school. We provided books, maps, cod liver oil capsules, a duplicator, an organ, and a piano. We also supplied a music teacher and electricity, and cleaned, scrubbed, and painted the school several times.

We also took part in education programs for our members. We took sewing classes and courses in first aid, home nursing, and money management. We provided dancing lessons and exercise classes. For several years, we provided salary and board for a swimming instructor in our own community.

As well as working for our own community, we have participated and helped in cooperative community efforts such as providing time, money, and supplies to the South Shore Sportsman's Dinners, Englewood and Bluefield Schools, Crapaud Rink Canteen, the restoration of the old stones in the Argyle Shore Cemetery, and the Mammography and Catscan machines at the Queen Elizabeth Hospital. We provide our Community Centre for the swimming instructors in the South Shore area every year.

Each year we arrange for Santa Claus to visit every child in our community on Christmas Eve, and present each with a candy cane.

We enjoy many fundraising activities such as fashion shows, concerts, crokinole parties, lawn parties, lectures, take-out lobster suppers, catering to weddings, and running a fast-food booth at the Crapaud Exhibition. Our annual strawberry festival is one of our most popular fundraisers, held in the first week of July every year. We have also written and published three cookbooks – *Country Kitchen I, II,* and *III*.

Along with our hard work, we have had a lot of fun and enjoyment over the years. We enjoy the company of many of our neighbouring Institutes, and we celebrate our anniversary every year in an enjoyable manner. We have also had some overnight slumber parties, travelling dinners, and we even held a meeting at Government House in May of 1986, when the Honourable Lloyd and Helen MacPhail were in residence. This year we chartered four of our members – Beverly

MacPhail, Dorothy MacPhail, and Roma MacDougall, who are also Life Members, and Ruby Seller.

Our greatest achievement to date has been establishing a place for our community to gather. In 1973, we bought the Argyle Shore School, and in 1977 we drew up a 99 year lease to move the Argyle Shore Hall to its present location beside the school. In 1978, the two joined to make the Argyle Shore Community Centre. We have provided for various renovations over the years and today we have a beautiful Centre that is used for all community activities. We organize showers and anniversaries, and in later years have held a "Meet your Neighbour" pot-luck supper every year. At this event we present a gift to each new family taking up residence in our community. Our Institute is the glue that holds our community together.

On a wall in our Centre we hung a plaque which will hold the names of members of our WI who have passed away. By doing this we will have a permanent record of the women who have been so important not only to the history of our WI, but also to our community.

Arlington

Miss Windsor organized the Arlington WI in 1927. The first officers were Mrs. Seaman Ford, President; Mrs. Artemas MacArthur, Vice-President; Miss Edith Phillips, Secretary-Treasurer.

The Arlington WI was very active in providing for their school and their community. They installed a pump, painted the interior and exterior of the building, and provided treats for the school children and shut-ins. During the war years this Institute branch donated their time and their talents in giving assistance to the soldiers overseas.

Arlington WI was active for almost sixty years before disbanding in1996.

Augustine Cove

Miss Mary G. MacDonald, general organizer from the Department of Agriculture, established the Augustine Cove WI on October 27, 1939. The first roll call showed the following ladies as members:

Priscilla MacFadyen, Bessie Cameron, Louise Howatt, Jean Carruthers, Mrs. Major Carruthers, Daisy, Edna and Kate MacFarlane, Mabel Wadman, Mabel Newsome, Myrtle, Ada and Bertha Peters, Doris Webster, Kathleen MacFarlane, Geraldine Darby.

Our branch quickly put the WI motto "For Home and Country" into action, as World War II had just begun when we first organized. Although our main interests were our school and community, during the first years war work was of primary importance. We made quilts, socks, mitts, and vests, and sent these items overseas. In 1943 our branch completed thirty quilts, three of which were made in one day.

When the school was remodeled and enlarged in 1952, the WI took on the project of installing a kitchen and dining area in the basement and completely furnishing it. The WI also assisted in landscaping the grounds, including erecting a fence and planting trees. For our effort we received a prize in the Rural Beautification Contest.

Our branch contributed financially toward having music taught in our school, a 4-H Garment Club and a Calf Club, Dental Clinics, Red Cross Swimming, and other initiatives.

Our community erected a War Memorial following World War I. The Augustine Cove WI continues to maintain this memorial.

Today our branch assists in the roadside clean-up, canvasses the district for charities, welcomes new babies, supports community showers and other celebrations, and visits the sick and shut-ins of the community. Each year we host annual events such as a Christmas Party, a Meet Your Neighbour night, an ice-cream social, and a bean supper. These events take place at the former two-roomed schoolhouse that the WI maintains as our Community Centre.

In the early 1970s, in compliance with the wishes of the Provincial Board of the PEIWI, the Augustine Cove WI compiled a community history, *Augustine Cove (1800-1973)*. This book includes information on early settlers, family histories and other items of historical interest.

It is worthy to note that one of our valued members, Joan Dawson, held the office of President of the Federated Women's Institute of Prince Edward Island from 1995 to 1997.

The Augustine Cove Women's Institute has ten members in 1999 and meets on the second Monday of each month. Our present officers are Marjorie Inman, Janet Quigley, Myrna Murray, Grace MacFadyen, Joan Dawson, Bethany Dawson, Lillian Cutcliffe, Myrtle Ceretti and Brenda Lawson.

Avonlea

Mrs. Robert MacKenzie held the first meeting of the Avonlea WI on November 10, 1920 at her home. The first officers were Mrs. Jeremiah Simpson, President; Mrs. Robert MacKenzie, Vice-President; Miss Mabel Woolner, Secretary-Treasurer.

In the early years, the Avonlea WI focussed its attention on their community school. Also active in the war effort, this branch donated much time and effort to the Red Cross. The Avonlea WI contributes to their community and participates in provincial projects.

The Avonlea WI is still active today.

Baltic Lot 18

These have been interesting and challenging years for our Women's Institute. For forty-two years we have followed in the footsteps of those who preceded us, "For Home and Country".

Our membership remains on par with earlier years, but now our members come from outlying districts as well as our local area, and we welcome their support.

The lifestyle in rural areas is very different today than twenty-five years ago, but our objectives remain the same. Our meetings are always very interesting, we discuss many things regarding our local community and our country at large, and we express our concerns as needed.

We support three charitable organizations each year. We volunteer and support Kensington Intermediate Senior High School by giving prizes and working at school lunches. Until recently, the Kensington Clothing Depot was a great source of income and a very demanding project that required more volunteers than were available. This was a great outlet for people wishing to dispose of good used clothing and especially helpful to those on lower incomes, since they could obtain clothing for children and adults at a nominal fee. We divided the money from this project between several organizations. Our WI continues to support the Red Cross by providing a Christmas fruitcake made and donated by a member each year, and we continue to supply knitted articles.

When our one-room school closed, we bought the building for one dollar and turned it into a Community Centre. This was one of our greatest accomplishments. In 1978 we opened one of the earliest Craft Centres in the area; this proved to be a very successful venture for eight years. Beautiful quilts, mats, woven articles and many other locally crafted items were in great demand by tourists and local people. WI members and local ladies gave generously of their time to staff the Centre from July to mid September. In 1986 we sold the property and invested the money – now the interest is divided annually between Kensington Intermediate Senior High School's Safe Grad and providing driving education to a student from Baltic district. The furnishings and records of the old school found a home in the Malpeque Museum and are available for anyone to view.

We have compiled the Baltic Lot 18 District's history. This proved to be an interesting endeavour. All families participated, and with the help of two students we completed and published the book in two years. It still sells readily and is a source of income for our local WI.

In 1995 we celebrated the 60th anniversary of Baltic WI, which was a great time for former members to come together with present members. Virgine Cole, a provincial representative, presented Life Memberships to several members, and others received WI stickpins. Our program that evening included musical entertainment by Mary Cousins and Ed Matthews, who in years gone by were always there to cheer the heart with their toe-tapping music. We also enjoyed an interesting display of Cavendish figurines.

We are especially concerned with the environment. We participate in the roadside clean up, and we were instrumental in preventing the CIC from placing a garbage disposal site in a very public area in our district.

We have twinned with several WI groups, Summerside, St. Eleanor's, New London, Hazel Grove and Fredericton, and we always enjoy being together.

We have a special member who is an MS victim. She was able to attend meetings regularly with the help of her faithful husband and sons. Now she is our honorary member. We meet at her home in the spring and fall and have a happy time together, and in gray November we pack a Sunshine Box for her, which she and her family thoroughly enjoy.

Our most recent act was to recommend Life Saving Awards to three of our fishermen for saving the lives of two others. These men were the subjects of a presentation at Government House in 1996.

We hold our meetings on the first Tuesday of each month, except for during July and August when we visit a place of interest and enjoy a meal out. We extend a friendly welcome to all new comers and residents alike. We hope we can continue to create interest, and that WI work in the area will progress. This is our link with the past and our hope for a friendly and generous future.

Bayview

The Bayview WI first organized in September of 1928. The first President was Mrs. Walter Simpson, and the Secretary-Treasurer was Mrs. James R. Stewart.

This branch disbanded in the early 1970s.

Beach Point

Beach Point WI first organized in 1943. During the war years our branch was closely connected with the Red Cross; they knitted, send parcels to soldiers overseas, and held fundraising concerts for the war effort. Our branch also contributed to community needs, donating to the orphanage and the local school.

In 1955 Beach Point WI disbanded, but we reorganized eight years later. Since then our membership has ranged from seven to twenty. We have always supported our community's needs, and FWIC and ACWW projects. We also supported our local school until it closed in the early 1970s, and in 1976 we bought the old school as a WI building. We have since renovated the building, and use it for various community events.

We have raised money to fund our projects through bazaars, "bring & buy" fundraisers, flea markets, bake sales, and canvassing the community. We use the money to donate to such organizations as the TB League, the Mental Health Fund, scholarships, the Kings County Memorial Hospital Building Fund, UNICEF, Pennies for Friendship, the Salvation Army, the Christmas Seal Fund, the Red Cross Swimming Program, the Northumberland Arena, Transition House, the Murray Harbour War Memorial, and the Stereotactic Mammography Fund, to name a few.

We are also active in organizing community events. For instance, each year we make Christmas tray favours for the hospitals, and lay a wreath on Remembrance Day.

We at Beach Point WI are glad to be a part of the WI, working and learning, "For Home and Country."

Bear River South

The Bear River South WI organized in 1926. Mrs. Vernon MacIsaac served as their first President, Mrs. James Chaisson, Vice-President, and Hilda O'Donnell served as Secretary-Treasurer.

The Bear River South WI was active in their community for over sixty years before disbanding.

Bedeque

Jean Bowness

The Bedeque WI organized on November 8th, 1937. At that time there were almost twenty members. We held meetings at members' homes on the first Tuesday of each month.

Our main project in the early years was to ensure that the school had the necessities. During the war years we also knit articles, sent boxes of chocolates, food and candy to the soldiers overseas, made sheets-pillows for hospital use, and adopted a needy family in Britain. We raised money by holding bean suppers, ice cream socials, and moonlight skates. At that time we also made and donated six quilts to the two orphanages, and donated to other various institutions.

In 1947 our members hooked a nursery rug for the annual convention. That same year Professor Jones introduced music in the school, and the children attended the Music Festival. We saved old woolens for blankets, kept a sick room supply cupboard, and continued to contribute to the school. We bought a projector, black out curtains, a table and chairs, 100 folding chairs, a teacher's desk, a book case, and books. To fund these donations we held "bring and buy" sales, pantry sales, yard sales, card parties, and catered to the RT Holman picnic at the beach. This was a lot of work, fun and money for our WI.

In 1954 we bought a second hand piano for school. The piano sold in 1982 when the school closed during consolidation. We celebrated our 25th anniversary by donating a plaque to the 4H for the best overall student. In 1950 we began girls sewing classes at the school; these classes still run as part of the 4-H. Many girls learned to make clothes for themselves, and the children participated in Schurman's school parade on CJRW for a number of years. To raise funds we had home parties and prepared banquets in the schoolroom for the Credit Union pantry sale.

In 1970 our WI branch entered a float in the Centennial year parade, sponsored a bicycle rodeo and provided for swimming lessons. We participated in the unofficial WI broomball league. We bought the school for $1 in 1984, made it into a Community Centre, and turned it over to the village commission in 1992.

We remember the sick and shut-in in our community with treats, flowers and cards. Over the years, we have made many quilts, and we give them to the needy and fire victims. We also give a cookbook to every newly married person in the community. We held a "welcome home" party for a member's daughter who participated in Olympic Games. One of our members received the Citizen of the Year award in 1994 for the surrounding districts. In 1995 we presented her with a plaque from our WI as a sign of our gratitude for her dedication and years of work in WI.

In 1997 we have eleven members. Three are Life Members, and we still meet the second Tuesday of each month to work for "Home and Country".

Belle River

Christine N. Gillis and Marsha Myers

On November 19, 1937 a group of ladies from Belle River met at the Belle River school. Supervisor Jean Rodd presided, and helped them to organize a Women's Institute. The ladies decided to name the branch Belle River Women's Institute.

The first officers were Mrs. Kenneth Nicholson, President; Miss Flora Stewart; Vice-President; Miss. Vergene Stewart, Secretary-Treasurer; Mrs. M. F. Riely, Mrs. Norman Bell, Mrs. Kenneth MacKenzie, Directors; Mrs. Craig Matheson, Miss. Margaret Riley, Auditors.

Mrs. Benjamin Miller held the first regular meeting on December 16, 1937 in her home. Each month two members visited the school to see what items they needed. On special occasions, members would give candy treats to the children. The Institute paid for scrubbing the school, and two members visited the sick each month and brought a treat worth $0.35. The collection for each meeting was 5 cents per member. In the first year the membership was twenty, and six of these members are still living.

During the war years Belle River WI members were very busy knitting for the Red Cross and sending parcels overseas to members of the Armed Forces from the district.

Today we count sixteen members, and we hold our meetings at different member's homes on the first Tuesday of each month. We try to have interesting meetings with special speakers, WI kits, and demonstrations, followed by a social hour.

Our WI donates to school, hospitals and charitable organizations. We raise funds using various means, such as collections, penny ticket articles, donations, auctions, raffle tickets, a travelling apron, dances, card parties, catering to weddings and anniversaries.

In the summer of 1996, the Belle River WI operated a canteen at Northumberland Park. This canteen raised funds that we put back into the community.

We enjoy a Christmas dinner each year at the home of Sadie Bell, and from time to time we treat ourselves to dinner at a local restaurant.

We in Belle River are proud of our community spirit.

Belmont

The Belmont Women's institute first organized on June 17, 1931 through the efforts of Marion Hardy, a local schoolteacher. Mrs. Ernest Inman was the first President, and Minnie Simpson served as the first Secretary.

Our WI continues to be an organization providing education, leadership opportunity, and social interaction for our members. The whole community recognizes the first Thursday in each month as "WI night". Because our community no longer houses only farm families but a diverse mix of occupations, Women's Institute is the common ground on which we meet and work together. We sponsor an annual Meet-Your-Neighbour Night with our two sister communities.

The role of our WI has changed through the years. During World War II we provided care packages through the Red Cross for the enlisted men and women. The one-room school was also our focus until its closure in 1972.

We give financial support to our community hall, hospitals, schools, USC, Salvation Army and many other worthwhile causes. We raise funds by quilting, catering, roll calls and various other ways as opportunities present themselves.

We are now twenty-three members strong, and we are privileged to have three charter members that are still active. We are "indebted to the past and committed to the future."

Bideford

Miss MacDonald organized the Bideford WI in 1944. The first officers were Mrs. Keith MacDougall, President; Mrs. Ivan Millar, Vice-President; Mrs. William Grant, Secretary-Treasurer.

This WI branch was instrumental in promoting the erection of a Regional High School and the Stewart Memorial Health Centre. They sponsored swimming classes and devoted their efforts towards the general improvement of their school.

The Bideford WI remains active in their community today, with thirteen current members.

Birch Hill

Mary Montgomery

On November 1, 1922, ten ladies met at the home of Mrs. Leslie MacLean to discuss forming a Women's Institute in Birch Hill. After contacting the Department of Agriculture, fifteen ladies met with Mrs. Betsy Carruthers, Supervisor of WI, on the evening of November 20, 1922 Mrs. Edgar Doherty's home. The Birch Hill WI came into being. Mrs. Robert Yeo served as our first President, Mrs. John Maynard Sr. first Vice-President, Mrs. Leslie MacLean second Vice-President, and Mrs. Ruby Dennis Secretary-Treasurer. Two ladies, Mrs. Yeo and Mrs. Dennis, had been members of the Lot 16 WI, formed in 1917. Our WI is a daughter of this earlier group.

The Institute members began to work immediately for improvements in the school and cultural life of the community, and this role continues today. They made repairs to the school, purchased much needed equipment for it, and donated to various charitable organizations. By 1924 our membership had reached thirty, the highest ever recorded, and at one meeting held at the home of Mrs. John MacLean on July 16, 1924, seventy-five people were present.

Programs were both enjoyable and educational with readings, recitations, songs, skits, debates, guest speakers, and demonstrations of skills. From the earliest years, one of the main objectives of the WI was to improve educational facilities in the area. When the new school opened in 1950, our WI contributed $1000.00 towards the building fund, and helped with wiring and equipment expenses. We also lobbied for a consolidated school, which we hoped would eventually replace the small community school. This dream became a reality when Ellerslie Consolidated School opened in Ellerslie in 1972.

In May of 1951, the new Stewart Memorial Health Centre opened in Tyne Valley. This Centre was the result of the combined efforts of 18 surrounding Women's Institutes, including Birch Hill. The hospital guest book pages from 1953 contain signatures of international delegates to the ACWW conference in Toronto, who took a tour of the Maritimes and visited our community. Ladies from India, Ceylon, Africa, Haiti, Norway, Rhodesia, Australia, England, Scotland and the US stayed as overnight guests in surrounding homes.

From the earliest years, Birch Hill WI has participated in many projects in the community and in the surrounding districts. We have celebrated several anniversaries with banquets and special events. Our Charter Member, Mrs. Enid Birch, cut the cake at our 75th anniversary in 1977, and she still attends our WI celebrations. This past summer we honoured three women who have been members for fifty years or more: Enid Birch, Jeanette Birch, and Eliza Newcombe. We currently have twelve Life Members.

Birch Grove

The Birch Grove WI of Freetown, PEI organized on February 4, 1932 at the home of Marguerite Schurman. There were fifteen charter members, and Mrs. Schurman served as the first President.

The early minutes tell of many interesting activities. In 1933 a parlour social at Bertie Jardine's raised $11.80. Ice cream and pantry sales realized approximately $20, and the average monthly collection was 90 cents.

Our members were busy with "Home and Country". We purchased new books for the school library each month, along with the large never-ending supplies of necessities such as toilet tissue and paper towels. We also paid for the spring cleaning of the large two-room school, which cost $2.50 each time. We gave fruit baskets to the sick and shut-ins, and supported the hospital, donating one bedspread and a pair of pillowcases.

The WI played a large roll in the social life of the community. To raise money, we rented the Community Hall and put on plays, socials, and concerts. In 1934 we purchased a piano for the Hall. By 1935 our membership had grown to thirty-five.

We continue to support "Home and Country" with regular contributions to various WI projects. We also make donations to hospitals and high schools, fire and accident victims, cancer patients, special Olympic participants, and figure skating groups. We remember the elderly, sick and shut-ins at home, in hospital, in the manors, and in institutions.

Our present fundraising events include card parties, auction, luncheons, and our annual variety concert.

In 1956 our branch took over the Birch Grove Community Hall, which had fallen into disrepair. We paid off the mortgage in 1957. The upkeep of this 1919 Community Hall is a large financial commitment, with maintenance, fuel, electricity, taxes, insurance, painting, grass cutting, and planting and tending flower beds. Several years ago we undertook major renovations from the foundation up. We restored the hall to its original beauty inside and out, and won several Rural Beautification Awards for our efforts.

The Birch Hill branch supported the community when we launched the Freetown history, *Freetown, Past and Present*, and nominated Robert S. P. Jardine for the Les Corbot Award, which he received for his work on the history. We also supported Mr. Jardine in his effort to add a cenotaph to the Freetown People's Cemetery.

After 68 years, our membership has declined. We only have seven members, all Life Members, but we are still very active.

In 1997, our President was Jean Schurman, daughter-in-law of the first President of 65 years ago. Our current members are Connie Reeves, Vice-President; Joyce Simmons, Secretary; Kay Baglole, Treasurer; Blanche Jardine and Lois Paynter, directors; Vivian Drummond and Joyce Simmons, auditors.

Bloomfield Corner

Miss Haszard organized the Bloomfield Corner WI on May 7, 1930. The first officers were Mrs. Urban Pineau, President; Mrs. Joseph Wedge, Vice-President; Mrs. Urban Pineau, Secretary-Treasurer.

The Bloomfield Corner WI was always interested in health and education. They improved the school with a new floor, new ceiling, new seats, septic toilets, and many other projects. They enlarged and fenced their schoolyard. This WI was also very conscious of the need for various services, and assisted in canvassing for the Red Cross, Handicraft Van, Home Nursing Courses, First Aid classes, and swimming classes. They contributed to a scholarship fund, assisted a refugee child, and encouraged good reading material. At Christmas, Bloomfield Corner WI members would visit all sick and shut-ins and give them "special treats". They also entered their school in the Rural Beautification contest.

The Bloomfield Corner WI was active through the 1960s, but there is no record of them since then.

Bonshaw

The Bonshaw branch of the WI organized in August of 1928. They enjoyed over fifty years of membership before disbanding in 1981.

Brackley

A group of women residing in the Brackley district met in the schoolhouse with a Women's Institute supervisor on October 2, 1947, and banded together as the Brackley Women's Institute. The first officers were Bertha Pierce, President; Gladys Carr, Vice-President; Gladys MacKay, Secretary; Pearl Jackson, Treasurer.

Our monthly meetings are educational, social, and well attended! Our main objectives were to beautify the school property, provide school playground equipment, and teach highway safety to our boys and girls. We provided sewing classes for the girls of our community. We also provided musical instruction and equipment at the school, and children of all ages still enter the competitions at the Provincial

Music Festival, with excellent results. Uniting with a neighbouring WI group, we enjoyed classes in adult sewing and handicraft instruction. We also sponsored First Aid classes for the community. We found the skills we learned in quilting classes most interesting. Most members readily shared their talents and provided for those less fortunate by participating in Red Cross knitting and sewing. On the lighter side, we had fun get-togethers, card parties, cake sales, talent shows and games. Although our men were not WI members, we could not have accomplished all our many activities without their support and help over the years.

We help those who needed special care, and we helped our teachers and pupils during the years that our local school was open. We share our wealth, whether monetary or our personal talents, by responding to the welfare of others such as orphans, sick and shut-ins, the bereaved, newborns and newlyweds, and less fortunate people across our province and country. We assisted the Red Cross to solicit for blood donor clinics and we volunteered during the clinics. We collected more than 100 books of all types, and forwarded them to a university in the far north of Canada that had lost their library in a fire. We always contributed to Pennies for Friendship and our adopted child, both projects of the PEIWI. Our branch and individual members give generous support to the QEH.

We tested our talents by participating in the Prince Edward Island Drama Festival, but we were quite successful according to the judges' findings, as we portrayed the life of women in the years of our Women's Institute founder, Adelaide Hoodless.

One major undertaking of the Brackley Women's Institute was to provide a history of our community, entitled **Brackley Past and Present**. We had some assistance, but our branch did most of the hard work! Some copies of this history have traveled as far as New York, USA and Western Canada.

Brackley WI received a Community Improvement Award in 1993 from the Rural Beautification Society, for our efforts in making our community more appealing to the eye of all who travel through our district. Brackley Women's Institute also participates in the Rural Beautification Pilot 80 Project together with several other communities across the Province. This helps to keep our community clean and an inviting place to live. This project started in 1980 and continues until the year 2000.

A few special events brought honour to individual members of our Institute branch. In 1988 the first Adelaide Hoodless Award of Honour went to Bertha Pierce for her service. Bertha Pierce, a strong advocate of rural beautification, was also the first recipient of the Rural Beautification Society's award for her flower garden display, and she won Provincial honours for this same garden in 1990. Our branch was also successful in having Mrs. Pierce, who is a nursing sister, presented with a tulip tribute. The Dutch royal family gave this tribute to nursing sisters across Canada, as a "thank you" from Holland to Canadians for our efforts during the during the Second World War. Mrs. Pierce also received a Governor-General's Commemorative Medal, in celebration of the 125th Anniversary of Canadian Confederation, for her outstanding contribution to her fellow citizens, community and country. Catherine Callbeck, a former Premier, presented the medal to Mrs. Pierce.

Glenn Younker received the Canada Voluntary Award of Merit for her life's dedication and immeasurable hours of service to her community through her work with Women's Institute and the United Church Women. Our branch nominated her for this award, presented by Catherine Callbeck. Our branch also presented Mrs. Younker with her Life Membership at the same time.

Brackley Beach
Ellen Cudmore

In 1995 we celebrated our 50th anniversary at Brackley Beach WI, and this occasion caused us to reflect on the initiatives and accomplishments of this group of women. 1945 to 1995 represents five decades of our commitment, dedication, and continuous work for "Home and Country".

Between 1940 and 1945, the women in Brackley Beach were organized as a Red Cross Society, and worked to raise money and provide knitted items, quilts, and boxes of food and soap for the war effort.

On the evening of October 19, 1945 nineteen women met at the home of Catherine and Edward MacCallum, and agreed to organize as a Women's Institute. As the world returned to peacetime in 1945, efforts turned to home. The renovation of Howe's Hall was our first major project. Improvements included everything from the installation of electricity to providing a pump, oil furnace, paintings and furniture. The WI and members of the community contributed much planning, work and cooperation to this initiative.

Our WI also supported the local school. We supplied musical instruments, assistance to hire music teachers, and treats for the children. We also provided necessities such as tissue, drinking cups, and even yeast, until our school amalgamated with Brackley in 1973. In March 1974 our WI purchased the school property from the Unit 3 School Board, and renamed it the Brackley Beach Community Centre.

From 1982 to 1984 the old school received a new lease on life as we remodeled, roofed, lifted, gave it a new foundation, and added on until we had the building that we meet in today. This was only possible with the help, support and dedication of community members, not to mention the dinners served, wood cut, card parties and auctions held, donations, and hours upon hours of labour volunteered. The Centre has weathered and witnessed celebrations such as New Year's Eve, Canada Day, anniversaries, receptions, Meet Your Neighbour Nights and Halloween. It is the meeting place for the North Shore Lion's Club and for the Playschool, which is now in its 15th year, and we are very pleased that the young mothers and preschool children continue to meet there.

Our outreach to the community continues as we remember and visit the sick and bereaved, and welcome newlyweds, new families and babies. Our WI also fulfills its commitment to provincial, national and international WI projects. We have supported many worthwhile Island causes and have completed many canvasses. We contribute to the Queen Elizabeth Hospital.

In June of 1994 we were pleased and honoured to host an Island wide reception for Valerie Fisher of Australia, World President of the ACWW. On her brief visit to the Island Mrs. Fisher was very impressed by the friendliness of the people and the beauty of the land.

She was especially pleased when our own "Anne", Kirsten MacCallum, gave her a special welcome.

Fundraising is a major part of our work and has taken every form available to us. We have fed everyone from the birdwatchers at sunrise to the fire fighters at Christmas. We have hosted. We have auctioned everything except our mates and our homes. We have worked together as a team. Our Christmas Luncheon and Bazaar has become an annual fundraising event for the upkeep of the Community Centre.

The care for and appearance of our community has been a major commitment, and has resulted in many years of successful competition in the Rural Beautification Society. We appreciate and acknowledge the participation of all community residents and landowners. To commemorate the 50th anniversary of our WI, we purchased a new entrance sign for the community, and a canvass of the community made the purchase of two additional entrance signs possible.

While we can look at the concrete accomplishments of our group, we also know of the intangibles – the deep friendships which have developed, the care and concern for others, the knowledge that we have friends who are there to help and support us, and that heavy burdens can be shared. We also know that each one has something to contribute and that everyone benefits when we pull together. We know it is possible to have fun preparing potato salad for 200, and that laughter makes washing mountains of dishes easier.

Education takes many forms, from practical experience to programs and guest speakers, and is a cornerstone of each meeting. The leadership given by women, their dedication to its principles, the many hours of volunteer work, and their commitment to continue to work for "Home and Country", is fundamental to the life or our WI.

These are some of the areas where our WI has been involved. There are many more. There are many projects to undertake and support. Many tasks have been accomplished and no doubt many have been left undone. We have done everything we could with those who were available to carry out the tasks. There is no question that there is a role for the WI to play in keeping this community vital and alive.

In concluding, we add Margaret Mead's comment on teamwork. "Never doubt that a small group of thoughtful, committed people can change the world. Indeed, it is the only thing that ever has."

Breadalbane

The Breadalbane WI branch first organized in June of 1933. The first officers were Mrs. Hedley Woodside, President, and Mrs. Pomeroy Murray, Secretary.

The Breadalbane WI was active in their community for almost fifty years. They contributed to the upkeep of their community cemetery, hall, and school. The Breadalbane WI disbanded in 1981.

Bridgetown

Bridgetown WI organized on August 23, 1926. The first officers were Mrs. Hodgson MacDonald, President; Mrs. Laughlyn McKay, Vice-President; Mrs. George Ross, Secretary.

The Bridgetown WI enjoyed more than fifty years of activity in their community. They contributed to their schools, and gave to many charitable organizations. The Bridgetown WI disbanded in 1980.

Brooklyn

The Brooklyn WI first organized in February of 1930. The first officers were Mrs. Edgar MacArthur, President; Mrs. J. Fred White, Vice-President; Mrs. James Hodgson, Secretary-Treasurer.

The main efforts were to help pay for their new school and to assist with general upkeep. They supplied desks and sanitary toilets, storm windows and installed electricity. The Brooklyn WI disbanded in 1995, citing a lack of members as their reason.

Bunbury

The Bunbury WI first organized on June 8, 1949. The first President was Mrs. Harry Wood, and the first Secretary was Mrs. Cyril Wood. This branch was active throughout the 1960s, but there is no record of them since that time.

Burton

Burton WI was established in 1953. Their first officers were Mrs. Peter Dalton, President; Mrs. Loretta Collicutt, Vice-President; Mrs. Coleridge Rogers, Secretary; Mrs. Harold Howard, Treasurer.

The Burton branch provided prizes and treats for school children. They remembered the sick and shut-ins, contributed to all worthy causes, and sponsored a First Aid course, swimming classes, and a 4H sewing club. This branch also sponsored a scholarship fund in their convention area. The Burton WI was active through the 1960s, but subsequently disbanded.

Cable Head East

The Cable Head East WI first organized on December 3, 1958. Their first President was Mrs. A.J. Larkin. This branch has disbanded.

Caledonia

Caledonia WI began in May of 1932. Mrs. D.L. MacPherson was its first President. This branch is no longer active.

Cambridge

The Cambridge WI first organized in February of 1949 by Supervisor Maylea Boswell. The first officers were: Mrs. James Lanigan, President; Mrs. Clyde Kerwin, Vice-President; Mrs. Mary Giddings, Secretary-Treasurer. In February of 2000 our Institute will be fifty-one years old. In 1981 we set our branch record for membership, thirteen. We now have eight members, and two are Life Members. One of these Life Members was sixteen years old when she joined.

In the early years, Cambridge WI held concerts, dances, auctions, pantry sales, and chicken suppers to raise money. Our branch supported the school, gave to charitable organizations, and looked after the needs of our community. Our WI owned the Cambridge one-room school, and sold it for $1000 in 1980. The school now sits at Seal Cove Campground in Murray Harbour North.

Since November of 1980, we sponsor winter card nights at the Cambridge Hall. We later added summer card nights. With the card plays, raffle tickets on different items, and the annual Christmas Box, we fundraise for our various activities. The Cambridge Hall Committee has recently taken over organizing the card nights. We have also catered to a few wedding and birthday parties, and occasionally we get together and have concerts and crokinole parties.

We have donated to the Cambridge Hall many times for upkeep (for example drapes for the windows, paint for the floors and hall, organ fund, refrigerator for the kitchen, and fire insurance). We also still make charitable donations. We still donate to some of our older charities, and we have picked up some new ones as well. We also donate to our community, whether it is to a family for a loss of their home due to fire, newlyweds, babies, or to the sick or shut-ins, or whoever needs help.

Over the years we always made time to go out and relax from a year of hard work, whether we go to the King's Playhouse in Georgetown to see a play or just out for a meal. It is a lot of work, but we all say it is worth every breath of air we take. It makes us feel good to do all of these things.

Canoe Cove

Rhoda MacKinnon, Velma MacPhee, Florence MacCannell

Canoe Cove Women's Institute first organized on September 15, 1950. Twelve members were present at that first meeting, and two of the original ladies are currently active members. Before the formation of Canoe Cove WI, several women in the district met frequently to assist with the needs of the school. This was similar to a Home and School group. This group expanded and evolved into a Women's Institute, which has flourished for several years.

When the Prince Edward Island government consolidated the public school system, most of our community's students were bussed to other schools. In 1973, Canoe Cove Women's Institute members made the wise decision to purchase our venerable school building, and this provides a center for Institute meetings and community gatherings.

As society changed and time passed, our community's interest in Women's Institute declined, and the remaining members formed a Community Group. This group met periodically and still opened meetings with the Mary Stewart Collect and paid WI dues for several years.

Interest for an organized Women's Institute revived in the late 1980s, and on October 15, 1988 Canoe Cove Women's Institute reorganized and continues to thrive. We have had many interesting meetings and members contribute to various worthwhile causes. Two of our present members, Florence MacCannell and Marty MacFadyen, deserve special mention. Florence wrote *A History of Canoe Cove*, published in 1992. In 1994, Marty won first place provincially and nationally in the Women's Institute Tweedsmuir Competition for her entry, "An Album Tour of My Community."

Cape Traverse

The Cape Traverse WI first organized on September 10, 1931. The first officers were Mrs. Louis Muttart, President, and Mrs. Gordon Harvey, Secretary.

No other information is available on this branch. They disbanded in 1970, citing a lack of members as the reason.

Cape Wolfe

Mary Robin, Supervisor of Women's Institutes, first organized the Cape Wolfe WI on May 18, 1950. Mrs. Lloyd Cook served as first President, Mrs. Alvin Costain as Vice-President, and Mrs. Annie DeMoss was Secretary-Treasurer.

The main activities of this group were to sponsor swimming classes for all children of the community, and to give leadership to a 4H Garment Club. Active in the 1960s, the Cape Wolfe WI later disbanded.

Cardigan

There is no information available regarding exactly when the Cardigan WI first organized or disbanded. They were active in the

1920s and the 1960s, and they are also known as having been one of the early branches to support the efforts to build a provincial Sanatorium.

Carleton Siding
Lorraine Lowther

Carleton Siding Women's Institute has twelve members, and seven of these are Life Members. We hold our monthly meetings at one of the member's homes. We have wedding showers for couples getting married in our community, and send "get well" cards, sympathy cards, cards to welcome new babies born in the community, and "thinking of you" cards to any shut-ins. We also decorate, fill and deliver decorated Christmas Boxes for anyone age 80 and over.

We have donated books to Sherwood Home, white gift boxes for Hillsborough Hospital, and collected canned goods and paper products for Anderson House. We give used clothing to the Family service Bureau and the Salvation Army. We donate cleaning supplies to the East Prince Committee on Family Violence. We donated a case of baby food to Bosnia. We knit for the Red Cross, and make baby quilts for Prince County Hospital. Each year at Christmas, we make little party favours for the hospital trays at Prince County Hospital.

We donated $200 to the Endoscopy Equipment and $500 to Catscan PEI. We were also involved with the "Man in Motion – Rick Hansen" campaign, with a small reception at the Borden Legion Home. We sponsored a walkathon for Terry Fox. We give to different organizations, such as the Water Project in Kenya, Sudan Project, Mann House, Victoria General Hospital, Isaac Walton Killam Telethon, Nova Scotia Miners' Relief Fund, Amherst Cove Library Fund, the High School Graduation Funds, Senior Women's National Baseball Championship, Jillian Larkin Leukemia Fund, and various Fire Victim Funds. We also donate to the Holland College Graduation Fund at the Summerside Division.

We collect for different organizations, like the Heart and Stroke, Cancer and Salvation Army, to name a few. Our Institute won second prize for an album we made which included the houses in our community. We also started the local Community School program, which is still active and held in our new Amherst Cove School. Our Institute also started the Foot Clinic in our area for problem feet for seniors and others in the community and surrounding areas. As usual, each year we are still responsible for the Annual Roadside Cleanup.

Central Bedeque

The Central Bedeque WI first organized in 1918, with Supervisor Hazel Sterns presiding. In 1928 our branch participated in the movement to establish a provincial sanatorium.

Central Bedeque WI always supported the school, providing items such as hardwood floors, a pump, a flag pole and flag, Christmas treats, an organ, a music teacher, a stove, and desks. During the Second World War, our branch contributed sewing, knitting, quilts, pajamas, and Christmas boxes for soldiers to the Red Cross.

Our branch has supported many other organizations, such as the Prince County Hospital, the TB League, the Polio Foundation, the Cancer Society, the Salvation Army, Ambulance Fund, and the Alexandra Orphanage in England. We also support FWIC Projects such as the mobile kitchen, Pennies for Friendship, the Infirmary, Food Bank, Kinsmen's Club, Milk for Britain, and Baby Food For Bosnia. Locally, we support Summerside Meals on Wheels, an area kindergarten, the Music Festival, prizes for Three Oaks Senior High School, the Roadside Cleanup, and the Stereotactic Mammography machine.

During the years 1941-1948, records indicate our branch made at least 86 quilts either for sale or for donation to someone in need.

A number of our members have received Life Memberships, including Ruth Schurman, Ethel Hogg, Mabel Dawson, Ruth Callbeck, Gertrude Webster, Jean Green, Norma Reid, Jean MacCaull, and Martha Waugh.

One of the highlights for our group in recent years was a visit to the boardroom of the Executive Council of the PEI Government and the Premier's Office.

We erected two signs on the north and east entrances to Bedeque, with the words "Welcome to Central Bedeque" on them. We also helped with the Bedeque Canada Day festivities in 1998 and 1999, and contributed to Operation Christmas Child boxes in November 1999.

Central Lot 16

The Central Lot 16 WI first organized in 1917. The first officers were Mrs. Will Cotton, President, and Lulu MacLean, Secretary.

This branch centered its early efforts on improving their school, and assisting in all charitable causes.

Although not a large group, the Central Lot 16 Women's Institute was involved in community activities and supported many WI projects. In August of 1957, Central and Southwest Lot 16 Women's Institutes, at that time a single branch, celebrated their 40th anniversary with a banquet for members and husbands at the Lot 16 Community Hall.

In 1976 Central Lot 16 WI published the history of their community, **Pages From the Past,** which received recognition from the Heritage Foundation. For her efforts in spearheading this project, the Women's Institute made Mrs. Eileen Manderson a Life Member, and gave her the Heritage Plaque to place in her new home. Mrs. Manderson again brought honor to the Women's Institute and community when she became "Woman of the Year" at the 1977 Summerside Lobster Carnival and Livestock Exhibition.

Central Lot 16 WI had one of their members, Mary MacLean, serve on the provincial board for ten years, two of which she was provincial President (1975-1977). This stimulated interest and kept the members in closer contact with provincial, national, and international activities.

The Central Lot 16 branch disbanded in the 1980s.

Central Royalty

Central Royalty WI first organized in 1921. The first officers were Myrtle S. Harper, President; Mrs. James Roper, Vice-President; Mrs. Myrtle Ross, Secretary-Treasurer.

The Central Royalty branch built a one-room school in their district, and when that was no longer big enough, they built another two-room school. They instituted annual "School Fairs", and two of their members were the initial driving force behind the Music Festivals in PEI.

The Central Royalty WI was active throughout the 1960s, but subsequently disbanded.

Chelton

The Chelton WI first organized on October 20, 1926. The first officers were Mrs. Earl Pearson, President; Mrs. Charles Schurman, Vice-President; Mrs. Henry Affleck, Secretary -Treasurer.

Most of the Chelton WI's efforts centered on the school. They painted the interior and exterior of the building several times. They erected fence and donated seats, a teacher's desk, chair, blackboards, and many other necessary articles. This branch ensured that at Christmas shut-ins received boxes and the sick received fruit. The Chelton WI assisted with Red Cross work, and contributed to worthy appeals.

Active through the 1960s, the Chelton WI later disbanded.

Cherry Valley

The Cherry Valley Women's Institute began with their charter meeting on December 18, 1945 at the home of Mrs. Trueman Jenkins. Two charter members, Mrs. Hazel Ings and Mrs. Katherine Ings, are still active members.

Our 35th Anniversary took place at the Kirkwood Motel on April 4, 1981, and seven members received Life Memberships at this event – Mrs. Hazel Ings, Mrs. Ruth MacLeod Sr., Mrs. Elsie MacDonald, Mrs. Katherine Ings, Mrs. Norma Hayden, Mrs. Mary (Reg.) McInnis, and Mrs. Ruth MacLeod Jr. On October 30, 1985, we held our 40th anniversary at the newly renovated Cherrycliffe Community Centre, where Mrs. Bertha Young received a Life Membership. Mrs. Wanda Ings received her Life Membership in 1987. On November 7, 1995 Cherry Valley WI celebrated our 50th anniversary at Cherrycliffe Community Centre.

Cherry Valley WI helps support the upkeep and financing of the Community Centre, our home for many community activities and meetings. We donate annually to many local, provincial, and worldwide organizations. We give sick treats and Christmas treats as needed to the sick, elderly and shut-ins. We enjoy "Secret Pal" card and gift exchange.

We use programs of information on agriculture, health issues, environment, education, and safety at monthly meetings. These programs inform members of ways to improve quality of life for themselves, their families, their communities, and the world.

Chestow

The Chestow WI organized in 1951, and was for at least twenty years before disbanding.

Clermont

Mary Robin organized the Clermont WI on May 13, 1953. The first officers were Mrs. Edson Rayner, President; Mrs. Cecil Mill, Vice-President; Mrs. William Mill, Secretary-Treasurer.

In 1954 the school won 2nd prize in the Rural Beautification competition and the R.T. Holman trophy. The school closed in the 1960s, and students now attend in Kensington. The Clermont WI remained active through the 1960s, but later disbanded.

Clinton

In October 1939, many ladies from our district felt they could work more effectively for "Home and Country" if they became organized and worked with Women's Institutes. On October 16th, 1939, at the home of Mrs. Lottie Paynter with supervision from Mrs. Mary MacDonald, WI Provincial Executive, thirty-two women sat down together and held the first meeting of the Clinton WI. Of those thirty-two women, five are still living, and eighteen were with us in 1989 to celebrate 50 years of working together "For Home and Country". Margaret MacKay deserves honourable mention, since she has continued to be a member, and for many of these years she had 100% attendance at meetings.

Clinton WI worked in close cooperation with the Red Cross, knitting socks, sweaters and sewing children's clothing. We sent many boxes to soldiers overseas. The main goal was to work for the betterment of our children. We accomplished this by working together with the school. We financed our endeavours by voluntarism, government grants, card parties, grab bags, pantry sales, suppers, afternoon teas, ice-cream socials, potluck suppers and many more activities.

Clinton WI donated Kleenex, Band-Aids, paper towels, dishes, and many other items to the school. We provided school lunches, treats and prizes. Our branch purchased a piano and funded a music teacher. We helped to organize swimming classes, 4-H, Halloween parties and school picnics. When the schools consolidated, we voiced our opposition. Consolidation took place, however, and we automatically added the Kensington schools to our list. For years Clinton WI members took their turn and accepted the responsibility of serving hot lunches at the school. We also volunteered at the Community Gardens. When electricity came to our area, the WI covered the cost of installing electricity in both the Hall and the school.

Over the years Clinton WI has contributed to the community and to many charitable organizations, either by canvassing the district or donating directly from our own funds. After the New London Rural Fire Department organized, the WI collected membership dues. One of our members, Marion Woodside, tastefully painted three "Welcome to Clinton" road signs. We were instrumental in having the mobile x-ray unit come to the area, and for two years we had sewing instructors from the WI office give instruction on basic sewing. The Community Gardens Beauty Pageant has many times had a beautiful contestant from the area, partly funded by the WI.

For entertainment, we hold contests, give readings, welcome special speakers and we entertain our twin WI. We remember the sick and shut-ins at Christmas. Since Panorama Park opened at the top of the hill overlooking Hardings Creek and the South West River, a committee from the WI sees that flowers are planted.

Our members have participated in many worthwhile projects. This would not have been possible without the support and co-operation of our spouses, for which we are very grateful. At one particular time, we were asked to draft a plan for a modern farm home. With the assistance of Mr. Bruce Clark, Clinton WI won a $25 prize.

Clinton WI members have received a number of honours for their efforts. One of our members, Nina Pickering, won a prize in the Coats Embroidery Contest. She also won first prize for the Island in the Tweedsmuir Cup Contest for her entry of six hooked chair seat covers. Lieutenant Governor Hyndman saw them, and suggested that the one with the Island Crest on it would make suitable chair seat covers for the dining room chairs in Government House. Ms. Pickering hooked the twenty-eight chair seat covers in 1964. A few years later she hooked treads for the steps leading to the bed in the Queen's bedroom at Government House.

Two of our members, Enid MacKay and Phyllis Paynter received the Kensington Recreation Association Volunteer Award. In 1992 Phyllis Paynter received the Lescarbot Award presented by the Government of Canada for her "Outstanding contribution to Cultural Activities". In 1996, Mary Sullivan received an Award from the New London Tourist Association in Appreciation of her many years of Service and Support to the Tourist Industry. One member received a prize at the Lobster Carnival for a log cabin quilt she had made. On November 12, 1974, we honoured a senior member of our WI when she reached her 90th birthday. She was present for the occasion, which we celebrated at the home of Mrs. Enid MacKay.

In 1972 our WI selected a committee to write the history of the community. The chairperson of the committee was a senior citizen and she, along with other senior citizens and two WI members, Edith Woodside and Mary Sullivan, compiled the history. For a number of years we prepared floats for the Harvest Festival Parade, capturing first place in the WI competition in 1988, and in 1989 we won first place in the WI competition category in the Fireman's Parade. Each year we help with the Fireman's concert by supplying one or two numbers. We have a WI member on the Management Committee of the New London and Area Fire Department.

We have organized several community picnics since the change in the school system resulted there not being a school picnic. We have also had "Meet Your Neighbour Nights", and we present new residents with a history book of Clinton.

In October 1981, Nina Pickering, Alma Henderson, Margaret MacKay, Blanche Heaney and the President, Janet Cotton met for the regular meeting. Because our membership was getting small, they took a vote at that meeting as to whether to disband Clinton WI. The vote was in the affirmative. However, since several members were absent and one or two of them were on the executive, some felt the decision was unfair. In January 1982, because of the energetic willpower and foresight of some, we held another meeting. The purpose of the meeting was again to decide whether Clinton WI should continue. Mrs. Mary Palmer from the Provincial Board, was present at that meeting, and she read a letter from Doreen McInnis. In this letter Doreen quoted from the immediate past President of the ACWW, Dame Reigh Roe of Australia, who said, "It's not quantity that makes an organization, but quality". The members all voted in favour of continuing. We now have fourteen members.

In 1994 our WI was instrumental in organizing a district "Home Coming", and approximately 275 residents and former residents attended.

In preparing this report I could not help noticing the harmony, good will and the hard work that prevails among WI members. The Women's Institute in Clinton has been and still is the main chain in our Community, and the members are the links. Keep up the good work.

I end with a quotation:

"Alone our work is of little worth

Together we are the Lords of the Earth,

So its all for each, and each for all

For united we stand, divided we fall."

May we all continue to work together for "Home and Country."

Clyde River
Helen M. MacPhail

The Clyde River Women's Institute organized in 1950, and continues to be a vibrant and interesting branch. In recent years, our annual membership has ranged from twenty-three to thirty-one members, with an average of twenty-five. Attendance at regular monthly meetings averages seventeen, with full participation in special events and fundraisers. Seven charter members received Life Memberships at our 40th anniversary, and seven more received Life Memberships in 1990. Our branch holds monthly meetings, a summer outing and several fundraisers each year.

A primary goal of the Clyde River WI is maintenance of the Riverview Community Centre (formerly the Clyde River School), of which we are the proud owners. The Centre is the home of many community-based activities. In 1984, our Institute applied for a Canada Works Project to renovate and upgrade the building. We completed the project in 1986, and with a community canvas and several fundraisers, we paid off the mortgage for the work in 1988. Fundraising is an ongoing task, with a new furnace, a new well and a complete interior and exterior decorating accomplished in five years. Clyde River WI also donates annually to various provincial, national and international Women's Institute projects, and we donate to various local requests.

Riverview Community Centre is the location for many community events. In the last twenty years, events such as the annual Christmas parties and Canada Day celebrations have been very successful opportunities to enhance community spirit. For the last three years our activities now include the children's Christmas party, staged in the afternoon. This has proven to be very popular with the kiddies. We also have a new "Keep in Touch" committee, formed with the purpose of visiting former members who no longer attend meetings. Visiting with some faithful ladies who supported the Clyde River WI over the years is indeed a rewarding event.

The Riverview Community Centre is used by the Presbyterian and Baptist churches in the community, and by community family groups, private parties, wedding showers, craft activities, Community Council meetings, and of course, Women's Institute meetings.

In 1996, Clyde River hosted the District 9 Convention, and in 1997 we hosted a busload of WI members from Great Britain. We made many friendships that day, and since that meeting, we now carry on a regular correspondence between several new English and Canadian friends.

Several members of the Clyde River WI have taken leadership roles at a provincial board level. As we now go forward into the new millennium, we can look back with pride at the many achievements we have made "For Home and Country".

Coleman

The Coleman WI first organized in September of 1921. The first officers were Mrs. J.B. Crozier, President; Mrs. James Arsenault, Vice-President; Mrs. C.W. Williams, Secretary-Treasurer.

The Coleman branch focussed their efforts on their school, before disbanding in 1972.

Conway

The Conway WI organized on September 1921. The first meeting was held at Mrs. W.J. MacKay's home on October 4, 1921. Bessie Carruthers was Supervisor of Women's Institutes at that time. The first officers were Mrs. David Smith, honorary President; Mrs. W.J. MacKay, President; Mrs. Elige Palmer, Vice-President; Miss Katie O'Halloran, Secretary-Treasurer.

The Conway WI made the school their chief project since they organized. They bought books and supplies, and furnished a room. They erected a monument and plaque in memory of the soldiers who fought in the First World War. They also sponsored collections for charities and helped those in need in the district.

The Conway WI was active through the 1960s, but later disbanded.

Cornwall

The Cornwall WI first organized in conjunction with York Point and Marshfield in 1913. These three branches separated in 1955.

Since the 1970s the Cornwall WI participated in a variety of activities, some of which include collecting for the cancer fund, United Appeal, and other charitable organizations. Our members also attend District Conventions and other WI related activities. We donate to school libraries, remember shut-ins at Christmas, and provide gifts for the hospitals.

Cornwall WI has enjoyed numerous presentations and speakers on various topics. Some of these have included women and the law, drugs and their availability, life on Baffin Island, and numerous talks on health issues such as cancer. We have also enjoyed many demonstrations on topics of interest to members.

Over the years, we participated in the Roadside Cleanup, and assisted at the Provincial Exhibition at the WI building and at Blood Donor clinics.

In July 1972, one of the founding members of Cornwall WI died, and in December of 1978, another founding lady, Mrs. Gordon MacMillan died. In 1986, Mrs. George MacMillan, a lifelong member, received the Islander of the Year award. Mrs. MacMillan died this year.

Coronation

Coronation WI organized in 1913, and held their first meeting in the French River Hall. When the First World War broke out the Institute changed to a Women's Patriotic Association (WPA), and the members did work for the Red Cross such as sewing and knitting. The Institute meetings were thought to be "a great advantage to the women of the different districts, because of the social spirit of helpfulness and by the exchange of ideas which broadens the mind." The WPA disbanded after a few years, and so on February 23, 1937 the Coronation WI re-formed. They decided on that name since 1937 was the coronation year of King George VI. Early members held their meetings in the French River Hall, but with the Hall gone, we now hold meetings in our homes.

In the early years our Institute looked after the Park Corner school, supplying them with a music teacher, having fundraisers to help with the upkeep of the school, and buying school supplies. Today we still maintain the school, and hold some of our regular meetings there. Many in the community use the old school for 4H meetings, wedding showers and receptions, pancake breakfasts, suppers, and in 1996 Paula Clark rented the school for the summer to open a language institute to teach English to Japanese.

Our Institute has been actively involved in the community. We help out with the New London Fire Department's annual concert, the lunch program, the Queen Elizabeth Elementary School, Clinton View Lodge, Anderson House, the New London kindergarten, and the hospitals. In the 1970s Ralph Hostetter donated land to the Institute for a dump site, which we maintained until 1997.

The first school reunion of the Park Corner School was held on June 27, 1987. In 1988 we celebrated the 75th anniversary of the provincial WI, and participated in a new WI activity called twinning. Our first twin Institute was Rennie's Road. In 1991 one of our members, Brenda Montgomery, received the Volunteer of the Year award at the Kensington Festival. We give treats, cards, flowers and memorials to members in times of sickness and bereavement. Many of our members have enjoyed the WI workshops and conventions. Today our Institute continues to learn new things through workshops, kits available from the WI office, and guest speakers.

With so much changing over the years, the Institute has continued to maintain its place in the community, always there to lend a helping hand.

Covehead Road

Covehead Road WI continues to follow the example set by the founding members in 1931. In doing so, we remain committed to fulfilling and upholding the aims and objectives of our organization.

Our branch makes a conscious effort to meet and address the needs of our members and their families. As well, we play a significant and vital role in the life and growth of our community, which holds us in very high regard. We also enjoy a wonderful working relationship with the local Fire Department, each supportive of the other's endeavours.

During the past twenty years, there have been a number of achievements and accomplishments, highlights and honours. For instance, as a result of a resolution submitted by our branch in 1980 and supported by all levels of Women's Institute, the visually impaired now have access to Canadian paper currency that they can easily identify by distinctive markings.

In 1981 Doreen B. MacInnis, a third generation member of Covehead Road WI, was elected President of the PEIWI. In 1996, she was the recipient of the prestigious Adelaide Hoodless Award of Honour. In 1999 Loretta Van Ekris was elected to the Provincial Board of Directors as Convener of Agriculture. Patricia Morrison was named first runner up in the 1982 PEI Woman of the Year competition. In 1986 she received the Health and Welfare Canada Lifestyles Award for her outstanding voluntary contribution in the area of Health Care.

Doreen MacInnis, (1980), Grace Worth (1989), Muriel Doyle and Katie VanEkris (1997) have all received Life Memberships. Six members received Certificates of Appreciation from the Red Cross Creations Program. With seven new members added to our roll, we placed first in Queens County in the membership recruitment campaign, and in 1996 captured a Rural Beautification Award in the small community category.

We at Covehead Road are active in our community. With assistance from the Community Council, we were successful in our efforts to secure two old abandoned open wells located in the neighbourhood. We also expressed concern about the availability of explicit pornographic films presented on First Choice TV through a letter writing campaign to provincial and federal government officials. Covehead Road WI erected "Welcome to Covehead Road" signs at both approaches to the community, and this worthy 1993 project received much appreciated monetary support from the residents.

Members have been involved in many other exciting activities. We have observed the 50th and 60th anniversaries of our branch, and we hosted a visiting International Farm Women's group, an FWIC

Convention Bus tour, a Canada 125 Celebration, and a recognition party for a former member, school teacher and resident, Mrs. Jeanette Marshall.

With assistance from a Triennial Conference Fund, established in the 1970s by Convention Area 10B, several members have had the rare opportunity of attending an FWIC conference. We were actively involved in the planning of the 1995 Covehead Road School reunion and we participated in the 1989 "Festival of the Descendants". The most memorable activity occurred when members formed a "rap" group entitled "Old Girls from the Road". This group performed at three WI functions, one of which was the 1994 Provincial Annual Convention.

Our current officers are Pauline Moase, Past President; Loretta VanEkris, President; Sheila Jewell, Vice-President; Joanne Lewis, Secretary; Sybille Jones, Treasurer.

Given the diversity of our group in terms of age, talents, skills, and interests, our twenty-one members look forward to the future with both optimism and enthusiasm.

Crapaud
Marion MacDonald

The Crapaud Women's Institute first organized in 1928 and throughout the years has worked "For Home and Country". During the early years and for many years to come, the first interests of our group were the elementary school and the building of the community hall.

Crapaud WI contributed over $2000 to the Hall, and also donated curtains and the piano. Our group claimed the kitchen as their room, and held meetings there for a number of years. Other worthy causes receiving support included the Music Festival, the Crapaud Library, the Red Cross, Dental Clinics, and Water Safety courses. In 1954 the community skating rink opened. For many years our branch operated the canteen, and gave the profits back to the rink.

Beginning in 1954, our branch provided the meals at the Crapaud Exhibition, and for the past several years we have sponsored a craft fair at Englewood School. For many years we have furnished a room at the QEH, made donations to the equipment and Mammogram Fund, and given to the IWK Hospital, our local Medical Centre and the Fire Department and other worthy causes, and helped residents in time of sickness and fire.

We compiled a history of our community in 1956, then published Volume 2 in 1973, and Volume 3 in 1991.

It has not always been all work and no fun. We enjoy tours and outings, and eating out at various restaurants. We try to keep our meetings interesting with guest speakers, demonstrations, auctions, and other activities. We enjoy a close bond of friendship, fellowship and cooperation.

We have twenty-two members on our roll call and meet the first Tuesday of the month at the United Charge Meeting Room. In 1999, our President is Anna Stewart, Vice-President is Gladys Lowther, Secretary is Marion MacDonald, and the Treasurer is Shirley Nicholson.

Cross Roads

Women in Cross Roads first organized as a Women's Institute in 1916. One of the highlights of the early years was the annual "Apple Blossom Tea."

We continued to be active in our community. Having purchased the Cross Roads School in 1975 as a Community Centre, our members worked diligently to raise funds to maintain and upgrade the building. In 1981 we re-shingled the roof, and members and their spouses worked many long hours painting the exterior. Over the next number of years we had to direct most of our fundraising efforts towards repairing and replacing items in the Centre. The Cross Roads Community Centre was a focal point for many social activities and meetings for community groups. Due to the increasing costs of maintaining the Centre, however, the Cross Roads Women's Institute relinquished ownership to the Cross Roads Centre in 1992, with the understanding that the Hall would continue to be available for community activities. Since amalgamation, the Town of Stratford has taken over this responsibility.

Our branch was very proud to have one of its members, Beatrice Reeves, honoured in 1985. Beatrice Reeves has always been a very active Institute member, and has held many executive positions both on Prince Edward Island and at the national level, culminating in her appointment as President of the FWIC in 1985.

The Cross Roads Women's Institute continues in our service "For Home and Country" by assisting in various projects in cooperation with the Town of Stratford.

Cumberland - Rocky Point

Our Institute has been very busy since 1979. Members voted to change the name from Ringwood to Cumberland - Rocky Point. We made this decision because the historic name for our district was completely dropped when the school was closed and so the significance was unfortunately lost.

We purchased the old school building before 1979, and since then we have been engaged in renovations to make the building usable. We replaced the roof, moved the building onto a new foundation, added a new ceiling, and weatherproofed the windows. We then replaced the wiring and installed electric heat, plumbing, and a small kitchen and washroom. Finally we repainted the outside, and now the whole building is quite pleasant. We hold our meetings there, and the old school has become a small source of revenue through rentals for parties and elections. We use it in the fall for quilting bees, where we produce the beautiful quilts that we either raffle or make on order.

Our branch has other sources of revenue – we hold ice cream festivals, bake sales, tables at craft fairs, and we cater for groups such as the local pool league or wedding receptions. We contribute to various charities and causes, such as Anderson House, swimming classes, and gifts for the QEH, both financial for the new Mammography machine, and cooking for their spring fair. We also give Christmas gifts to the sick and shut-ins in our community.

Our membership now includes two Life Members: Cecil Hyndman, an active member for many years, and Marie Stretch, who follows her mothers' example in her interest in the local branch as well as in the whole Island federation.

Our branch is not all work and no play! Members have at least one yearly outing. We have visited many places, such as the gardens of Government House, a heritage home, the quilting store at Bedeque, and Fort Amherst Historical Park. This year our outing was a tour of the Fixed Link site, which we found very interesting and educational.

Cumberland - Rocky Point is a busy and productive group.

Darnley

On a clear and frosty night, January 28, 1935, the residents of Darnley gathered to welcome a new family to the district. The fellowship that they enjoyed led several of the ladies present to suggest a WI, and before leaving for home they had set up their group. Mrs. John MacNutt served as their first President, Mrs. Lloyd Adams their Vice-President, and Miss Annie Woodside their Secretary-Treasurer. Louise Haszard visited the group and outlined the aims and purposes of Institute work.

The Darnley WI's efforts centered primarily on the school and hall. They purchased fencing for both – the men erected the fences. They laid a tile floor the seniors' room, and they redecorated the interiors of both rooms several times. Darnley WI provided cod liver oil capsules for the pupils, and other necessary articles. They awarded a prize for general proficiency for each grade, and contributed to the District Convention Area Grade 10 Scholarship Fund.

This group took over the maintenance of the community hall, built and equipped a modern kitchen, redecorated the interior several times, provided new seats and chairs, purchased a piano, had the roof shingled, the walls painted, and electricity installed. Welcome signs mark the entrance to the district. They contributed to all worthy causes, and remembered the orphanages with quilts and gifts of toys. During the war years the Darnley WI women sent boxes to the soldiers overseas, and knitted and sewed for the Red Cross. Members conducted the district survey in advance of the mobile x-ray unit's visits, and remembered the sick and shut-ins with treats of fruit. Darnley WI raised funds by holding suppers, ice cream socials, and concerts, catering to organizations, and having card parties.

The Darnley WI was active in their community for more than thirty years before disbanding.

DeSable

The Desable WI first organized in March of 1948. Mrs. Melville Bell served as their first President. DeSable WI was active for almost fifty years before disbanding in 1994.

Dock

Delma Horne

Dock WI first organized in January of 1935. The first officers were Mrs. John H. Wells, President; Mrs. Howard Clark, Vice-President; Mrs. Chester Hayes, Secretary-Treasurer. The Dock WI originally formed as a Community Club.

Over the next fifteen years, although the Dock group was not officially affiliated with Women's Institutes they followed the same general plan, concentrating their efforts towards improving the school and the community. The women gave considerable thought to joining the provincial organization, and in May 1950 Mary Robin officially organized this group as a Women's Institute.

In 1953 we were happy to have one of our members elected to the Provincial executive, and she later became a Provincial President. In 1960, when a disastrous forest fire swept through many areas in the western part of the province, Dock WI women worked in conjunction with the Red Cross in preparing and serving food to the fire fighters.

Dock WI has continued to be an active force in our community. We hold our regular meetings from September to June, and often have guest speakers on different subjects of interest such as travel, special skills or achievements. At other meetings members make presentations, or show videos, slides, or photos of their area of interest. We donate money to UNICEF, the Music Festival, swimming lessons, the Salvation Army and several other charities. Members canvass the district for the Cancer, Heart and Stroke, and United Way Campaigns. Every spring we participate in the Roadside Cleanup. At least twice a year we answer roll call with a donation to the West

Prince Caring Cupboard (Food Bank). We also donate to Rainbow House or other women's shelters. At Christmas, we pack treats for shut-ins.

We call on newcomers to our district and present them with a small gift. This year we have been giving Women's Institute cookbooks to our new neighbours.

In 1974 we purchased the Dock (Union) School. When we later sold it, we decided to use the money for the benefit of the youth and the seniors of the community. We donated some of the money to the Western Hospital and to Lifeline, and invested the remainder to provide a Scholarship Trust Fund for students who have completed their first semester of post-secondary school.

In 1990 five members were presented with Life Memberships, pins and certificates.

In the spring of 1999, Dock WI decided to take on a literacy project. We prepared letters to parents of pre-school children, advising them to begin reading to their children at an early age. Public Health Nurse Anna Buchanan agreed to distribute these letters to parents of pre-schoolers at her annual clinics. We also contacted the principal of the elementary school, and he agreed to speak to parents on the importance of getting young children interested in teaching.

Our area sponsored four families of Kosovar refugees. Dock WI prepared and served the lunch at the welcoming party for this group, and we invited the three ladies to one of our meetings; they enjoyed it very much, and may soon become members.

For our enjoyment, we have a "Secret Pal" program. At our Christmas meeting, we each "pick names". The member whose name we each choose is our Secret Pal for the year. We do kind things for our pal throughout the year, ending with a Christmas gift at the December meeting. It's fun to find out who sent the gifts and cards through the year! Our February meeting is preceded by a candlelight dinner for our spouses (on Valentine's Day). During the summer we go on outings, visit places of interest in our province, and enjoy a meal at a popular restaurant.

We enjoy the fun and fellowship of our group. At every meeting we repeat the lovely Mary Stewart Collect and in our daily lives we strive to live up to it.

Dunblane

Women's Institute was already a strong unit in society when our group formed in 1928. Ethel Schurman came from Charlottetown on November 28, 1928 to organize a branch in our district. Our first officers were Mrs. Nellie Gorrill, President; Mrs. Elva Gillcash, Secretary. The ladies held their meetings on the first Saturday afternoon in each month.

In the 1920s and 1930s, there were very few cars and no paved roads - very few families could afford telephones in our area. Women in our community welcomed the formation of Women's Institutes groups in rural areas of the Island. Institute was a means of getting together once a month to discuss mutual interests, and the social aspects were especially important. It was this group of ladies, the members of Dunblane WI, who remembered the sick and the shut ins in our district; a committee visited them once a month, and brought a bit of cheer into those lives. Tuberculosis, a leading cause of death, sent many to the sanatorium in Charlottetown. Our group remembered those dear folk, many of whom were from our community.

Farm taxes paid for some school expenses, such as teachers' supplements, wood for the school and janitorial services, but school buildings needed much more. Our Institute furnished chalk, brushes, maps, fountains, stove, flags, and other necessary items. Later, we financed the digging of a well when water was unavailable elsewhere for school use. We always remembered the school children at Christmas and in June.

It was in the early years that our Institute sponsored four years of sewing club work for girls, led by Mrs. Ella Boulter. The club had financed its own expenses, but also had the interest and cooperation of the members of the Institute.

During the war years, our efforts to relieve suffering were tremendous. Many will remember the knitting and the quilting. We made knitted articles and quilts by the dozens to aid in war relief. We remember Victory certificates, Milk for Britain, Save the Children Fund, Chinese Relief and there were the Salvation Army, TB League, Red Cross and orphanages.

When the Community Hospital Ladies' Aid formed, our interest turned to service for others again. We helped furnish one of the hospital rooms, donated quilts and small items for patients' welfare, and gave financial aid as well.

Do you remember the 25 cent membership fee, or the 39 cent quilt batt? Do you remember the night in May we walked home from Mary Livingstone's, when the plant slips we were carrying froze? How many remember our Institute supper in Jim Stewart's home at West Point? Or the bean supper we held in Glenwood Hall to raise money for war relief? It was beans and tea that night. Then there was the $2 government grant. It did add to our funds. How many secretaries recall mailing the minutes of each meeting to head office?

We had lots of fun too. In more recent years, we hired cars and visited various parts of our Island. To pay for these expenses we set up a holiday bank and added our change during the year. During the past few years our group held yard and bake sales to add to our funds in aid of the Prince County Hospital equipment fund and the new equipment needed in the cancer unit of the Queen Elizabeth Hospital.

Since our ancestors named our district after the Scottish town of Dunblane, we held a memorial service in our local church for those dear children and teacher who were killed by a gunman. We forwarded over $600 to the suffering families.

We are grateful for all the help and encouragement we received from home economists in the O'Leary area. At present we have seven Life Members. We are indeed united in our efforts For Home and Country.

Dunstaffnage

In 1945 the Dunstaffnage WI reorganized after WW2. They adopted the name "District's Best Friend", to represent Dunstaffnage, Bedford, and Frenchfort. Suffolk later joined the branch when they had too few members to continue their own WI.

In 1995, DBF Institute celebrated our 50th anniversary of reorganization. The original meeting in December 1945 had sixteen members present. Of those sixteen, eight are deceased and seven were able to be present – three of them still live in the district and are active Life Members.

The local school was the focus of the WI, and our WI was a strong force in the over-all life of our communities. Most of our fundraisers centered on community events such as weekly card parties, box socials, suppers, dances, and lotteries of quilts. Our WI bought various pieces of equipment for the school, such as a first-aid kit, books of knowledge, water fountain, bicycle racks, and other items.

In 1950, a member donated an organ. At this time, under the direction of the teacher, Miss Betty King, the school choir received first prize at the Music Festival. Shortly thereafter we bought a piano for the school, and hired music teachers until the school came under the administration of the Unit Three School Board. We also organized a swimming program at a local shore, with a member, Mrs. Marjorie Dover, as teacher. Later we helped to subsidize the Red Cross swimming program. We still play a part in recruiting a coordinator for this program.

In 1983 the school closed its doors after serving four generations of students. Dunstaffnage WI organized a closing event and prepared a short history of the school. Former students and teachers were invited, and many were present for this event. We then bought the school for the required $1 and turned it over to a District Board of Directors. After extensive renovations, it became a very active Community Centre. Dunstaffnage WI donated the piano we had bought many years earlier.

Our WI members visit and deliver treats to sick and shut-ins from the four communities, whether they are at home, in nursing homes, or in senior citizen's homes. We also pack a box for a needy family. We organize wedding showers for the young people of the communities. We send cards to the sick, bereaved, and those with new babies in the communities.

Each year, we donate a prize to the handcraft section of the WI exhibit at the Provincial Exhibition. We also volunteer time to work at the WI exhibit. For many years Dunstaffnage WI collected fire protection dues from the residents of the communities. This was a big job, and we were thankful when the taxation office took over the responsibility.

We respond to appeals for worthy causes. We always support the QEH, Anderson House, USC and special WI projects. We held a number of fundraisers to support the Stereotactic Mammography project at the QEH, and we were able to make a sizable donation. Over the years, our WI has also supported the local Girl Guide and Brownie leaders.

In 1969 we were instrumental in getting flashing lights at the railway crossing on the Suffolk Road. Recently, after lobbying over a period of four years, we finally got a light at the intersection of the Frenchfort Road and the St. Peter's highway.

In 1997, one of our members, Mrs. Elsie Hill, was honoured after being employed for twenty-two years as assistant manager of the handcraft exhibit at the Provincial Exhibition. She handled this job very capably, and is still an active Life Member of our WI. At the WI Convention in May 1998, several of our members received Certificates of Appreciation for over fifty years of service. Maud Thompson, one of our Life Members, is in the Golden Book of Recognition. This year Maud, her daughter Glenda Mallett and her granddaughter Kathryn Mallett (three generations) rode on the WI float at the Gold Cup and Saucer parade. They were chosen because they have all entered exhibits in the WI exhibit at the Provincial Exhibition.

We have had twenty members (more or less) over the years. At present we have twenty-two members. We are proud to have had three members receive the Woman in Agriculture Award: Anne Boswall, Rena Thompson, and Willena Stewart. Two of our members have served on the Provincial board.

Our District's Best Friend WI is alive and well!

Duvar

Duvar WI first organized in November of 1932. Their first officers were Mrs. Simon Martin, President; Mrs. Alvina Gallant, Secretary;

Mrs. Peter Richard, Treasurer. Much of their work through the years was for the school. This branch is still active today, with ten members.

Earnscliffe

Earnscliffe WI organized on November 6, 1929, in our little red schoolhouse with Miss Mary MacPhail, Supervisor of Women's Institutes for PEI, attending. Miss Dora Doyle, a teacher in Earnscliffe, served as first Secretary and Mrs. Bernard Doyle the first President.

Mrs. Doyle held the first regular meeting at her home, and twelve members attended. In those days, transportation was by horse and buggy or sleigh, so the husbands always came to the meetings. They enjoyed a game of cards and told a few tall tales. There was no calorie counting then either, so members always served a big delicious meal.

The principle means of making money were card parties, dances, ice-cream socials, cake and pantry sales, and grab bags at the meetings. Each November members held a large auction at the school. Members sold aprons, pajamas, and other useful articles of clothing, all made from remnants donated by Simpsons and Eatons. Lots of baked goods, pickles, jams, and vegetables were all part of the auction.

During the war years the work of our WI was at a standstill, as members worked with the Red Cross to provide necessary articles for the men who were fighting for their country. Members knitted socks, mittens, and other necessary articles for shipping overseas.

When cars came to Earnscliffe ladies did not drive, so when Queenie Mutch obtained her driver's license she would take the ladies to conventions and meetings.

Earnscliffe WI has been helpful to many organizations over the years. Our branch donated to the Retarded Children's Association, TB League, March of Dimes, Salvation Army, Pownal Rink, community dump, UNICEF, and we gave out prizes at school closings, to name a few. We carry on this work today, as many of the members still collect in the district for various organizations. We give treats at Christmas time for all children in the district, up to and including children in grade six. We also have showers for all newly-weds in the community.

Many years ago, we entered the Earnscliffe School in the Rural Beautification project. Our WI put up a new fence, planted trees and flowers, put up a new flagpole and a flag. We received a prize for these efforts. Before the amalgamation of the small schools, the Women's Institute was very involved in providing the necessary items in the school such as toilet tissue, water fountains and cups, chalk, blackboards, etc.

In recent years, our Women's Institute has helped with various activities in the community such as the Roadside Cleanup, swimming lessons, and the local 4H club. We also donated a substantial sum of money to the QEH to help purchase a Stereotactic Mammography machine. We make tray favours for the patients' trays at the hospital and give gifts to the White Cross. We give treats to shut-ins at Easter, and donate to a variety of organizations.

In 1972 Earnscliffe and Cherry Valley Women's Institutes took ownership of the Cherry Valley School, which is now used as our Community Centre. To help pay the bills we hold barbecues, yard sales, New Year's Eve parties, and card parties. The Community Centre serves as a gathering place for many community activities such as the 4H Club, the Lions Club, bridal showers, and as a polling station for elections.

Over the years, membership in Earnscliffe Women's Institute has remained between twelve and fifteen members. As we enter a new millennium, may we, the members of Earnscliffe WI, continue to work "For Home and Country."

East Baltic

Inez Dixon

Our Women's Institute re-organized in 1942 when our country was in the middle of the Second World War. Consequently, our main efforts at that time centered on doing our "bit" for the war effort. We knitted and sewed for the Red Cross, and sent food parcels.

Our interest also focussed on the local one-room school. We provided all of the incidentals for the well being of our pupils. Our interest is still keen in our Eastern Kings Consolidated School. On observing that the stage of the school was badly in need of new curtains, we took on this project. We became engrossed in buying the material, measurements, cutting, and sewing it. When we hung the curtains, it was a very satisfying result to a mammoth undertaking! We also supply small items for the school – tissues, marking pencils, crayons, etc.

We support Health Care projects, both provincially and locally. Our members volunteer at Colville Manor and at the Home Equipment Loan Program store at the Souris Hospital. In 1993 our group received the "Organization of the Year" award in a competition sponsored in the Eastern Kings area.

For more than twenty years we have held an auction every fall; this is our main fundraising event. Members contribute everything from quilts to pickles, which Cindy Bruce, our competent auctioneer, auctions to the highest bidder.

These are some of the highlights of our organization. We have an average membership of twelve, and we meet on the first Tuesday of each month from September to June. We close for the summer months by treating ourselves to a dinner.

We hope to continue working "For Home and Country", and doing what we can to improve our world.

East Bideford

East Bideford WI organized in August of 1944. Active for over twenty years, this branch later disbanded.

East Point
Margie Stewart

East Point WI organized on July 6, 1917. Our branch remains strong and vibrant. The East Point branch now embraces members from North Lake and South Lake.

In recent years, our major project has been the acquisition of a vacated one-room school (North Lake School) which we restored and renovated. North Lake Place now serves as a Community Centre. We share it with the East End AA Group. Our Institute holds weekly card parties to have fun and raise money for the numerous charities we support.

Fourteen members meet in our homes monthly, and we make sure to mark notable birthdays and anniversaries with a beautiful rose and an appropriately decorated cake. Two members, sisters Beatrice and Rita MacDonald, have served the WI for 65 and 54 years, respectively. They are now Life Members. We plan to present Life Memberships to all eligible members.

Once a year we reward ourselves with a ladies night out – a relaxing dinner and social hour at a local restaurant, compliments of our card party fund.

Our fundraising for 1997 focussed on a new Stereotactic Mammography machine for the Queen Elizabeth Hospital. In a house-to-house canvass, we raised $1,500. We also lend strong support to our elementary and high schools, community school and 4-H Club.

Overall, the community knows our group as always being ready to help whatever the cause. We see a strong future for our expanded group serving "Home and Country".

East Royalty

East Royalty WI first organized in October of 1925. The first officers were Mrs. Alex Janie MacNevin, President; Mrs. John E. Holmes, Vice-President, Emma Holmes, Secretary.

This branch remained active in their community for more than forty years before disbanding.

Ebenezer

Kay MacRae

The history of Ebenezer Women's Institute dates back to 1926. The first members met at the home of Lois MacDonald. Mrs. MacDonald received a gift at this event. Lois died in 1999, our last charter member to pass to her eternal rest.

In those early years, the men would usually drive the women to these meetings. The men would then socialize in the kitchen while the women held their business meeting in the parlour. The practice of meeting in our homes continues.

During the war years, Ebenezer women knit for the soldiers and assisted the Red Cross with other projects. Today we still work diligently with hand and heart for such endeavours as Anderson House, decorations for hospital trays, and making blankets for the Red Cross, to name but a few. We also give financial support to the Adelaide Hoodless Homestead, Bail Out Bucket, Women Feed The World, Salvation Army, and others.

In the early 1970s we bought the Ebenezer Schoolhouse and later sold it, which enabled us to give $2,000 to the Pediatrics Unit of the Queen Elizabeth Hospital. In 1997 we held our first annual coffee party, and raised $350 for the Stereotactic Mammography machine. In 1999 we erected new community signs and a new sign at the small cemetery in our community.

Each year we enjoy "an outing", when we visit a place of interest giving us further knowledge of our community. We participate at both the local and provincial levels, and have had members on the provincial board.

We have ongoing projects, and enjoy programs provided by our provincial office. For instance, we care for and maintain a small Pioneer Cemetery in our district.

We share our skills and abilities, working for the good of home and country. Since no other organization or institution in our district bears the name "Ebenezer", we play a very significant role in the preservation of our community.

Eglinton and Howe Bay

Eglington and Howe Bay WI first organized with the assistance of Helen Harper on June 6, 1923. One of our first projects was to provide new seats, blackboards, maps, and other items to Eglinton

School. In later years, we helped in building a new school at Howe Bay. We have financially assisted all worthy causes through the years. We send memorials, cards, treats, and other items to sick, shut-ins, and other people in the community.

Regular fundraisers and community activities include selling lunches at Bingo, catering to weddings, knitting and selling tickets on Afghans, collecting for cancer, taking an active part in the Roadside Cleanup, collecting food for the local Lions Club and the food bank, and entertaining and serving lunch to patients in nursing homes. In June 1993 we celebrated our 70th birthday at Coville Manor and presented five members with Life Memberships.

Over the years we have "twinned" with several Institutes, and enjoyed potluck suppers, line dancing, and other activities, and we often join our neighbouring Institutes, Fortune Bridge and Selkirk, for celebrations and social evenings.

In 1997 we raised and donated $700 towards the purchase of a new Stereotactic Mammography machine for the Queen Elizabeth Hospital.

Eldon

More than seventy-five years of service to home, school, and community has been the distinguishing mark of Eldon Women's Institute, organized in October of 1923. The first President was Mrs. T.F. West, the Vice-President Miss A. MacRae, and the Secretary-Treasurer was Mrs. F.S. Reeves.

Coincidentally, our WI organized at the same time that the community was busy building the Hall, and so our branch gave great support to that initiative. We held many fundraising events to contribute to the building fund, and held our first concert in the Hall in 1925. We continued to support the Hall, and also took up the school's needs. For instance, we installed the school's blackboard and window blinds – amazingly the school did not even have these items before the WI arrived! We carried on our support for the schools in our community and the consolidated schools throughout these past years.

We have also been concerned with public health. In the early years that meant supporting the Red Cross and its public health initiatives. Since then we have also contributed to the Cancer Fund, the Polio Clinics, the TB League, March of Dimes, and other health initiatives.

We also enjoy community activities. For instance, in 1957, Ezra Larrabee directed our play, "The Princess Gets a Kitchen," which we staged in several communities and at the PEI Drama Festival.

We would like to make special mention of Annie Gillis, who has been an active member of our Institute since 1928 – seventy years of service to her community!

Sweeping changes in technology, education, health, transportation, and communication have resulted in a changing emphasis for our Women's Institute. Although today's needs are different, they are still great, and the public-spirited women of today are just as ready as our pioneering women to take on the new challenges.

Ellerslie

Olive Dennis

Ellerslie WI first organized on May 16, 1927 with the assistance of Miss Evelyn Windsor. Our first President was Mrs. Roy Williams, and the Secretary-Treasurer was Mrs. Belle MacLean.

We have concentrated chiefly in helping our school and community. During the war years we did a great deal of knitting, presented gifts to the soldiers, and sent them boxes at Christmas. After the war ended many members continued to knit and sew articles for the Red Cross. From the beginning we worked for the school, had hardwood floors installed and the inside refinished, and we have kept it painted and in good repair. We also bought new desks and other necessities.

In 1958 the community built a new four-room school, and as always Institute members assisted and helped raise money for this major project. We bought desks, books, games, and many other articles. Part of the basement was made into a playroom for the small children; we painted this and made it attractive. Ellerslie WI contributed towards launching the Stewart Memorial Health Centre at

Tyne Valley, and assisted with upkeep of the Centre from time to time. We did this by answering roll call with donations of articles for the Hospital. During the fire disaster of 1960, our members helped in many ways and assisted in the preparation of food for the fire fighters. We contribute to many worthy causes.

Our members have received many honours over the years. We have always supported all community projects and appeals with donations and canvassing the district. The biggest changes over the years have occurred in our school. We started with a one-room school, and subsequently moved to a two-room school serving Ellerslie and Bideford. This was later enlarged to a four-room school, and finally, through consolidation, a beautiful open-area Ellerslie Elementary school now serves twenty-two school districts. Since consolidation we give a gift of money to the most improved grade six student every year.

What a change over the years from monthly scrubbing and carrying water in buckets and creamer to the water fountain, before a pump made water available at the school! We also supplied other necessities when the school committee reported the needs requested by the teachers.

We send get well and sympathy cards to WI members and families in the community. At Christmas we send cards signed by members to the sick, shut-ins, and former members who have moved away. We have showers for the newly married, and give WI cookbooks to new residents in the district. We sponsor contestants each year for the Tyne Valley Oyster Festival, and in the past we have entered a float in the parade, as well as a contestant and a citation for Lady Pearl and Citizen of the Year.

We support the Ladies Auxiliary of Stewart Memorial Hospital. We plant flowers at Green Park to help beautify the park, and provide lunch one night in the tourist season at the Yeo House. We fundraise by catering to various groups, making quilts and selling them, and recruiting donations. We've contributed to many community needs, such as fire victims, hospitals, swimming classes and day camps, the Community Hall, the kindergarten at Ellerslie School, the Tyne Valley Playschool, the White Cross gift box, the Tyne Valley Fire

Department's jaws of life, Community Living, the Stereotactic Mammography machine, Block Parents, playground equipment, the Ellerslie Legion (Cross or Wreath), the figure skating club, the IWK (flannelette and mittens), and the West Prince Music Festival.

When asked by the PEIWI, we have contributed to "Bail out Bucket", Women Feed the World, Transition House and Rainbow Residence, Chernobyl Children's Relief Fund, the Weanimix project for Novici, the USC for Bangladesh, and the Adelaide Hoodless Homestead.

We also do a few fun things. We attended a play at Jubilee Theatre, and a picnic at Legere Park in Summerside, on invitation from McNeills Mills-Poplar Grove Institute. At our Christmas meetings we exchange gifts with a secret pal, and Evelyn MacNevin treats members to Divinity Fudge and brown sugar candy, a real treat! We go out to dinner as a group in June, and at times we have twinned with another Institute, which helps us make new friends and become aware of what other Institutes are doing.

We have Convener programs at each meeting about other countries, and sometimes speakers and educational programs. We look forward to our monthly meetings as a way to keep in touch with our friends and enjoy a friendly get-together.

Let us keep our Institute going and strive to encourage new and younger members to become involved, for "home and country".

Elmira

Elmira WI first organized in 1917. Their first officers were Mrs. A.P. MacPhee, President; Mrs. Stephen Mellick, Vice-President; Josephine Campbell, Secretary.

This WI branch is one of the many that were responsible for the construction of a community hall in their district. They also supported their local school. Active in their community for more than sixty years, the Elmira WI disbanded in 1981.

Elmsdale

On a pleasant March evening in 1926, an enthusiastic group of women found their way to the home of Mr. And Mrs. A. L. Rennie. Mr. Rennie first voiced the idea of forming an Institute. In the absence of the Supervisor, Mrs. Rennie, with the Regulation Books she had received from the Department, proceeded to form the first Women's Institute in Elmsdale.

The community began to feel the need for an Institute when the School Trustees asked the women if there was any way they could help with the expense of adding a second room to their one-room school. The first officers were Mrs. Bruce Currie, President; Mrs. J. A. Callahan, first Vice-President; Mrs. E. W. Johnston, second Vice-President; Mrs. Hugh Williams, Treasurer. Twenty-four members were present at that first meeting.

Elmsdale WI's main objective was to aid in the building fund, which included the purchase of an extra half-acre of land for school grounds. Over time the efforts of their group focussed on the school and contributing to all worthy causes. They purchased flowers for departed members, provided treats for sick members and prizes and treats for the school children, and exchanged visits with other Institutes.

Elmsdale WI remained active for more than thirty years before disbanding.

Emerald

Emerald WI first organized in November of 1925. Mrs. Joseph Hughes was their first President. This branch remained active for more than fifty years before disbanding in 1978.

Fairview – New Dominion

Fairview-New Dominion WI held its first meeting as an amalgamated branch at the home of Beth Currie on January 27, 1985. The first officers elected were Helen Nicholson, President; Beth Clow, Vice-President; Karen Currie, Secretary; Joanne Meyer, Treasurer.

We spent our first years getting established, attending conventions, and supporting local projects. We raised funds at a Bake Table at Afton Hall in May, and a Pantry Sale at Dunollie Park in July.

Fairview-New Dominion WI continued meetings and a variety of programs and fundraisers. In September 1986 we started a drive to raise funds for a new Acton Community Centre. Two members of our WI, Sylvia MacEachern and Dorothy MacEwen (and their husbands!) were very instrumental in getting this major project underway, and the Afton Community Center is now a wonderful facility that is still well used. Each year, we raise funds by catering to banquets and weddings to assist in the upkeep of this facility. We call on WIs from around the area and neighbours to help at these events. We also fundraised by selling cookbooks and holding strawberry socials and bake tables. By January 1989, our WI had donated $1,277 to the Community Centre project. In April 1990, we donated another $685.00 to this fund.

In October 1990, our branch decided to start a social group at the Community Centre. This group meets in the mornings for ten weeks throughout the winter months. We serve tea and coffee, and this is an ongoing project with guest speakers, activities, and a potluck lunch. This program is called "Leisure Time".

In October of 1992, the Community Centre needed new curtains. We enlisted the aid of two other WIs – Nine Mile Creek and Rice Point. We three collaborate on many projects, since we all have relatively small memberships.

We now have four Life Members in the Fairview-New Dominion WI: Mary Currie, Katherine Lowther, Helen MacPhail, and Sylvia MacEachern.

Our Institute existed for a number of years in the 1930s and the 1940s. The war years brought about an interruption to the existence of our branch. There are four books of minutes for meetings in the early years, held by Mr. Bill MacEwen of New Dominion. Mr. MacEwen is writing a history of this area, and has been using them as a reference.

We have a number of annual projects, which include a donation to the Bluefield High Graduation Fund, a donation to the South Shore Red Cross Water Safety Program, items for tray decorations at hospitals at Christmas, White Cross gifts each Christmas, a wreath placed at Nine Mile Creek monument for Remembrance Day, Roadside Cleanup in May of each year, trays of sweets to the elderly in our community at Easter, cards, donations, and visits for getting well, sympathy, and anniversaries in the community, and a Strawberry Social and bake table in the summer as a fundraiser (a joint project with Nine Mile Creek and Rice Point).

Fanningbrook

This Institute branch first organized in 1939. Their first President was Mrs. Daisy Jay. Active in their community for more than thirty years, the Fanningbrook WI counted building a new school among their accomplishments. The Fanningbrook branch of the Women's Institute is no longer active.

Fernwood

The Fernwood WI first organized in 1921, with the assistance of Bessie Carruthers. Mrs. Edwin MacFarlane served as their first President. This Institute branch was active for over forty years before disbanding.

Fortune Bridge

On November 5, 1996, Fortune Bridge Women's Institute members celebrated 60 years of service with a banquet at Fortune Community Centre. Five members received Life Memberships on that occasion. We presently have fourteen members. Our current President is Tilllie MacEwen, Norma MacKenzie is the Vice-President, Joyce Dixon is the Secretary, and the Treasurer is Mary Burke.

Our branch conducted a very successful door-to-door collection for the Mammography machine. We collected a total of $1900 in the community and fringe areas, and gave $200 from our funds.

We host the residents of Colville Manor Birthday Party once a year, the Bayview Lodge once a year, and speakers from the Blood Plasma clinic and the Health Heart Nutrition. Members visit the sick and shut-ins in the area. Our Convener of Safety had an interesting guest speaker who spoke on safety in the home and community.

Our group supports the Consolidated School by donating supplies for their first aid kit, treats at Christmas, and prizes at the end of the year. We also donated towards the purchase of a baby simulator for the Souris Regional High School, and prize money at the end of the year. We give to the Area #12 scholarship fund and the Kings County Music Festival. We support the Lion's Club project for needy families in the area.

Instead of exchanging gifts at Christmas, we give to a needy person or family in the area. We contribute to the White Cross Gift for mentally handicapped, and to trays at the Souris Hospital. We support the Souris and Queen Elizabeth Hospital equipment funds, the Souris Emergency Shelter for women and men in violence, and Anderson House in Charlottetown. We participate in the Roadside Cleanup, and many members recycle articles on a regular basis.

We raise money by having pantry sales, catering, bingo lunches, and taking collections each month. For our June meeting, we go out with Selkirk and Eglinton-Howe Bay Institutes for a meal and social hour.

As a group, Fortune Bridge WI feels very much a part of the Women's Institute organization, working together to improve the lives of families, "For Home and Country."

Fortune Cove

Fortune Cove WI first met at the school on November 21, 1933. The teacher, Miss Eva Sabine, called on the women of the community for their help. The first officers were: Mrs. Lester Wallace, President; Miss Eva Sabine, Secretary-Treasurer.

Over the years Fortune Cove WI provided small articles for the school such as a dictionary, drinking fountain, map of the Maritimes, prizes for attendance, and Christmas treats, and made payments to the local Grade X Scholarship Fund and the Provincial Home Economics Scholarship Fund.

During the war Fortune Cove made many quilts for Red Cross work, and did some knitting. They donated to many appeals for war services, and sent boxes regularly to soldiers from the district. One boy writing from Italy expressed his sincere gratitude for some toilet soap that was in his box. Apparently he had never realized the importance of soap until he found himself without this necessity.

One of the very active members, Mrs. Vernon Metherall, moved from the district after the Institute had functioned for 13 years; she had served as President for seven years. Mrs. Lester Wallace presented her with a gift. Another President, Mrs. Charles Yeo, was remembered with a gift before she left to live in Pembroke, Ontario.

Since several families moved from the district, and it was very difficult to interest younger women in Institute work, Fortune Cove WI decided to disband in November 1962, after 29 consecutive years of Institute work.

Fortune Road

Fortune Road Women's Institute first organized in 1945. Their first officers were Mrs. R.L. Burge, President, and Mrs. Fred Ross, Secretary. The major concern of the Fortune Road branch was their community school, and they made it their responsibility to provide for many of its needs. This branch was active in their community for over twenty years before disbanding.

Fredericton & Hazelgrove

Fredericton WI organized in 1921, and the neighbouring Hazelgrove WI followed a year later. Since their beginning, both groups worked enthusiastically to improve the way of life in their communities. Our two Institutes amalgamated in 1978.

One of the early main initiatives was the upkeep of the school in each community. Committees formed to visit the school regularly to determine needs, our WIs provided Christmas gifts for the students and teachers, and contributed to the events held at the end of each school year. Our WI's have also taken on the responsibility for maintenance of the community hall.

We have assisted many charitable causes over the years. Our records indicate that members made quilts and raised funds for the orphanage in Mount Herbert, and we carried out fundraising for the Salvation Army, hospitals, YMCA, Canadian Cancer Society, and others. When the province needed a sanatorium, our WI canvassed the area and made sheets, pillow cases, bedjackets and other items. We also donate handcrafts to the Red Cross and to a local seniors' community care facility.

Our Institutes paid for the first inoculation clinic against diphtheria in 1930, and we have since sponsored many other clinics. During the Second World War, we packed used clothing, blankets and baby layettes for overseas relief, and sent boxes of foods and fruits to local soldiers serving overseas. When the soldiers returned, we celebrated with a banquet in the Hall.

Our Women's Institute has always considered community activities very important. We have initiated variety concerts, meet-your-neighbour nights and Canada Day picnics. We participate in the Roadside Cleanup, and encourage non-members to join in.

Over the years we have had first aid demonstrations, ice cream and box socials, auction sales, candy-making demonstrations, flower arranging, cake decoration, bean suppers, Halloween parties, bake sales, crafts, visits to residents in the community who were ill, and we send cards for various occasions.

Programs have always been an important part of each meeting, and members always have the opportunity to learn more about many areas of interest to Island women. We also invite other people in the district to various meetings when the topics might be of interest.

Our 70th Anniversary in 1991 was a highlight for our group, and we were delighted that some of our past members were able to celebrate with us in having a lovely meal and time of fellowship. We have also enjoyed meeting with our various twin Institutes over the years. Some of our members have served on the Area Executive, and we are pleased to have a number of Life Members.

Just as we benefit from the dedication of the Women's Institute members of the past, we hope that future generations will benefit from our efforts in this worthwhile organization, "For Home and Country."

Freeland

Freeland Women's Institute was inaugurated in September 1921. There were approximately eight members in the beginning, and our membership grew to twenty-two. Many came from surrounding communities to join until they had enough members for their own Institute.

The first and foremost objective of Freeland WI was to provide items needed for their community schoolhouse. Once those needs were met, our Institute worked for Red Cross, prepared packages for returning soldiers, and organized community concerts. We still support the Health Centre, the school, hospital equipment funds, and much more, including fundraising suppers. We try to stress the need to improve quality of life not only for our members, but for every individual in the community.

We found some interesting insights into the past in our old record books. In July 1926, six members and sixteen visitors attended the Annual Picnic at Mrs. Ernest Hardy's summer home. On September 8, 1926, seven members and thirty visitors held a regular meeting at the home of Mrs. JC Tuplin, Murray Road. The reports indicate having raised $14.28 at the Ice Cream Festival held in August.

In this age of technology and multi-media one must listen closely to understand the needs, hopes and aspirations of our individual family members as well as our Institute members. I hope that this involvement and care will encourage our future generations as the founders of the Women's Institute encouraged us.

In 1973, after school consolidation, Freeland WI obtained the school we worked so hard for over the years and thus continue to this day to contribute to Home and School. Many local activities take place in the Freeland WI Community Centre. We often let the building at subsidized rates in order to accommodate non-profit and self-help organizations.

In September of 1996 we celebrated our 75th anniversary. Still committed to self-improvement through education and community involvement, this Institute wishes to instill in its members a great sense of place, love of neighbour, and above all, pride in "Home and Country".

Freetown

Freetown WI first organized in January of 1932. Mrs. Austin Scales served as the first President. Active for forty years, the Freetown branch later disbanded.

Gasperaux

Jean Llewellyn

Gasperaux's first WI organized in January of 1926 by Margaret Gordon, the schoolteacher, but we do not know how long they stayed together. The name of the Institute was the "Money Makers" at that time. They used the money they made to maintain the one-room schools from grades one to ten.

The branch started up again in 1948. The first President was Mrs. Austin Davey, the Vice-President Mrs. Everett Dixon, the Secretary-Treasurer was Mrs. Harry Graham, and as far as we can tell from the old books, it has been going ever since.

Our Institute now has twelve members. We have 10 meetings a year, none in May or June. We have four Life Members at present. Mrs. Ethel McCarthy is our President, Mrs. Jean Llewellyn our Secretary, and our Treasurer is Mrs. Roger Palmer.

We have different moneymaking projects; we sell tickets on a lobster draw in June, and in December we sell tickets on a complete turkey dinner for Christmas. We have penny auctions every month. We give to the Cancer Society, the Heart & Stroke fund, the crippled children's auction and others.

We have two members on a sick committee for our district. We put on a cold plate dinner for seniors and a party for the children at Christmas, and Santa attends both of these. We also own and maintain our Community Centre.

All and all, we have an active WI.

Gowan Brae

Gowan Brae WI organized in March of 1925, with Mrs. Alex McGillivary serving as their first President. This branch remained active in their community for more than forty years before disbanding.

Graham's Road

The Graham's Road WI first organized on December 4, 1914. The first officers were Mrs. John A. Brown, President, and Miss Laura MacLeod, Secretary-Treasurer.

This branch worked for the Red Cross work during wars. They won first place in the Rural Beautification contest in 1957 for their work on the school grounds. Graham's Road WI sponsored a music teacher for the school and participated in the Music Festival. They contributed to the upkeep of their community hall, and provided a piano, a science chest, a flag and flagpole, swings, tilts, slides, a bicycle stand, and many other articles to their school.

The Graham's Road WI was active in their community for over fifty years before disbanding.

Greenvale

Jean MacRae

Supervisor Evelyn Windsor organized the Greenvale WI on March 30, 1925. The first officers were Rita Carew, President; Mrs. Gordon Brown, Vice-President; Winnifred MacDowell, Secretary-Treasurer.

In the early years, Greenvale WI directed their efforts towards the district school, which housed grades one to ten until the early 1970s. They supplied many needs and comforts for the students. They also learned crafts and needlework, and educated themselves about better ways to care for their families. In 1976 we bought the one-room school and converted it into a Community Centre. Since then much of our efforts have been focussed on renovating the building and maintaining a picnic site. In 1996 we covered the roof in steel and painted the building.

During World War II, our branch put forth a valiant effort to send many socks, mitts and quilts as well as letters to the soldiers from the district who were overseas.

Greenvale WI holds celebrations to mark special occasions. We have given sixteen Life Memberships.

In 1990 we donated $1000 to the QEH toward the purchase of the Catscan machine. We raised the money by selling tickets on a quilt, and by holding a flea market and bake sale. In 1997 our branch received the first prize of $50 for the greatest increase in membership during the 1996/97 year.

Our WI holds regular meetings, have guest speakers, visit points of interest, remember sick members, provide treats for Halloween parties, hold community showers, remember new babies, visit twin Institutes, and donate to many worthy charities and medical emergencies.

We keep in mind the motto – "For Home and Country". We learn, share, contribute and give to make our community a friendly and caring place to be.

Greenwich

Greenwich WI first organized in November of 1925. The first officers were Mrs. Earl MacEwan, President, Mrs. Ambrose Rattory, Vice-President; Ethel Sutherland, Secretary-Treasurer.

The Greenwich branch made many contributions to their school and their community. When they first organized, the branch comprised three school districts – Grandview, Lyndale, and Uigg. Eventually their membership increased, and the Grandview and Uigg districts formed their own branches. Greenwich WI was the driving force behind the installation of power lines throughout their district, the hard surfacing of their highway, and the installation of all-night telephone service. This branch remained active for more than forty years before disbanding.

Haliburton

The Haliburton WI organized for the second time on May 6, 1958. Their first officers were Mrs. Charles Riz, President; Mrs. Raeford Locke, Vice-President; Mrs. Eliza Collicutt, Secretary-Treasurer.

This branch was active in their community for over ten years before disbanding.

Hamilton

Hamilton WI organized in 1936, and our membership has ranged from twenty-seven to nine members.

We have used our fundraising for projects such as community social activities, assisting fire victims, remembering sick and shut-ins, welcoming newcomers, supplying extras to the local school (such as a music teacher, sewing club instructor and materials, hot lunches, and cod liver oil capsules), hospitals and local charities, and prizes at the consolidated school.

During the war years we saved our medicine bottles for the local doctor, knitted and sewed for the Red Cross, sent fruit cakes to the soldiers, knitted and sewed baby clothing for the hospital and Afghans for seniors. We donated to the Russian relief, Greek relief, Chinese relief, milk for Britain, crippled children, Save the Children, hospital equipment, community rink rebuilding, Bob the Beaver, improvements to our hall.

On several occasions we have had a visitor, Eileen Crozier, bring greetings from the mother Institute in Stoney Creek, Ontario. To mark our 60th anniversary we sent greetings and thank you to our former members, now separated by distance, and received many appreciative replies.

In order to fund these projects, we hold lunches at the local race-track, concerts and dances in our Hall, parlour socials, and we hook and quilt items for sale.

The Red Cross recognized our first President, Ella Ramsay, for her 25 years of volunteer service. All of our members of 25 years have received Life Memberships. Of our charter members, Evelyn Simpson now resides in Alberta and Marjorie Ramsay is very active in our branch as we meet the present-day challenges "For Home and Country." Several members received the fifty-year Certificate of Appreciation at the Annual Convention in 1998.

Since the amalgamation of our schools, we have focussed our fund raising energies on our Community Hall (1889-1999), which the Department of Education declared a Heritage Place and listed in the Provincial Registry. This is a commendable incentive to preserve and maintain community halls as meeting places at the local level.With monetary assistance from trustees, the Hamilton Heritage Alert Club, our WI branch and a government grant, we have painted the exterior of our hall and redecorated the interior.

We look forward to serving "Home and Country" in the new millennium.

Hampshire

Women's Institute arrived in Hampshire in 1945, with the help of Miss MacDonald from the Department of Agriculture. Eleven members joined at the first meeting at the home of Mrs. John Edwards and Mrs. Chester Edwards. Mrs. Evelyn (Heath) Larter continues to be an active member in our organization, which has helped to develop and maintain a strong community.

Until the Hampshire school closed, our WI was supportive of the school. We purchased maps and supplies, gave treats at Christmas and the year's end, purchased an organ, and obtained music lessons for the school. We also provided cod liver oil capsules for many years. Today we donate money to Bluefield Senior High and East Wiltshire Junior High as graduation prizes. We also support our community's youth in attending out of province competitions.

Over the years our WI has supported many causes, including the Red Cross, the TB League, the White Cross, the North River Fire Department, Anderson House, PEI Exhibition Handicrafts, Catscan at QEH, Cancer Society, QEH Baby Blanket Project, Bicycle Rodeos, PEI Music Festival, and the Hampshire 4H Club. Our group is always ready to aid residents in time of illness or tragedy.

We have invited many speakers to promote education in the areas of health and home care.

Our group shows pride in our community. We have been winners in the Rural Beautification competition, and we take part in the Roadside Cleanup each year. We present babies born in Hampshire with a silver spoon, and new community residents have the opportunity to get acquainted at a WI sponsored, "Meet Your Neighbour Night" each July. Our WI members lobbied to have a flashing light erected at a blind intersection in the community.

In 1955 we purchased the former Warren Grove School, moved it to Hampshire, and converted it into a Community Hall. WI members worked hard to provide a heating system and supply the hall with tables and the necessary supplies. This building provided a location for many community events. In 1972 when Hampshire School amalgamated into Unit 3, our WI acquired that building. This building serves as the present Community Centre, and we continue to improve the facilities and grounds.

Eighteen members continue to meet at the Hampshire Hall on the second Monday of each month for a time of education and fellowship. Our group has honoured the WI motto, "For Home and Country."

Hampton

Kim Matters

Hampton WI first organized in 1947. We still have thirteen members.

Over the years our WI has made some significant contributions to the area. In 1978 our branch was responsible for having the Department of Highways install a double yellow line throughout the village of Hampton, and a street light at the corner in Hampton.

In 1985 we donated funds toward the installation of a fire exit and wheelchair ramp at the Hampton United Church. In 1986 our donations went towards an EKG machine for Dr. Hank Visser's office in Crapaud, and fire equipment for the Crapaud Fire Department. Some other groups that have benefited from our donations are the Victoria Kindergarten, Englewood Science Fair, Crapaud Fancy Dress Carnival, Bluefield High School graduates, IWK, Anderson House, Red Cross Water Safety and the Mental Health Association.

Hampton WI is very active within our own community. We send sympathy cards and get well cards to residents in cases of sickness or a death in the family. We purchase diapers for each new baby in the community. When a new resident or family moves into the community, one or two of our members deliver a plant to welcome them. We organize bridal and baby showers, and every December we hold a Christmas Party for the children. There are crafts to make, snacks to eat, and of course a visit from Santa Claus with a small gift for each child.

In June of 1995 we won the Queens County award for recruiting the most new members. In December of 1995, we were saddened by the death of Valerie Smith in a car accident. In February of 1996 Annie Ferguson was presented with her Life Membership pin.

Harrington
Valerie Phillis

Originally organized with Winsloe in July 1913, Harrington WI is still an ongoing and influential concern in the community. Although our membership numbers have fluctuated over the years, we hold regular monthly meetings throughout the winter months, and we undertake various beautification projects in summer. Harrington has been the recipient of PEI Beautification's Community Honour Award for many consecutive years.

Over the past four years several land-mark changes have taken place in our community. In 1992 our very attractive church was closed and taken to a new location in Sherwood. Reverend Scott gave the last service. In 1993 we erected a monument in the Harrington Heritage Cemetery, and in 1994 the Community Hall was auctioned off and removed from its location. It was indeed very sad to see the end of an era in the life of the community, with the removal of these once-active community buildings. Members of the WI worked hard to create a Community Park with well maintained flowerbeds, grassy areas, and erected a flagpole in 1994.

Harrington WI has also assisted the QEH Hospital Equipment Fund with fundraising activities. We remember and visit the sick and shut-ins, we make quilts and sell tickets in aid of a variety of community projects, assist the Red Cross in their yearly blood donor phone campaign, deliver Christmas Platters to seniors, and cheer the patients in the QEH with Christmas tray stockings. In the 1980s we held variety concerts and plays in the Community Hall; these were a source of raising funds for various community causes. We also entertained and provided lunch in senior complexes over the Christmas season.

The loss of the Community Hall has not meant any change in the community spirit generated by the Harrington WI. In April 1994 we held a hastily prepared but successful take-out supper to assist a new member of the community whose basement was at risk of flooding during the spring run-off.

In October 1998, members of Harrington WI rallied to assist a member of the community who was in great need of a car chair lift. This lift would enable him to access his specially designed vehicle, and thus lead a more mobile lifestyle. With a mammoth effort from all members of the WI, we prepared and delivered 620 cold plate suppers and raised $5,300.00. The many donations and offers of assistance received from members of the community demonstrated their great community spirit.

Harrington WI remains a busy, vibrant community, and we are proud of having had one of our members, Joyce MacKenzie, stand as Provincial President for the years 1985-1987.

Hazelbrook

Hazelbrook Women's Institute first organized on April 17th, 1928, with nine members. Our membership fee was 25 cents.

Our main emphasis in the early years was maintaining the local school, until it closed in 1973. We raised funds by holding ice cream socials, grab bags, crokinole parties, and auction sales and bake sales. Our Institute supported the League Of Mercy, Navy League, TB Sales, The Campaign Against Tuberculosis, Cod Liver Oil capsules, Provincial Sanatorium, Children's Aid, PEI Hospital, Charlottetown Hospital, White Cross, Protestant Children's Orphanage, St. Vincent's Orphanage, Red Cross, Music Festivals, 4-H, Sherwood Home, Brownies, Girl Guides, Cross Roads Fire Department and the Cross Roads Lions Club.

Although our membership has been inconsistent over the years, the Institute continues to support Pownal Sports Centre, Glen Stewart School, Queen Elizabeth Hospital, Provincial Exhibition, Pat & the

Elephant, Salvation Army, United Way, CBC Turkey Drive, Anderson House, Hazelbrook Baptist Church, Emanuel Cradle and the local Kindergarten. We welcome new homeowners to our district with a gift. We honour all newlyweds and grade twelve graduates. We remember our sick, shut-ins and elderly at Christmas with food baskets. We continue to support Women's Institute projects on all levels – local, provincial and worldwide.

In 1978, we made and sold a quilt that won second prize at the Provincial Exhibition. We hooked and raffled a new rug in 1992, and this won third prize in the Exhibition. We compiled a cookbook in that same year to help celebrate Canada's 125th Birthday, and we have sold all 900 copies. We have an annual Christmas raffle of fruitcakes and plum pudding.

In 1998 we celebrated our 70th anniversary at Joseph's Restaurant in Charlottetown. We were honoured to have our only living Charter Member, Miss Helen Chandler, in attendance, and members of Crossroads and Earnscliffe Women's Institutes joined us as well. We compiled the second volume of a cookbook to celebrate our seventy years "For Home and Country".

We are pleased to have two sixteen-year-olds, daughters of two of our members, join our Institute.

Heatherdale

Heatherdale WI organized in March of 1928. Their first officers were Mrs. S.M. Martin, President, and Mrs. W.A. MacPhee, Secretary.

In 1933 the Heatherdale school was destroyed by fire. Heatherdale WI concentrated their efforts on having a new school built, and when they had accomplished that goal, this branch focussed on maintaining their community hall.

Heatherdale WI was active in their community for more than forty years before disbanding.

Head of Hillsborough

This WI branch first organized in May of 1932. The first officers were Hilda Douglas, President; Mrs. H. Lodge Birt, Vice-President, and Margaret Birt, Secretary-Treasurer.

Head of Hillsborough WI focussed their efforts on their school and their community. They were most proud of having moved the schoolhouse to a new site and completely renovating it, inside and out. The Head of Hillsborough branch remained active for more than forty years before disbanding.

Highfield

Connie MacLeod

Highfield Women's Institute first organized in October of 1948. Our branch consisted of ladies who were former members of South Milton, South Winsloe and West Royalty Institutes. There was a great need and interest to form a WI in Winsloe (or Highfield, as it was sometimes called) at that time, as the rural school needed help. The first President was the late Mrs. O. W. Campbell, the Secretary was Mrs. Perley Taylor, and the Treasurer was the late Mrs. Doris Stockman.

Our Institute sponsored many events in order to make money for the school and the hall, which we maintained until the Winsloe Lions Club took over the task. We gave to many organizations and collected in the district for Red Cross, Salvation Army, Cancer Society and others.

At one time our membership was as many as twenty-six, but now we are eight, all Life Members. One Charter Member remains active, others have left Highfield, and some have passed on. We are proud to say we have one Life Member who is 103 years old. We all celebrated her big birthday with her.

We continue to give to many worthwhile causes. The QEH is our main objective at the moment. We find that great get together on the first Monday every month is most enjoyable.

In December of 1999 we had our 50th anniversary party, a turkey dinner with forty in attendance. We presented a Life Membership to one of our members at that time, Roma Francis. Roma has been a member since she was fourteen years old, and was on the provincial board at one time. She was totally surprised by our presentation.

Each winter our main project is to make a quilt. We don't even have to move it from the place that we make it now, our quilts sell by word of mouth.

High Bank-Little Sands

High Bank-Little Sands WI first organized in 1925. Their first officers were Mrs. John D. Livingstone, President; Mrs. Peter MacLean, Vice-President; Mary Smith, Secretary. This branch was active in their community for more than forty years before disbanding.

Hopefield

The women of Hopefield first formed a Women's Institute in October of 1934. Their branch remained active for over thirty years before disbanding.

Hunter River

Hunter River WI first organized in February of 1948. The first officers were Mrs. Cyril Smith, President; Mrs. J.L. Lepage, Vice-President; Miss Marion Gillis, Secretary-Treasurer.

Hunter River WI has been active in their community for over fifty years. They have sponsored many community improvements, and won a Rural Beautification award for their efforts. They provide for their school, their community, and various charitable organizations.

Hunter River WI is still active today.

Indian River

Indian River WI organized for the first time in November of 1925, at the home of Miss Hilda Cameron. Their first offers were Mrs. Joseph MacLellan, President, and Evelyn Pillman, Secretary-Treasurer.

This group disbanded in 1935 and re-organized in 1952. One of their members, Mrs. Ramsay, held convenerships at the provincial and national level.

The chief interest of this group was their school and community. They were active in their community for over twenty years before disbanding.

Irishtown

Irishtown WI organized in July of 1937. Miss Alma Campbell served as their first President. Active for more than thirty years, this branch later disbanded.

Jubilee

Evelyn Windsor, Supervisor of Women's Institutes, first organized Jubilee WI in December of 1927. Their first officers were Mrs. Sterling M. MacKay, President; Mrs. J. Lloyd Jelly, Vice-President; Mrs. William P. Cameron, Secretary-Treasurer.

The school was the chief concern of this group, and Jubilee WI supplied much equipment. They engaged a music teacher for several years. Their members were represented on the provincial executive and in the TB League. They contributed to all worthy causes and assisted fire victims —Jubilee WI reported good cooperation in community projects.

An "autograph quilt" sent to Prince County Hospital in 1933 delighted many patients. Jubilee WI sponsored a banquet for the hockey team and gave assistance to them as well. During the war years, they sent boxes to the soldiers overseas, and worked for the Red Cross.

This branch remained active in their community for over forty years before disbanding.

Kelvin Grove

Mary Picketts

Miss Jane McKenzie, Assistant Supervisor of Women's Institutes, organized Kelvin Grove WI on May 9, 1927. Our records show that our group has participated in many projects. We have tried to carry out the aims and objectives of WI by having programs that relate to the needs and interests of the women. Meetings are study groups as well as social outlets.

Our first President was Mrs. Harold Laird. Elsie actually had two terms as President, was Secretary for four years, and went on to become a provincial President. She was an editor of the *Federated News*, and she produced four issues of PEI's *Institute News* in 1968. Two charter members remain of the twenty-seven who joined the first year. Today we have eighteen members, fifteen of which are active.

Early records show that Kelvin Grove WI was very active working for the school. They purchased many articles, provided hot soup and treats, scrubbed the school and kept it clean. In 1950 the WI installed two indoor septic toilets at the school, and paid $50 towards having a pump installed inside the school. Our WI sponsored a Girls' Sewing Club, and home nursing classes. They supplied a music teacher for the school as early as 1935, and this included providing transportation for her.

During the war years our branch did much sewing and knitting, which was then sent to the sick and wounded of the armed forces and refugees. The minutes of every meeting from that period have long lists of Red Cross knitting and sewing passed in. We sent boxes of food and other items to the soldiers overseas, and our WI purchased several Victory Bonds.

When the local school closed, Kelvin Grove WI transferred its attention to the Regional Schools. We recently donated towards the purchase of new instruments for the band, and we support the Safe Grad Project. We have worked on the Hot Lunch Program, contributed to the Music Festival, and support swimming and water safety and the Figure Skating Club. Our group entered several Drama Festivals. The play committee enlisted many in the community, and put on plays to raise money.

A big project came following the building of the new school in 1949. Improvements such as leveling the yard, planting flowers and shrubs, building a new fence, etc. were completed at a "Community Bee". We received a prize from Rural Beautification for this effort.

Mrs. Laird stated that the winning of the prize was not as important as the splendid community spirit behind the effort. We have entered our community in the Rural Beautification Competition every year since 1982. At present, we are one of the ten districts in their Community Honour Award Competition. We look forward to adding tabs to our plaque each year well into the next century. We have taken part in the Roadside Cleanup every year since its inception, and pick up truckloads of garbage every year to help make PEI a cleaner place.

In 1991 we erected six signs to welcome visitors to Kelvin Grove and placed individual signs with wrought iron bases at each residence.

We have made many quilts, and give them away as needed. From 1960-1964 we adopted an Indian Girl through the Unitarian Service Committee named Bakkiam. We recently adopted a local family through the Salvation Army program, and have given them many items, including a hand-made quilt.

Over the years we have canvassed and donated to literally dozens of worthy causes. We remember the needy, bereaved, sick and shut-ins, placed toys and books in the Children's Ward at the hospital, and one Christmas we bought a tricycle for Sherwood Home. We give to Meals on Wheels, and one member has been President of this organization.

We have participated in many of the projects of both the provincial and national WI, such as furnishing rooms at the QEH, purchasing Mammography equipment, Buckle-Up-Baby, Anderson House, Pennies for Friendship and many others. In December 1928 a request came from Charlottetown asking for the assistance of our WI to support a sanatorium. We donated $25 in 1929 and for many years following. We were proud to play a small part in the fight against Tuberculosis.

We have volunteered at the Community Gardens and at the Used Clothing Depot. Our members have held executive positions in these organizations and as a branch we give financial support. One of our members is the President of KARA (Kensington Area Recreational Association).

In July 1992 our community held a reunion. Over 200 attended this weekend celebration. Former residents and schoolteachers were invited, and our WI was involved in organizing and carrying out this event.

A number of our members have won awards. In 1973 Elsie Laird received the Woman of the Year award, and in 1984 Wanda MacMurdo, won the PEI Figure Skating Association Volunteer Award. Wanda also won the PEI Figure Skating Association's Section Judges Award in 1990. In 1995 Sandra Caseley received the Canadian Figure Skating Association Volunteer Award, and in 1996 the PEI Rural Beautification Society named a new award after Nina Crozier. Mrs. Crozier's interest in the flower garden section of the competition prompted the Society to create the Flower Gardens for Seniors category. Mrs. Crozier has been a Rural Beautification winner thirteen times, and five of these were first place honours. Her flowers are truly beautiful.

Through the Institute, we have endeavored to unite the community for the good of all, and to create a closer fellowship among the women of Kelvin Grove. We had three new members join recently. We hope to continue to carry the torch "For Home and Country" into the future, and to continue the splendid work begun by women who resided here before us.

Kilmuir

Kilmuir WI first formed in 1932 with 14 members. Over the years our membership has varied, and now stands at 10.

We support the PEIWI's projects. For example, we participate in the Roadside Cleanup, conventions, workshops, scholarships, the fund drive for the Mammography unit, Adopt-A-Child, twinning, and others. In addition, we have provided support for the residents in our own district.

In the 1960s, our Institute helped the community to purchase the church hall as a Community Centre. We also helped our local school. We supported 4H Clubs, and raised money for the Kings County Memorial Hospital Building Fund, the Music Festival, and other organizations. We celebrated the 70th anniversary of Women's Institutes by holding a potluck supper for members and guests. We held card parties, dances, suppers and raffles. We made quilts for donations, held bridal and baby showers, welcomed new residents to our district, and provided for those who were sick or shut-in.

In 1967 the Island Centennial baby was born to one of our members, and we presented a $50 bond to the baby.

In the 1970s, we continued the above activities, and provided support to the library. We celebrated the 60th anniversary of the PEIWI by holding a potluck supper. In 1979 we almost disbanded, but were successful in recruiting new members instead!

The 1980s saw our Kilmuir WI expanding again. We held "Meet Your Neighbour" nights, supported the Terry Fox Run, and added a number of new service organizations to our list of donations. The Lions Club, Salvation Army, Meals on Wheels, food banks, Anderson House, Red Cross swimming program, Lifeline, QEH Foundation, IWK, United Way, and Riverview Manor all received our support during this period. We celebrated our 50th anniversary by presenting three of our charter members with gifts.

We lobbied our local government to clean up an old abandoned gravel pit. We donated wall clocks to the KCMH, in memory of deceased members. Kilmuir WI held special events with other Institutes in the area, and shared guest speakers with them. In March of 1988, we celebrated the 75th anniversary of the PEIWI by hosting our "twin" Institute, North Pinette, at the Regional Service Centre. All enjoyed the cake decorating and flower arranging demonstrations.

In 1987 we hosted two WI members from Devon, England for a week. We held a reception at the home of Lorna McGowan for the members and visitors.

In the 1990s we have continued supporting the PEIWI and our community. We still fundraise by holding potluck suppers, flea markets, raffles, bring and buy sales, and other fun activities. We now make blankets for babies at the IWK and the QEH, and have taken ownership of the Community Hall from the now defunct Hall Committee. We placed a plate commemorating the 100th anniversary of WI in the Hall, in memory of Angus McGowan.

One of our members, Georgia MacTavish, recently received the USC pin in recognition of thirty years of outstanding service to the Unitarian Service Commission.

Kingsboro

We at Kingsboro WI held our 85th anniversary on October 4, 1999, exactly 85 years from the date our Women's Institute was organized. We have active third and fourth generation members.

It is quite a different era today than it was when we first began. Members worked for the war effort in 1914 and again in 1939, but from the very beginning they did not forget the "home" they worked for – community and schools.

We still help our community and schools, and not just in our local area. There are so many people in need these days, it is difficult to choose any certain one. We support swimming classes, Lions club, MacIntyre House, Souris Hospital, White Cross, and fill shoeboxes for Samaritans' Purse, to name just a few. We don't forget those who cannot get out due to one thing or another. We have birthday parties at Colville Monor Nursing Home; we provide cake, ice cream, cards and entertainment. This year we were at Bayview Lodge. Everyone is so glad to see us come; it makes us feel ashamed that we do not go more often.

These places did not exist 60 years ago or more, and neither did line-ups for food. I wonder what our pioneer ladies would think.

Some thought that school consolidation would be the demise of the Women's Institute. Well we had news for them. We supply everything from Kleenex to money for special projects for Eastern Kings Elementary, and prize money for them and for Souris Regional High School and District Area #12. We also give to whatever the provincial Women's Institute is currently supporting. There are so many calls for money; we try to do our best. One would think that in this day and age we wouldn't have so many people here in PEI and other places in so much need.

We make most of our money from Good Used Clothing sales and pantry sales, which we hold twice yearly.

We look back at our pioneer members, who had so little ways to make money, yet they did so much. We don't know how much longer we can keep going; the younger generation has no interest. What they don't know is how much we do "For Home and Country."

Kingston

Kingston WI first organized in October of 1936. The first officers were Mrs. MacSwain, President, and Miss Mabel Auld, Secretary-Treasurer.

Kingston WI is still active in their community today.

Knutsford

Betty Sweet

Knutsford Women's Institute first organized on November 28, 1928. Thirteen members were present for the first meeting at the home of Mrs. Vera Smallman. The membership had increased to thirty-two by 1929. Mrs. Smallman is our only surviving charter member.

During the early years Knutsford WI's efforts were directed mainly at improving conditions within the local school. They purchased maps, globes, brooms, paint and a water fountain. They awarded prizes to students with high academic standing, and organized a Junior Red Cross. At the end of the school year, the WI treated the children to an afternoon at the beach with refreshments provided. They also organized a sewing circle for girls.

In 1931 Knutsford WI cooperated with Institutes across the Island in providing furnishings for the Provincial Sanatorium. Our members raised funds for this by directing and presenting plays and concerts to surrounding districts.

During the Second World War, Knutsford Institute members worked closely with the Red Cross in support of the war effort. Our branch knit sweaters, stockings, caps, gloves and mitts, and sewed and donated many other items of clothing. They packed boxes for soldiers and prisoners of war, and made quilts for refugees and air raid victims. In addition, our branch contributed to Milk for Britain, Greek Relief and The Department of National War Services. We raised funds by presenting plays and variety concerts featuring local performers. These social functions served a two-fold purpose, drawing communities together for the common good of the war effort and providing emotional support during a time of world crisis.

In the post-war years our efforts again turned to the community and to the province. Knutsford WI established a school committee to monitor the needs of the local school and the well being of the children. The opening of the Community Hospital in 1957 opened a need to have representatives of the Institute on the Ladies Auxiliary. From the beginning our Institute has acted as a liaison between the Auxiliary and ourselves. In addition, members have donated time, money and much-needed items for the hospital and its patients.

Knutsford members also supported the community rink by staffing the canteen as volunteers, one night a week, for several winters. They hired students under a Summer Student Employment Program, who compiled a history of the community. We have participated in "Roadside Clean-Up" each spring since the PEIWI introduced the program. We have supported most provincial projects, including the Mammogram Fund, Ultrasound Fund, Red Cross, Water Safety, Music Festival, Cancer Society and the Heart and Stroke Foundation.

Internationally, our Institute donated layettes to the Unitarian SerVice Committee, and adopted a son through the USC Foster Parent's Plan.

Following the consolidation of the rural schools in the 1970's, our members decided after careful deliberation to purchase the local school. Like so many other communities, we shared the concern that our autonomy would be lost if our central meeting place was abandoned. Provincial and federal grants were supportive of the need to retain a Community Centre in rural areas.

Adopting such an ambitious project required a great deal of time, energy and money. We installed running water and electricity, painted the interior, and converted one of the classrooms into a kitchen complete with cupboards, dishes, fridge, stove, table and chairs. We furnished the other classroom to provide space for social gatherings, including community bridal showers and Women's Institute Meetings. We shingled and painted, replaced windows and doors, erected a new fence, and planted tree shrubs and flowers. We had entered the building in Rural Beautification Competitions since 1949 as a school, and now as a Community Centre. The Community Centre, the local cemetery, and the district have all been entered in their respective categories, and we have been rewarded with a number of first place finishes.

Since our beginning sixty-eight years ago, Knutsford Women's Institute has raised nearly $50,000. We have done this by catering to banquets and bake sales, selling quilts, using hire-a-student programs, Community Pride Project and the Secretary of State Project, collecting prize money from the Rural Beautification competition, and canvassing for donations from the community.

We currently have nineteen members and we meet ten months of the year. Our meetings follow the usual order of business after our traditional devotional period at the beginning of each meeting.

It is the sincere wish of our present membership that we will honour the efforts of our founding members by continuing to build upon their foundation, and that our endeavours "For Home and Country" will be a lasting memorial to them.

Lady Fane

Lady Fane WI first organized in July of 1946. Mrs. Gordon Cotton served as their first President. Active for more than twenty years, Lady Fane WI later disbanded.

Lake Verde

Lake Verde WI organized on February 3, 1953. The first officers were Mrs. Raymond Wood, President; Mrs. J. Curley, Secretary; Mrs. Ira Redmond, Treasurer. This branch remained active for more than twenty years before disbanding.

Linkletter

Organized on April 2, 1918, Mrs. Alfred C. Linkletter served as the first President of Linkletter WI. Mrs. M. A. Linkletter was the Vice-President, and Mrs. Lloyd Linkletter, Secretary-Treasurer.

Linkletter WI made many contributions to their school and their community. They were particularly active during the Second World

War, cooperating with the Red Cross in all needed activities. This branch remained active for over fifty years before disbanding.

Lincoln

Lincoln WI first organized on January 12, 1937, with Mrs. George Myers serving as their first President. This branch was active throughout the 1960s, but later disbanded.

Little Harbour

Little Harbour WI organized in March of 1921. Their first officers were Mrs. Louise MacDonald, President; Mrs. Fred Rose, Vice-President; Edna MacDonald, Secretary-Treasurer. This branch disbanded in the 1930s, and then re-organized in 1952. Little Harbour WI remained active through the 1960s, but later disbanded.

Little Pond

The women of Little Pond first organized a Women's Institute on November 7, 1929. Mrs. Elliot Dingwell served as their first President. This branch was active in their community for more than thirty years before disbanding.

Long Creek

Organized in 1924, Long Creek WI has always worked hard to support our community school, provide for the sick, and donate to various organizations. We held quilting bees and either donated the quilts to the needy, or sold them to raise funds. We placed road signs at all entrance points to the community welcoming visitors, and with the help of seniors we renovated our Community Hall, installed a bathroom, added a kitchen, and installed a new furnace. We hold showers for the newlyweds in the community, and have a committee to welcome all new residents.

Long Creek WI was instrumental in drawing up the original resolution to build the provincial sanatorium.

Our ladies continue to be very busy in the 1990s. We still hold community showers, an ice cream social every summer, weekly card parties, and we sell community birthday calendars each fall. Long Creek Day is the most attended day of the year. Our Institute holds Long Creek Day for all current and past residents of the area. It starts with a pancake breakfast, contests, hayrides, face painting, lunch, a car rally, games, supper, and a beauty pageant. After a very full day, prizes are awarded.

On the first Thursday of every December we hold our annual Christmas party, and invite all the ladies of the community to dinner and a gift exchange. Later in the month we light our community Christmas tree. All residents are invited, and we provide hot drinks and cookies. Just before Christmas we have an outdoor decorating contest for the entire West River area. A person outside the community judges the entries, and the top three winners receive prizes.

Long River

Miss Katherine James, Supervisor of Women's Institutes, addressed a group of women organizing a WI in Long River in 1913. Mrs. Dunbrack and Miss Helena MacDonald, who were in charge in 1914, finally established the WI here. Mrs. Dunbrack's demonstration was about pastry, and Miss MacDonald gave a very interesting demonstration on millenary. Mrs. Dan M. Johnstone served as our first-President, and Bessie Johnstone was Secretary-Treasurer.

During World War I we formed a Red Cross Society, and by 1916 supplies were badly needed so we dropped the Institute for the war. We contributed hospital supplies and made socks, sweaters, gloves, and other items for the soldiers, and packed boxes of food for the soldiers of our community.

Long River Institute re-organized in 1931, with Mrs. Ernest Dunning as President and Carrie Woodside as Secretary-Treasurer, and immediately started working on improving the school. Over the years the small schools consolidated into larger ones, and now our children bus to Kensington. We still support our students, however. For example, when we sold our Community Hall, we used the proceeds to establish a scholarship fund for high-school graduates from our community.

We have also taken on a number of other projects over the years. We knit for the Red Cross, make quilts for fire victims or to sell, give to the Hospital Equipment Fund, and collect for the Cancer Fund, Heart Fund, Diabetes Fund, and many others.

Our members attend the WI conventions and workshops, and volunteer their time to community projects. We give Life Memberships to our older members, and have a Christmas Party at our December meeting, husbands invited!

We still work "For Home and Country".

Lower Freetown

Dorothy Stavert

On May 25, 1923 the women of Lower Freetown met in the "Old Hall" to organize a Women's Institute branch. Bessie Carruthers served as organizer. During this meeting, members voted to pay $15 on the teacher's salary, buy supplies for the school as needed, and planned an ice cream social to raise money. Nine members joined the Institute at that meeting. By the end of the first year, they had gained ten new members.

Lower Freetown WI reported a very busy first year, making quilts for the needy in the community and knitting socks, mitts, and scarves for the Red Cross to ship overseas. They reported $31 raised at the August meeting. Later that year the school children put on a Christmas play, charging 35 cents admission for adults and 20 cents for children.

In 1953, three charter members, Mrs. Lottie Cairns, Mrs. Winnie Cairns, and Mrs. Ina Stavert, all now deceased, received Life Membership pins in recognition of their many years of service. While members these women were very busy with many activities and projects.

In 1976 our Institute decided to buy the local school – we paid $55 for the building. We received a grant from the New Horizons program, and renovated the building extensively. The Lower Freetown Community Centre is now home to senior citizen monthly meetings, birthday parties, card parties, suppers, showers, 4H Clubs, political meetings, and many other activities.

On May 24, 1993 we held the 70th anniversary of Lower Freetown Women's Institute at the Centre, with twelve members and ten former members attending. Marion Hammil, a former member, thanked the members for inviting them and said they enjoyed the meal and friendship, and were honoured to help us celebrate such a special occasion. We had a pot luck supper, Jessie Burns read her poem entitled "Now and Then", and eight members were surprised when Betty Millar presented them with their Life Membership pins. Mrs. Gladys Paynter, 57 years of membership, Mrs. Florence Reeves, 53 years, Mrs. Doris Cairns, 51 years, Mrs. Bertha Gardiner, 50 years, Mrs. Etta Gardiner, 34 years, Mrs. Georgie Cairns, 31 years (now deceased), Mrs. Dorothy Stavert, 23 years, and Mrs. Eunice Simmons, 23 years, received their pins that day.

Our Institute remains very busy – there are so many needy people in the world. Through our weekly card parties we are able to assist the Prince County Hospital Equipment Fund, the QEH, Hospice, Salvation Army, Anderson House, Sudan Project, Three Oaks High School, Pennies For Friendship, Athena School Band, and our seniors in the community. At present, we have nine members. Old pictures and books dating back to 1923 are at the home of Dorothy Stavert.

Lower Montague

Christine Ellsworth

Lower Montague WI has been active since 1922. We support all groups seeking help and funding, such as Anderson House, the Music Festival, IWK Children's Hospital, Lions Club Christmas Fund, Meals in Motion, Lung Association, MS Society, Cancer Collection, Crippled Children's Auction, Kingswood Centre, Montague Regional High grad class, certain projects at KCM Hospital, the wheelchair fund at QEH, knitted squares to Zambia, lunches for the Red Cross, and swimming instructors.

We hold a twinning party each year, sent treats to sick and shut-ins in our area, hold showers for newly weds and new babies, have speakers at our meetings, take part in the Terry Fox walk and

Roadside Cleanup, and support our hall in Lower Montague and keep it in good repair.

Our WI has received two certificates of merit from Kingswood Centre in Montague. We average twelve to fourteen active members, and ten are Life Members. We are an active group and really enjoy the social part of our meetings every month.

MacNeills Mills

The MacNeills Mills WI organized on December 2, 1929. Their first officers were: Mrs. D.H. Smith, President; Miss Manderson, Secretary Treasurer; Mrs. R.C. MacDonald, Vice President.

This branch worked for their school and community for fifty years before disbanding in 1975. The remaining members unofficially joined the Poplar Grove branch, and the two branches officially amalgamated in 1985.

Malpeque

The Malpeque WI first organized in April of 1913. The first officers were Mrs. Thomas MacNutt, President; Mrs. James Keir, Secretary Treasurer.

A lot of our work in the last twenty years has focussed on our Community Hall. The Malpeque Community Hall reopened in the late 1970s after our WI completed a number of improvements. We had taken out a loan to complete these renovations, and for the next few years we fundraised in order to pay back these funds. We entered our Hall in the Rural Beautification Program in the 1980, and continued to improve the property as a Canada Community Development Project in 1981. We continued to work on the Hall throughout the 1980s, and were successful in again receiving government support for this in 1986 as a Winter Works Project.

We began discussing purchasing the lot next to the Hall in 1991, and finally did this in 1993. Again the fundraising began, since we had new loans to pay off! We also continued to make improvements, such as installing a new picture window and planting trees on the property in 1996. By 1997 the Hall needed work again, so we applied for and received an infrastructure grant from the federal and provincial governments. This allowed our WI to proceed with a new round of major renovations. Beginning in October, we painted the inside, installed new flooring, stabilized the floor and insulated under the stage, built a platform to store chairs under the stage, shingled the roof, and installed new windows, siding, shutters, a wheelchair ramp, an outdoor tap, and a flag pole. In 1998 we erected the flagpole and the new sign – Malpeque Community Centre. We won first prize in the Rural Beautification for the work done that year.

The Malpeque Community Centre has been home to all kinds of community activities. Triple Threats Theatre Company has performed their illiteracy program there on more than one occasion, as has the Youth Awareness Program. In order to pay for our work, our fundraising events included dances, flea markets, BBQ and bake sales, community concerts, a BBQ at the Superstore, and ceilidhs held in the hall each week throughout the summer, which we cater. We have also sold tickets on handmade items such as table cloths and baby quilts.

The Hall has been one of our ongoing projects, as has the Fanning Scholarship. In 1979 Malpeque WI signed the deed to sell the old Fanning School. We invested most of the proceeds from that sale, with the intention that after two years we would use the money earned for a scholarship that would preserve the Fanning name. In 1982 we presented the Fanning Scholarship to its first recipient, and we continue these presentations today.

We are also active in other areas of community work. For instance, we supported the new elementary school in Kensington in 1980. In 1996 we erected Welcome to Malpeque signs in two areas of the community. In 1997 we placed new banners under our Welcome to Malpeque road signs that read "Home of Emily of New Moon." We have also helped a candidate in our area to attend the Forum for Young Canadians in Ottawa.

Malpeque WI members participate in joint projects and those of the PEIWI. In 1985 we cooperated with Women's Institutes in New Brunswick, Nova Scotia, and PEI in adopting a village in famine-ridden Ethiopia. We participated in the PEIWI fundraising campaign for the Stereotactic Mammography machine, and we support the Hoodless Homestead Upkeep Project. We celebrated the 70th and 75th anniversaries of the PEIWI, and we were honoured to receive a gavel at the 70th anniversary. We lend our voice to issues of national concern, by, for instance, sending a letter to our Member of Parliament to protest the proposed licensing of Bovine Growth Hormone.

In 1989 a decline in membership prompted the remaining members to send an invitation to attend the next WI meeting to all the ladies in the community. This initiative was a resounding success, since one year later eight new members had joined the Malpeque Institute, doubling our membership! By 1993 we had seventeen members paying dues, and we presented a Life Membership to Connie Auld that year.

Last June we held a buffet for members and spouses, and invited the ladies in the community. On this occasion we presented George MacKay with the Erland Lee Award, as thanks for all of the work and support that he has given to Malpeque WI for so many years – thanks George!

Maple Leaf – Traveller's Rest

This WI first organized July 25, 1913, and included Traveller's Rest and Sherbrooke districts. In 1921 the members decided to separate and form two Institutes. The first officers for the Maple Leaf group were: Mrs. Harry Walker, President; Mrs. J. W. Hall, Vice President; Miss E. S. Marchbank, Secretary; Miss Etta Walker, Treasurer.

Maple Leaf WI was always very active. In 1913, our branch sponsored a petition against running automobiles on the Island! After World War 1, we erected a monument on our Hall grounds to honour the many soldiers who sacrificed their lives. We sadly added new names after the Second World War. In 1926 we built and maintained an annex to the Community Hall. The entire community used this as a clubroom.

In 1959, we received third prize in the Provincial Tweedsmuir Competition for an "Institute Song" that we composed. In 1960-61 we received third prize for Mrs. John Marchbank's chair seat covers, and had special mention at the FWIC National Convention. We have received numerous other prizes for our members' handicrafts. One of our members, Mary Baker, brought honour to our midst when she won two national awards for plays and an Honourable Mention for an essay.

Safety has been one of the chief concerns to the members of Traveller's Rest WI. We lobbied to have directional signs and lights installed where needed, and have had improvements made on the Traveller's Rest hill. Until 1993 we gave grade twelve prizes to the students in our district. At this time we decided to donate to the Safe Grad Program instead, as this is a worthwhile project to support. We continue to be conscious of safety on our highways, and we often voice our concerns and objections to circumstances that we feel are unsafe.

In 1973 we compiled a history of Traveller's Rest district. Since the publication of the Centennial History Project in 1973, our members have faithfully collected facts about the district, and a historian has recorded this data for further use. We also compiled pictures and data of all members of our WI, since its beginning in July 1913. Since we are a combined group with Sherbrooke, we collected similar photos and information from them for the years 1913-1921.

In June 1976, our WI tore down the dilapidated Hall. We had the grounds landscaped, erected a flagpole, and put up a sign, "Traveller's Rest Memorial Grounds". We designated the land as a park and added a picnic table. In 1977 we purchased the Traveller's Rest school property adjacent to the Memorial Grounds. These two parcels of land together provide our growing community with a place for fun and recreation.

Our members also participate in many health projects, such as donations to the Mammography machine and Prince County Hospital Equipment Fund, entertainment for residents at Summerset Manor, and sponsoring a lecture on Cancer.

Louise Marchbank, has served on the Provincial Board since 1963 serving as Provincial President 1969-71.

To commemorate our 75th anniversary, Maple Leaf Women's Institute erected a cairn on Traveller's Rest Memorial Grounds. We were fortunate to obtain a huge granite stone on the shores of our own district. We affixed a bronze plaque to the cairn with the following inscription: "1913-1988, Commemorating 75 years of service for 'Home and Country'; Erected by Maple Leaf Women's Institute of Traveller's Rest, July 1-1988."

In 1978 our WI held a community picnic. We made and delivered flyers to each household in the community. This proved very successful, and so by popular demand it became an annual event. Usually 125 - 130 people attended! In 1993 we decided that we could no longer sponsor this picnic, and we made this known to the community, with the suggestion that maybe some younger residents could get together and organize future community picnics. The community missed the get-togethers so much that in 1996 some younger residents, with encouragement from the WI, held a very successful outing.

In 1988 we entered the PEI Community Entrance Enhancement Competition which added greatly to the beautification of our community. We were pleased to have won first prize. We were also honoured to win first prize in the contest "Programs, Make Them Count".

In June of 1997 we celebrated our 84th anniversary by motoring across the new Confederation Bridge to the beautiful new home of Claire Dyke-Patriquin, a former member now living in Wentworth, Nova Scotia. We were welcomed to NS by another former member, Wanda Seeley, now living in Amherst.

It was an honour when one of our members, Louise Marchbank, won the 1986 Adelaide Hoodless Award of Honour. In 1998 another member, Alma Adams, a former board member of PEIWI, won the Adelaide Hoodless Award of Honor. Then in 1999 Phyllis MacInnis, won the same award. This makes three members of our branch as winners. How honoured we feel to have these talented ladies in our membership.

Margate

Isabelle Picketts

Margate Women's Institute first organized on May 12, 1930. Our first officers were Mrs. F. D. Marks, President; Mrs. Harry Brown, Vice-President; Mrs. Heath Mayhew, Secretary-Treasurer.

In our earlier years we sponsored plays, and in 1945 we entered the Drama Festival. We also entered the Music Festival each year. During the Second World War we knit for the Red Cross. In our community, we contributed to a scholarship fund, sponsored the Handicraft Van, home nursing, and First Aid classes. We entered and won the Rural Beautification contest for our school in 1958. We also gave to the Tuberculosis League.

In more recent years, we have remained very active in our community – the list is long, but worth telling. We collected fire dues from the community, and give quilts to fire victims. We hosted a family night for all members of the community for several years. We give to the Figure Skating Club in Kensington, and to the local rink. We give treats to anyone in our district that is in hospital, to the shut-ins at Christmas, and we visit our nursing home once a month and make something for their trays at Christmas time. We also worked at the Used Clothing Depot in Kensington, and one of our members was on the executive of this organization for many years. We have helped with the blood donor clinic over the years. We had a light installed at Margate Corner to try to prevent the many accidents that had occurred over the years, and erected road signs at the entrance and exit to Margate. All brides in our community receive a WI cookbook and a history of the community.

We help needy families in our area. We have made layettes for needy children. We had an adopted child, helped the Lion's Club with gifts for Christmas Daddies, had a travelling apron, helped mentally handicapped children, and always give Christmas treats to the children at our school. We gave a donation to two Margate students who attended a seminar at the Terry Fox Canadian Youth Centre in Ottawa. We kept the school in supplies and looked after swings in the playground. We gave to the music teacher, purchased books for the school, helped with Water Safety, and worked at the Blood Donor

Clinic. We always gave school prizes at both the Elementary and High School levels, the Music Festivals, and to the Safe Grad program and Helen Herring Scholarships. The annual Roadside Cleanup is one of our more successful latter-day projects.

On a broader level, we also contribute to provincial, national, and international endeavours, such as World Vision, the PEI Council of the Disabled, CUSO, the Adelaide Hoodless Homestead, the Prince County and Queen Elizabeth Hospitals, and the Salvation Army. We donate towards the rent of the WI booth at the Harvest Festival in Kensington, and to 4H, Anderson House, the Heart Foundation, the Flowers of Hope campaign, the water supply in Kenya, Multiple Sclerosis, the IWK Hospital, the Riverside Hospital, Easter Seals, and Heart Foundation.

All of these activities require money! As fundraisers we have held baseless sales, bake sale, card parties, white elephant sales, and auctions at our meetings, just to name a few.

Our branch is not all work and no fun. We enjoy our twinned Institutes, and have visited sites of interest such as Government House, the Heritage Foundation, and Jewels Country Gardens. We have an annual luncheon in April, and a potluck supper at Christmas, where we exchange our "Secret Pal" gifts. We also very much enjoy our correspondence with a member of a Margate WI in England, and another one in British Columbia.

One of our highlights was winning the PEIWI's Community History Competition in 1973. Over the years, we have celebrated our various anniversaries, the last one being our 65th in May of 1995. Fourteen of our members have received their Life Memberships.

Marshfield
Doris Wood

Marshfield Women's Institute organized on April 1, 1913, under the supervision of Katherine James and Mrs. A.F. Dunbrack. The Marshfield group was the first branch officially affiliated with the PEI Department of Agriculture. Eleven members joined at that time, with the following officers elected: Mrs. L.H.D. Foster, President; Mrs.

Charles Robertson, Vice-President; Miss Bessie Crosby, Secretary; Miss Norah Ferguson, Treasurer.

In war years, our branch set aside home and community affairs in order to support the Marshfield soldiers "at the front". When the war ended and the soldiers returned home, one set of minutes reads, "It was decided to present each soldier who had been overseas with three pairs of sox and two pair for the boys who did not go across...." We shipped socks, Afghans, shirts, and many other items overseas and raised funds by innovative means to give to the Red Cross.

Our group's achievements have been many over the years, and we remain a constant in our community. We supplied music to the school, and sponsored sewing classes, first aid, swimming and water safety, and handicraft courses. In recognition for our accomplishments, our branch received the "Best Community Effort" award from the PEIWI in 1955.

In the early sixties, our members conducted an extensive highway safety project, which we then entered in a national competition. In late March of 1963, on the eve of our 50th anniversary, the Canadian Highway Safety Council advised us that our project had achieved first prize, and we would receive a bronze statuette and $1,000. This was the first time in the history of this award that a Maritime group had won, and was a fitting climax to our first 50 years. Part of this project was our design for a "Slow Moving Vehicle" sign, which is widely used today. The committee chairperson was Mrs. W.R. Godfrey, and Marshfield WI won this competition for three successive years.

In 1958 we became the owners and caretakers of the Marshfield Hall. Built in the late 19th century, "The Hall" was the center of our community – from the days of the Farmers' Institute to political meetings, elections, concerts, wedding receptions, showers, fashion shows, turkey dinners, card parties Boy Scouts, Girl Guides, 4-H activities, and of course WI conventions and meetings. In recent years, the building had experienced a gradual decline due to lack of use. We finally decided to dispose of the contents, and we dismantled the building in December of 1999. Another chapter in Marshfield history has closed, leaving behind a lifetime of memories for those dedicated people who worked to provide this facility for Marshfield and area for so many years.

In 1990, we formed a Community Pride Committee under the auspices of the Women's Institute. This led to the formation of the Pioneer Cemetery Trust Fund Committee, with Vera MacDonald serving as chairperson, for the long-term maintenance of the Five-Mile House burial grounds. A sub-committee is presently researching the families of those buried in the Pioneer Cemetery, and other historical interests of the community.

In this the year 2000, our enterprising group of ladies will present the fourth annual Variety Concert. These concerts have raised $7,000 to date for the Queen Elizabeth Hospital Equipment Fund. We hold our concerts at the Carrefour Theatre, and Velma MacDonald is the chairperson of the concert committee.

Several of our members have achieved recognition for our individual efforts. Doris MacBeath is a winner of the Adelaide Hoodless Award, and Helen Stetson is a winner of the Tweedsmuir Competition and the author of two books of poems. In 1997, Marshfield WI won the FWIC Special Project prize at the Women's Institute Centennial Celebration in Hamilton, Ontario for our collection of artifacts in use at the turn of the last century.

Doris Wood is the first member of the Marshfield WI to serve on the Provincial Board.

As a new millennium gets underway, the ladies of the Marshfield Women's Institute will continue to serve our community with emphasis on education, family life, personal growth, and community action.

Mayfield

Mayfield WI first organized in April of 1926. The first President was Mrs. Blair Andrew, and the first Secretary-Treasurer was Mrs. Willard Nicholson. Mayfield WI disbanded in 1967.

Meadowbank

Eileen Drake

Meadowbank WI first formed in December of 1938, with the first meeting at the home of Mrs. Carrie Drake. Meadowbank had previously been a part of the York WI.

Our WI has remained a popular meeting place for women in the community. We enjoy a variety of social outings across the province, and have organized all sorts of community events, ranging from wedding showers to Christmas parties to summer picnics.

We take part in various charitable activities, including collecting clothing for people in need, knitting for the Red Cross, and door-to-door fundraising. We continue the tradition of community service through activities such as providing a wreath for the memorial service at the Cornwall cenotaph, donating to the Upper Room Angels and Anderson House, and canvassing for groups such as the Canadian Cancer Society and the Salvation Army. Meadowbank WI also has a long tradition of sending messages of congratulations, get well, and sympathy to people throughout the community.

No group can survive without dedicated members, and we are fortunate to have had many such women. One charter member, Flossie Hyde, still lives in the community and remains active in WI. Another, Eva Hyde, served for many years as Secretary-Treasurer, and although she still lives in Meadowbank she is no longer an active member.

The challenge for us today is to continue the work that those dedicated women began so many years ago. With a current membership of eighteen, it is especially gratifying to see several new and young faces that have the potential to bring new life to the branch.

Melville

The Melville WI first organized in October of 1946. Their first President was Mrs. Alex K. MacKenzie. This branch remained active in their community for almost thirty years before disbanding in 1974.

Mermaid

Mary McIsaac

Mermaid WI formed on February 2, 1950. The residents of Mermaid felt the need for a new school for many years, but there had been no progress on this until an energetic teacher, Alice McCarthy, saw that a Women's Institute could get the job done. Alice discussed her idea with several residents in the district, and they put invitations in the mailboxes. They held their first meeting in the old school, and each lady brought a lantern. Although some people in the district had electricity, there were no lights in the old school. Thirteen ladies joined, and their first President was Mrs. Joseph Matheson. Within two years, they had a new school.

Card parties, suppers, concerts, ice cream socials, bake sales, and other activities helped provide funds for school furniture, library books, a piano, and even the services of a music teacher.

When the schools consolidated in 1972, our Institute acquired the deed to the old school and it became Mermaid Hall. We renovated extensively in 1981-1982, and the Hall continues to serve the needs of the surrounding area for community functions and meetings such as 4H and others. The Mt. Herbert-Bethel WI has been supportive in helping to maintain the hall.

The function of our Institute has shifted from school needs to community needs. Our membership now stands at fifteen.

Middleton

Bessie Carruthers organized the Middleton Institute on September 21, 1921. Their first officers were Mrs. Clifford Wright, President; Mrs. John McCardle, Vice-President; Blanche Roberts, Secretary-Treasurer.

Middleton Institute remained active in their community for more than forty years before disbanding.

Milburn

Milburn WI organized on December 6, 1946. Mrs. Rose Barbour served as their first President. Active for over twenty years, the Milburn WI later disbanded.

Millcove

Millcove WI first organized in October of 1951. This branch remained active through the 1960s, but later disbanded.

Millvale

Millvale WI first organized in 1930. Their first officers were: Mrs. Alfred Murphy, President; Mrs. George Murphy, Vice-President; Mildred A. MacDonald, Secretary.

This branch focussed their efforts mainly on the local school, particularly after the school itself fell victim to two fires. The Millvale branch was active for more than thirty years before disbanding.

Millview

On November 7, 1929, Millview Women's Institute first organized. Members were soon busy working for "Home and Country", whether by sewing sheets for the Sanatorium, collecting for Red Cross, or providing needed items for the local school such as a piano and salary for a music teacher. During the war years, members kept busy knitting for the Red Cross, sending boxes of various items to the local soldiers overseas, and supporting other overseas projects.

Millview WI often combined fundraising with community social events such as dances, card parties, concerts, and plays. Always a strong supporter of 4-H, our members often became 4H leaders. We also purchased such things as a sewing machine, project prizes, and we sponsored Achievement Days.

As the years passed, members supported other community projects, such as local swimming lessons, collecting for various charities, cleaning roadsides, erecting community signs, donating White Cross gifts, sponsoring Terry Fox Runs, supporting hospitals, and assisting in the financing of the local Pathfinders' trip to England and the First Aid Team representing Prince Edward Island.

In 1980 we received an award certificate for quilts donated to USC. Individual members have also received recognition for their work. One member was nominated for the "Woman of the Year" award at the Summerside Lobster Carnival, and another was featured in "Women in Business". In 1996 we honoured a member in the "Golden Book of Recognition" for her sixty years of service.

Members and community residents support all Institute projects generously. We are currently assembling a written history of Millview. This project is part of our ongoing desire to preserve the heritage of our community.

Millview Women's Institute is an integral part of our community.

Milo

Milo WI first organized on May 27, 1928. The first officers were Ruby MacLean, President; Mrs. Ivan MacLean, Vice-President; Pearl Craig, Secretary-Treasurer.

Milo WI sponsored Sewing Clubs, music lessons, and hosted the Handicraft Van in their community. They also assisted with the Public Library in O'Leary.

The Milo WI was active in their community for over forty years before disbanding.

Mill River

Louise Haszard first organized Mill River WI on May 19, 1931. Their first officers were Mrs. Rhoda Gard, President; Mrs. Gordon Metherall, Vice-President; Pearl Craig, Secretary-Treasurer.

Mill River WI raised money through lunch fees, fishing ponds, social evenings, and ice cream festivals on the members' lawns. They used their funds for school projects, such as a new floor and ceiling, wallpaper, and new windows. This group disbanded in 1936 and reorganized in 1945, with a membership of 21 at that time. In 1949 Mill River WI assisted in building a new school, and were subsequently responsible for maintenance.

This branch remained active for more than fifty years before disbanding in 1984.

Miminegash

Our Institute organized in 1946, and over the last twenty years we have had anywhere from 13 to 22 members.

We do most of our fundraising by catering – we do hot dinners, senior citizens banquets, and fire department banquets. We support various charities, including the IWK, Easter Seals, Children's Wish Foundation, United Way, the Stereotactic Mammography machine fund, Transition House, and many other organizations. We also donate to missionary priest Father Roy Shea, who is in Brazil helping poor people and teaching them about God.

Miminegash WI members visit hospitals and the manor, and play bingo with residents. We donate articles to schools and hospitals, and present senior mothers with roses on mother's day. Patsy Shea is writing to a WI member in New Zealand.

We usually have a nice meal together at Christmas and exchange gifts. Sometimes we dress up on Halloween, and we send out cards and flowers to those in need in the village. At our January 2000 meeting the board presented MaryAnn Gallant with an appreciation award and some flowers for over 50 years of service.

Montague

Montague WI first organized in May of 1914. Their first President was Mrs. David Wright. This branch was active in their community for more than fifty years before disbanding.

Montrose

Montrose WI first organized on September 27, 1950. Their first President was Mrs. Harry Pridham, and Mrs. Hubert Campbell their Secretary-Treasurer. This branch remained active for more than twenty years before disbanding.

Mount Albion

Mount Albion WI first organized in November of 1926. This branch remained active for more than forty years before disbanding.

Mount Herbert - Bethel

Joyce Wood

Mt. Herbert--Bethel Women's Institute first organized on November 7, 1935. Mrs. Earl Ings served as the first President.

Our membership has always averaged approximately twelve women. Much of their interest in early years focussed on the war effort. Our WI donated homemade mitts, pajamas, clothes for babies, money, Christmas boxes, socks, candy, cigarettes, and many other items to the Red Cross. We also gave coats to the Legion for the boys on leave.

In November of 1946, our Institute disbanded due to lack of interest. We reorganized in November of 1953.

Members put a lot of effort into the upkeep and support of the local schoolhouse. We also performed mending and patching at the Mt. Herbert Children's Home once a week. Our branch donated to local charities, and raised funds by means of suppers, crokinole parties, sandwich making for levees, and other activities.

After the local school closed, WI members put more emphasis on helping to sponsor Scouts, Cubs, and 4-H. We helped with an Adapted Aquatics program at the YMCA once a week, collected for charities, and kept in touch with the needs of our community. In recent years, we raise money by having suppers, bring and buy sales, bake and craft sales, and other various means.

Although our membership is small, we manage to support a number of projects, such as His Mansion in Pisquid, Mermaid Hall, Anderson House, Road Side Cleanup, Stereotactic Mammography Machine at the QEH, Upper Room Angel Program, Camp Gencheff, Pat and the Elephant, and the Singing Strings, to name a few. At present, our main project is erecting road signs in Mt. Herbert and Bethel.

We've had many speakers over the years, including Cindy Cousins from His Mansion in Pisquid, an Island Nature Trust representative, Lisa Garland from the PEI Association of Newcomers to PEI, a lady from the Cancer Society, and a speaker who informed us of the importance of organ donation.

WI is not just about work – we do have some fun activities. One of the things we really enjoy is getting together with our twin WI branch. It gives us the opportunity to get to know other members and have some fun, laughs, and of course delicious food. We usually start the year with a corn boil or a potluck supper, and end in June with a barbecue at a member's home. We've had a progressive Christmas dinner, pasta demonstrations, ribbon embroidery demonstrations from Needle and Nut, a visit to His Mansion in Pisquid, a Christmas Tea and toll-painting demonstration at Clark's Tearoom in Mount Stewart, a sleigh ride, guest speakers on Creative Colours, Microwave Cooking, and many more fun activities.

This is a short summary of some of the many things we participate in, and enjoy doing, as we continue to support home and country.

Mount Mellick

Mount Mellick WI first organized in 1930. Their first President was Mrs. W.J. Mutch, and the first Secretary was Hazel MacEachern.

Mount Mellick WI was very active in working for the Red Cross during the war years, and sponsored a community reception for each soldier that returned home, memorial services for those who did not.

This WI branch was also interested in the welfare of their school, sponsoring sewing clubs, garden clubs, a library fund, and a piano and a music teacher.

Mount Mellick WI is active in their community today.

Mount Royal

Mount Royal WI first organized in October of 1932. Their first President was Mrs. Thomas R. Palmer. The Mount Royal branch disbanded in 1977.

Murray Harbour North #110

Evelyn Windsor, Assistant Supervisor of Women's Institutes, organized Murray Harbour North #110 WI on November 10th, 1925. Our first officers were Emma Cook, President; Mrs. C.J. MacLure, Vice-President; Mrs. Irving Millar, Secretary-Treasurer. Mrs. William Kennedy held the first meeting at her home.

Over the seventy-some years of organization, we have had as many as thirty-one members (back in the forties), and we are now down to seven, with some meetings as low as five.

During the war years we knitted and sent boxes with cake and cookies to the soldiers overseas. For many years the children of the community were our big concern. We always supplied all the necessary items for the school such as fountains, chalk, library books, halibut oil capsules, picnic transportation, treats at Christmas, and sponsored Water Safety Programs. We also kept the schools scrubbed.

We have made quilts for Unitarian Services, and knitted for the Red Cross for many years. We now give donations to many charitable organizations and help with all community activities.

Our one remaining Life Member, Mrs. George M. Clow, has been a member for over fifty years.

New Annan

New Annan WI first organized on April 29, 1915, the sixteenth WI organized in the province. Eleven members formed our first WI. Our first President was Mrs. W.H. Moase, Vice-President Miss Alice Wright, and our Secretary Miss Ethel Duffy.

Our school was badly in need of repairs, and our country was at war. The women organized socials as fundraisers, some of which held at the then famous New Annan Racetrack. They bought wool, which they carded and spun into yarn. They knit socks and packed boxes of food that they sent overseas, and sent money for adopted prisoners of war. In 1918 New Annan WI had the honour of being the first Institute on the Island to merit a card of honour from the Canadian Fields Comfort Commission for knitted socks for Canadian soldiers – our branch sent over 200 pairs.

In honour of those that endured and sacrificed their lives for Canada, a soldier's monument was erected at Traveller's Rest. Our Institute shared in building the monument, unveiled on September 14, 1921. Each Remembrance Day we place a wreath in memory. We had our Honour Roll re-furbished and placed in the Royal Canadian Legion in Kensington in 1984.

We supported our schools by supplying cod liver oil capsules, soups for lunches, library books, and other necessities. Since consolidation we have volunteered at the school lunch program, donated prize money at year's end, and donated toward computers and playground equipment.

In 1971 our WI published a history of New Annan. M. Louise Moase, a member of our group since 1927, compiled the research for this project. We also purchased our local school that year, and we maintained it as a Community Centre until we sold it in 1991.

We continue to participate in the annual Roadside Cleanup, and support all WI projects at various levels. We volunteer at the Kensington Community Gardens during the winter and participated in the Kensington Harvest Festival each fall. We donate to the prizes for handicraft and 4H classes. We participate in the Harvest Festival Parade by entering WI floats, and have won several awards for our efforts. We donated toward the purchase of a new ice-surfacing machine at the Community Gardens Rink. We donate to the Music Festival, various charities, make quilts for the needy, and contribute to other needs in our community. Our WI organized a sewing club for girls in 1941 and again in 1969. We also organized the 4H Club in our community, which continued until 1992.

In April of 1997, our Institute organized a "Time, Treasure and Talent" auction. This event realized a total of $2,670.00, which we then donated towards the purchase of a Stereotactic Mammography unit at the Queen Elizabeth Hospital. We have given to our hospitals for various equipment purchases over the years, and recently became an associate member of the Prince County Hospital Auxiliary. We also make tray favours at Christmas and at various times donate useful articles to the hospital, such as blankets, pajamas and other necessities.

In 1983 we donated our minute books to the Provincial Archives. This year we raised money to help with the Chernobyl relief fund that brings children to PEI for six weeks. We continue to support many worthwhile causes in our area. Our WI has made many quilts for fire victims and those in need.

We have celebrated our 50th, 60th, 70th and 80th anniversaries. Our group enjoys the sociability and educational opportunities that Women's Institute provides, and looks forward to the next century with enthusiasm. We presently have a membership of eighteen and look forward to the 21st century with enthusiasm, as we work "For Home and Country".

New Glasgow

Ann Francis

New Glasgow Women's Institute has enjoyed a long and colourful history spanning over seventy years. It began on a cold March 7th evening in 1924 at Mrs. George H. Stevenson's home. Miss Matheson, Supervisor of Women's Institutes, had come to speak to twelve women who wished to organize the 81st branch of the Women's Institute on PEI. They exchanged information, appointed a Board of Directors, elected the first slate of officers, and New Glasgow Women's Institute was born.

The first officers were Mrs. Percy Dickieson, President; Mrs. Brenton Dickieson, Vice President; Margaret Stevenson, Secretary-Treasurer,

New Glasgow WI's activities invariably reflected the times. During the 1920s socials and suppers were the main fundraising events. Emphasis was on community get-togethers, and the proceeds from these events supported community projects. The Institute was very active in this respect. Funds also went to support an orphanage, the cemetery, school fairs, a rink, the Red Cross, and the School for the Blind. By 1925, the newly formed Institute was thriving, boasting thirty-four members.

During the 1930s New Glasgow WI petitioned for and worked diligently toward the opening of the Provincial Sanatorium, raising money with "poverty socials" and plays. Support for the local school continued, and knitting and sewing for the Red Cross Junior Ladies became a new priority.

The 1940s brought the sobering war years to New Glasgow, and the motto "For Home and Country" took on new meaning for Institute members. Activities focused upon supporting our men and women overseas. The Institute continued to hold socials, concerts, and picnics, while sewing, knitting, quilting, and boxing food to contribute to the war effort. New Glasgow and two other communities also began showing films in the local hall. Support continued apace for the school and orphanage as well as the Kinsmen and the Greek Relief Fund. Following the publication of the first provincial WI cookbook in 1937, New Glasgow members sold copies, and provided lunches at the local hockey rink.

The 1940s brought a series of "firsts" to the province, and with these the sense of community in New Glasgow began to widen, fostering support for projects beyond the local boundaries. The PEI Music and Drama Festivals, and the Jubilee Endowment Fund for scholarship in Home Economics began in this period, and New Glasgow was honoured when Myrna Smith earned the Home Economics award.

With the WI's radio program came an ever-widening sphere of influence for Institute members. Consequently, the 1950's saw New Glasgow Institute's goals directed toward the improvement of the community's education and health. New Glasgow began a sewing class, and hired and paid a music teacher for the school. The proceeds from countless pantry sales, auctions, talent shows, and teas were targeted toward a Dental Clinic, the March of Dimes, the Ceylon Project, mentally handicapped children, and the Music Festival, in addition to local obligations. An increasing awareness of needs and concerns outside the immediate community demanded that Institute members contribute to society in an expanding capacity. The fact that in August of 1958 the New Glasgow WI had the highest number of blood donors in the province at their donor clinic, sponsored by the Junior Farmers, reflects this change in awareness.

The 1960s followed the continuing pattern of fundraising for worthy causes, again on an increasingly large front. Our Institute catered to Junior Farmers and 4H, held mother/daughter banquets and card parties, collected fire dues, and ran the canteen for the Maritime Holstein Field Day at Elmer MacDonald's farm. In the early 1960s we entered an agreement with the provincial government for the maintenance of the David Laird Memorial Historical Site in New Glasgow, an agreement which continues to the present. Meanwhile, there was the music teacher to pay and swimming lessons to support in Stanley Bridge – both items of great importance to the children of the community. We helped the Junior Farmers sponsor the community in the Rural Beautification Contest, and were thrilled to share the winning prize. We packed used clothing for the Unitarian Service Commission, and petitioned the Minister of Highways for a safety traffic light in the busy community.

New Glasgow lost its school during this decade, and with pupils attending school in Cavendish, the nature of Institute giving underwent a change. We bought a sewing machine for the Sewing Club, and gave education prizes to Central Queens Regional High School in Hunter River where our students graduated. When the neighbouring Institute in Mayfield disbanded in 1967, seven of their members joined with us. We also worked on a community history during these years, and erected new district signs.

The freewheeling 1970s ushered in a new stream of priorities for the New Glasgow WI. Canada was looking outward, and New Glasgow followed suit. In 1973 we hosted a wonderful "Centennial Party" and issued invitations to all district ladies to attend in centennial dress. We held Welcome Parties for the many new-comers to the community. Institute members traveled to Kensington to take turns working in the rink canteen, and we began a yearly outing for our members, with activities such as bowling and attending concerts or dining our to promote fellowship. New Glasgow shared in the 1976 FWIC National Convention in PEI by hosting a busload of delegates at the Shining Waters Lodge in Cavendish, owned and operated by one of its members. We also contributed to the new Dr. Helen Herring Scholarship Fund. The local Fire Department, in operation for approximately eighteen years, built a new Fire hall in 1977, with a meeting room that could double for community functions. The Institute helped to equip this hall with 60 chairs and an electric stove, plus numerous other items, including a piano. This hall gave us the facilities to sponsor a defensive driving course, a first aid course, and a safe bicycling course for school children.

In the 1980s our Institute directed more attention toward addressing social and environmental concerns in the province, while maintaining firm support for our traditional priorities. We began visiting other Institutes and inviting them to our meetings to hear special guest speakers. Reflecting the times, we supported new causes such as Anderson House, the Upper Room, and the Food Bank. We carpeted the local Fire hall meeting room and supported a local Kindergarten Program there. We encouraged environmental causes by participating in the annual Roadside Cleanup, and our members to endorse the slogan "Reduce, Recycle, and Re-use" through newspaper and bottle collections. In 1987 we raised money for a set of digital scales for the Queen Elizabeth Hospital Nursery, and we continued to support the hospital each year, donating $2,000 in that same year towards the heralded cat-scan purchase.

Several New Glasgow WI members have made significant contributions to provincial life through the Women's Institute. From 1985 to 1987, Esther Dickieson served on the Provincial Board, the final year as chairperson of the Provincial Exhibition. Margaret Sellar continues to be a Provincial Exhibition organizer with the committee. Mrs. Leta Andrew, now deceased, received the Adelaide Hoodless Award of Honour in 1991, bringing great honour to the organization in New Glasgow. This was followed by the Woman of the Year Award, presented to Mrs. Andrew in 1992. Mrs. Esther Dickieson was also the recipient of the Adelaide Hoodless Award of Honour in 1994, in recognition of her contribution to Island society.

The 1990s continue to place fundraising demands on the resources of New Glasglow WI, and we continue to meet these needs wherever possible. Several new initiatives have proven popular and rewarding. In the summer of 1995 we began hosting tour groups for a luncheon served in the Christian Church Fellowship Room, to allow visitors a taste of the sense of community the Island fosters and enjoys. The annual fall pot-luck supper continues to prove itself a valued social get-together. In 1996 we gave the proceeds from this supper, totalling

$1,000, to the Queen Elizabeth Hospital to aid their campaign to purchase a Stereotactic Mammography machine. Two youths from the community were able to participate in international projects with the help of New Glasgow WI – one to Costa Rica on an aid and work project, and one to Baltimore, Maryland, with a cultural theatre project. In March of 1994 we welcomed our 70th anniversary with a dinner celebration. In 1995-96, Ann Francis and Esther Dickieson composed a letter on behalf of the New Glasgow WI proposing to the Provincial Board that a general WI scholarship fund of at least $500 be established for students continuing their education. On-going discussions resulted in the passing of a motion at the provincial level, which brought into being the new WI Education Scholarship, our contribution towards recognition of the 100th Anniversary of the Canadian Women's Institute. We continue to supplement these initiatives with members' everyday volunteer efforts in so many areas – from visits to nursing homes to packing Christmas cheer boxes, and from catering to wedding and anniversary receptions to working at the Institute Building during the provincial exhibition. Institute women still open their homes to their fellow members for their monthly meetings, they support their neighbours in times of sickness and bereavement, and they share in the celebration of marriages and births.

The purpose of the Womens' Institute is exercised daily through the efforts of members such as those in New Glasgow. It is with a very real sense of pride in our history that New Glasgow Institute members dedicate time and resources to the betterment of "Home and Country", and will continue to do so in future.

New Haven

Phyllis Newman

Our Institute first organized on November 5, 1935, with sixteen members joining on that occasion. Three of these charter members are still with us, and a fourth resides in Charlottetown. At one point, our membership was as high as twenty-six members.

Our local school received many supplies and treats for the students, and we still contribute money to the schools. During the Second

World War years we knitted for local soldiers and the Red Cross. We remember the sick and bereaved, and families that experience fire loss. We contribute to many charitable organizations, and we assist in door to door collections.

Each November since 1967 the Riverdale-Churchill WI and we have hosted a party of dancing and a bountiful lunch to the residents of Riverside Hospital. Music is supplied free. We also invite the "Hillsboro Hospital" patients once a year to a dance with a live band and a bountiful lunch.

For the past few years we have invited our spouses and some neighbours to a potluck supper. This is our special yearly project for various charities such as the Mammography machine fund. In 1999 we presented the proceeds from our potluck, $200.00, to the Queen Elizabeth Hospital Foundation.

In the last few years our membership has declined due to death, and one other member is now unable to attend due to her health. At present, our membership is fourteen, and the majority is in the "elderly" age group.

We have celebrated our 30th, 40th, 50th and 65th anniversaries, and we look forward to our 65th in November 2000.

New London

New London WI organized in June of 1913, but disbanded six years later. The branch reorganized in 1934, and the President at that time was Mrs. Archibald Campbell, the Secretary Mrs. Walter Found.

During the war years our WI dedicated a great amount of time and effort to knitting and sewing for the Canadian Red Cross. We continued to work for the Canadian Red Cross after the war, and we co-sponsored the Red Cross swimming classes while held at "The Swimming Rock" in Stanley Bridge. We also supplied layettes for UNICEF.

Our Institute was responsible for having a traffic warning light installed at the New London intersection. We also erected nicely painted signs on each of our four roads leading into the village. We supported the appeal for construction of a new Lion's building in

1980 after fire destroyed the original one in 1979. Together with seven surrounding districts, our WI continues to maintain the New London Rural Community Fire Company by having a representative on the board and assisting in purchases, taking part in their annual concert, and helping out at "New London Days". We also freely gave of monetary and voluntary assistance in aid of the new rink in Kensington when the old one burned down. We provide for both Prince County and Queen Elizabeth Hospitals. We supported the clothing depot until its closure by volunteering help and providing items for sale.

One of our members donated land for a seniors' apartment building, and through the efforts of our WI the Murray MacKay Court was built. We remember the seniors, shut-ins, and those in nursing homes with cards throughout the year, and we provide treats at Christmas.

Once a year we enjoy tours. We have toured the Veterinary College with Dr. Tim Ogilvie, Government House when Marion Reid was Lieutenant Governor, and Kensington Towers and Water Gardens with Senator Johnstone. We toured the South Shore Villa, Cavendish Figurines, ADL, Elmer's Dairy, the Cheese Lady, and other tourist attractions. We have had a great number of guest speakers, including an RCMP member, a fire safety speaker, an Anderson House representative, a bee grower, a lawyer, and speakers from different charities. One of our most enjoyable and rewarding events occurs when we host our twin and neighbouring Institutes.

We maintain our WI hall and keep repairs up to date. We have a hot air furnace, washroom facilities, and a well-equipped kitchen. Many events happen here, such as card parties, concerts, suppers, and meetings. We do some catering, and were honoured to supply old-fashioned cookies, tea, and coffee in celebration of the 125th anniversary of Lucy Maud Montgomery's birthday.

Although many young people in our area are not interested in becoming WI members, we continue to be an active group, and were pleased to have three new members join in 1999. We will continue to work "For Home and Country" by focussing on family, community, and personal growth.

New Perth

Beryl Diamond

Bessie Carruthers organized New Perth WI on September 22, 1920.

The school was the focus of many projects of our WI, beginning in 1948 when we solely financed the installation of plumbing. New Perth WI also played an important role in organizing 4H Clubs. Still, we on many non-school related projects, such as the Program Planning Contest, sponsorship in Handicraft Courses, Red Cross First Aid, Healthy Aging Course, and Cancer Clinic for Women at the Kings County Memorial Hospital.

Two members of the New Perth Institute have served as provincial Presidents – Mrs. George Martin and Mrs. Lincoln Dewar.

In 1995 our WI released **Link With The Past**, a 269 page book detailing the history of the New Perth. On September 22, 1995 we proudly celebrated our 75th anniversary.

Newtown Cross

Newtown Cross WI first organized in August of 1953. Their first officers were: Mrs. Eunice Ross, President; Mrs. Charles MacEachern, Vice-President; Mrs. David Gillis, Secretary-Treasurer. This branch remained active throughout the 1960s, but later disbanded.

Nine Mile Creek

The first meeting of Nine Mile Creek WI took place on November 6, 1939 in the one-room school, as many of the meetings were in those days, with thirteen members attending. Florence MacDonald was our first President, Sarah MacDougall the Vice-President, and Jessie MacDougall was Secretary-Treasurer. They always started their meetings by singing the "Institute Ode" followed by the Woman's Creed, and the meeting always ended with our National Anthem.

Our Institute filled the following years with many activities that showed how important we are to the community. We provided many concerts with a sale of fudge made by WI members. There's no doubt that our one room school benefited from the WI. Our Institute members, young and old, spent many evenings spring cleaning the school, and even polishing the desks. Children always had treats at Christmas, swimming lessons in the summer, and even cod liver oil capsules in the winter, in spite of the children's dislike for the last item!

During the war years, the WI again rallied to the call and did their share of Red Cross work. They knitted, quilted and sewed. Each year they purchased a wreath for our war dead, and placed it on our memorial monument.

Friendliness and fellowship continues to be the key motto of our successful Institute. We continue to support our Community Centre and organizations. Our main objective is to improve conditions in the home life in our province, the conditions of schools, and anything that adds to the well being of the district. Each year we strive to become better citizens "For Home and Country".

Norboro

Norboro WI first organized in July of 1913. The first officers were Mrs. Patrick Hughes, President, Mrs. J.A. Harding, Secretary-Treasurer.

Norboro WI was active in supporting their local school, and other charitable organizations. They raised money by holding suppers, ice cream socials, pantry sales and plays. They used their funds to purchase all manner of supplies and furniture for the school, and they donated to various causes such as the TB League, the Red Cross, Salvation Army, March of Dimes, and the CNIB.

The Norboro WI disbanded in 1979.

Northam

The Northam branch of Women's Institutes organized on May 28, 1923 and has been active ever since. In earlier years our branch was mainly concerned with the Northam School, where one teacher taught grades one to ten. In 1948 the community opened a two room school, and our WI supported this school until the present Ellerslie Consolidated Elementary and Summerside High schools opened. We provided Red Cross cod liver oil capsules for the children in the community, and treats for the schoolchildren and pre-schoolers at Christmas and at school closing.

We hold our meetings in members' homes, with an average attendance of twelve to fifteen. Our ongoing challenge is to raise funds to support the school and various appeals. There was the Stewart Memorial Hospital tea to support and Christmas tray decorative items for the hospital. We WI provided a prize for decorative items for the hospital. Members canvass the district for the Cancer Society, support Red Cross swimming classes at Green Park, and canvass for Flowers of Hope, Heart & Stroke, and the United Fund. All participate in the annual Roadside Cleanup in the spring. We provide gifts for hospital patients, sponsor wedding showers, contribute to high school graduation prizes, enter a float each year in the Oyster Festival Parade, and sponsor a young lady from the district as a contestant in the Oyster Queen competition. Northam WI assists with Oyster Festival suppers, which support the Tyne Valley rink. We also support the Stewart Memorial Hospital Auxiliary in its activities, and donate to the school library. At Christmas we remember district seniors. In 1983, our WI assisted with plaques for framed paintings by local artists to be hung in Stewart Memorial Hospital.

Over the years, Northam WI has donated to Hillsboro Hospital, UNESCO, an adopted child, the Adelaide Hoodless Homestead Fund, Home Economics and Law scholarships, the White Cross, Pennies for Friendship, a Remembrance Day wreath, a fund to furnish three rooms at the Queen Elizabeth Hospital, the Tyne Valley figure skating club, Ellerslie Day Camp, the Red Cross Water Safety Program, UNICEF, the Salvation Army, blood donor clinics, the Family Service Bureau, Anderson House, the Music Festival, Allied Youth, the camp for disabled, Meals on Wheels, the Prince County x-ray equipment fund, a gift stall at the Provincial Convention, playground equipment, the Easter Seal fund, the Safe Grad dance, the Mammography fund, and the Hardy Boys Trust Fund.

After the schools consolidated in August 1973, we took title to the old school property, and we have continued to maintain this. Many renovations have resulted in a fine Community Centre, open from

April to November. We were very pleased to win a Rural Beautification prize in 1980 for our Community Centre. We also won a prize in 1981 for "Something for Everyone", sponsored by the Provincial WI. In 1982, four of our members received Life Memberships. To continue supporting various needs, we hold potluck suppers, sponsor a Spring Ball, cater to WI workshops, and hold auction sales, turkey suppers, card parties, bingo, and quilt raffles. We also cater to weddings and anniversaries, and we hold an annual goose supper.

In 1973 we celebrated our 50th anniversary at a nearby restaurant. In 1983 our WI celebrated our 60th anniversary by going out for dinner. Una Colwill Sanderson, a charter member, was present on that evening. We read highlights from the early years of our branch, and Eva Colwill composed a poem with something about each member. In 1998 we celebrated 75 years of organization with our provincial President Betty Millar as our guest. We toured the home of our original President, Lulu Yeo, which new owners have appropriately restored. We then enjoyed dinner at a nearby restaurant, where our current President, Norma Ramsay, reviewed a bit of our WI history.

North Bedeque

North Bedeque WI organized on June 25, 1946. Mrs. Brewer Waugh served as their first President.

This group was instrumental in helping to organize the North Shore Music Festival. North Bedeque WI provided a music teacher for the school, sponsored a hot lunch program, donated books to the school library in memory of departed members, and gave an Encyclopedia for use of the students. They also provided a Community Centre for their area by renovating the local hall and donating supplies.

North Bedeque Institute had the distinction of making more layettes for Unitarian Services Committee than any other group, and appeared as guests of CKCW at Moncton.

North Bedeque WI remained active in their community for more than twenty years before disbanding in 1972.

North Granville

We recently celebrated our 65th anniversary at North Granville WI with a potluck supper in the Centre. Husbands, families, and other community residents were present with our members. Following a most delicious supper, our President and our Secretary received their Life Memberships. Rowena Taylor read the President's citation, Helen Weeks presented the certificate, and Helen Parsons presented Mrs. MacWards, President, with her pin. Jennie Taper read the citation for Mrs. Beatrice Parson, Secretary, Aline Coles presented the certificate, and Maude Matheson presented her pin.

Although taken by surprise, each expressed their thanks to the members, and then we all enjoyed some slides.

North Lake

North Lake Women's Institute first organized in July of 1914. This Institute originally served three districts – Elmira, Lakeville, and North Lake. Elmira later withdrew and organized their own Institute branch, and in 1959 Lakeville did the same. The North Lake WI remained active for more than sixty years before disbanding in 1977.

North Milton

North Milton WI celebrated our 50th anniversary on November 18th, 1996. We honoured twelve living Chartered Members and twelve posthumously.

For fun and fundraising events we hold "Meet Your Neighbour" Nights, auctions, teas, yard sales, bake sales, lotteries on quilts and other items, and much more. We supported our school, providing music and other needs before amalgamation. Now we donate prizes to the high schools in our area. We also participated in the annual Roadside Cleanup. This proved to be too much for a handful of people, so we asked each person to look after their own frontage. This has worked out well.

You would think that all that ditch hopping, along with cleaning the school, cleaning the hall and our own spring housecleaning would have done a great deal towards narrowing our waist-lines. It didn't help much. We had too many scrumptious cooks, and too many community events with lunches! We tried to give up on or cut down lunches at our WI meetings, but to no avail. Our love of food won out. Being a miserly bunch, you would have thought that the idea of charging each member $0.01 for each inch of waistline would have deterred us, but No! We just kept on eating and eating, and getting fatter and fatter.

Also according to human nature, we kept growing older and older. We accepted that. Nevertheless, it was a bit annoying to be obliged to put one cent, for each year of our age, into a birthday box. It is bad enough to be getting fatter and growing older without being penalized for it.

We have had some pretty good roll call responses. One was "A suggested remedy for anything," or "A household duty that I enjoy," from December 1965. This one really made me snicker, because by that time most of us were busy washing, ironing cooking, cleaning separators and milk pails, and trying to raise a bunch of children. At the same time we may have been spending 3/4 of the day in the potato field, and in the other quarter we would be cooking for all the pickers, and trying to sweep a path through the house. What we enjoyed most was probably flopping into bed at night. Another good one was "What men think about women," or "What man would dare tell a woman, and what woman would really want to know."

We always try to have interesting and enjoyable programs and events. Some examples of programs include armchair travelling, Island touring, and social and health issues. One of our early programs was entitled Nursing in the Far North, while a more recent topic was Farm Marketing and Associated Stress. At one early WI meeting we talked about the idea of women serving on the Jury. The consensus was that jury duty was advisable for women, but should not be on a compulsory basis. (I do not think that the women of today would feel that they needed the special treatment.) Some of the events where members received honours included Woman of the Year Awards, Drama Festivals, Music Festivals, and Life Membership Presentations. Life memberships have been presented to Nanne

Garrham, Anna Thompson, Beth Neill, the late Mary Coles, Doris MacKenzie, Alesha Coles, Marjorie Leard, and Mary Hooper.

We are thankful for the direction of Provincial Board and the ACWW who have helped us to become more and more aware of the need for self education, and the need to recognize the problems of people in our community, province, our country and throughout the world. While keeping these things in mind in a fast moving world, as more and more people move into the rural communities we women of the WI must work hard to hold on to the close community spirit we have had in the past.

North Pinette

Kathleen Ross

Institute 153 formed on December 1, 1927 in Roseberry, PEI. Miss Saunders came from Charlottetown to a meeting at the home of Mabel MacEachern, and she explained the duties to a group of seven ladies, all of whom joined. Meetings were held monthly, and according to the minutes, they were quite entertaining. Members exchanged many household hints, home remedies, and recipes. In 1928 membership was 18, with the collection for the year amounting to $6.35. This group disbanded in October 1930.

In October 1928 the name Roseberry changed to North Pinette; this is still our community's name today.

In 1939 the WI group formed again; Miss Mary MacDonald came from Charlottetown to reorganize the WI. One of the members from this meeting now lives in Charlottetown (Tessie Ross, aged 95). There were many benefits held at the local hall to raise funds for the group, with a fee of $3.00 for the rent.

In 1968 we bought the former North Pinette school from the School Board, and now this building is very convenient for many functions in our community.

We are very proud to have all of our branch's minute books in our possession. We are still active, but our membership is down to eight. Our group doesn't have young members but we enjoy each other and working "For Home and Country."

North River
Margaret MacKinley, Erna Younker, Irma Gallant

As we begin to prepare this history, we think back to those eight farmers' wives who met in East Wiltshire schoolhouse in July 1913 and organized Harmony WI. They soon changed the name to North River WI.

Conditions were very different in rural PEI then. Money was scarce, but by working together they accomplished many things. School and community improvements were foremost in their minds. For some of them the WI meeting was a night out and many times they would take "the baby" with them rather than stay home.They found time to knit and sew for the Red Cross during the war years, and many a young bride received much instruction in home making from the older and experienced members.

In 1979 there were thirty-four members enrolled, thirteen of them Life Members. We now have twenty-nine, and sixteen are Life Members. We have made many achievements over the years. For instance, in 1979 we successfully lobbied the Department of Highways to install traffic lights at North River Corner. We maintained the WI Park at North River until the Town of Cornwall took over the task following amalgamation. In 1985 we received a citation for outstanding volunteer work with the Blood Donor Clinics, and in 1984 our WI purchased the Warren Grove School, which we later turned over to the CIC as a Community Centre.

We have made donations large and small, to initiatives such as the Adelaide Hoodless Homestead, the IWK Hospital, Mentally Challenged Children's Camp, Scouts and Brownies, Unitarian Services, and Sherwood Home. We donate money each year toward the prizes at Bluefield and East Wiltshire Schools. We made and donated a quilt to a family who had lost their home by fire. We knit for the Red Cross, supported MS, and the 1984 project for Clean Water. Since 1990 we have donated a special prize for a quilt at the Provincial Fair in memory of a deceased member. We support BOB, Pennies for Friendship, Transition House, Anderson House, Red Shield Campaign, Easter Seals and White Gift project. We knitted squares for Zambia, and gave donations to assist the children of

Chernobyl, The International Peace Garden and the Field House and Dream Park at East Wiltshire and Cornwall Schools. We remember our members on Golden Wedding Anniversaries, special birthdays, and give Memorial Gifts, and in 1993 we attended Lois Thompson's retirement party. Each year at Christmas we remember the older residents and shut-ins.

We raise money for these donations by catering to wedding receptions, anniversaries, levees, and banquets. We hold suppers, auction sales, and make and sell prize quilts.

We've had speakers from Transition House, Heart and Stroke Foundation, RCMP, Hospice, North River Fire Department, Partners For Living, and two exchange students who had spent months in France, just to name a few. Our community service includes sponsoring the Red Cross swimming classes and subsidizing each student from the community with $10, Roadside Cleanup, knitting mitts for the local firemen, and donating money to the Fire hall.

It hasn't been all work and no play. Each year in June or early July the group goes out to eat and then to visit something of interest. We've entertained our spouses, held "Meet Your Neighbour Nights", lawn parties, picnics, and attended craft demonstrations. Each year we go to one of the nursing homes to entertain the residents.

As we pause to think about our achievements we are quite pleased and hope our WI will continue to be active for many more years.

North Tryon

North Tryon WI organized on December 9, 1927. Eight women – Nettie Callbeck, Winnie Dawson, Minnie Delaney, Lila Gamble, Gertrude Inman, Margaret Johnson, Georgie Lefurgey, and school teacher Pearl Ramsay – met at the home of Lila Gamble. These ladies continued to meet on the first Wednesday of each month.

Records of meetings held during the first thirty years of the Institute were lost in a house fire. Members recall that in addition to supporting the local school and community, our WI also made quilts and knit socks, mittens and vests for the soldiers who served overseas during the war. During these years there were approximately twenty-one members in the North Tryon WI.

North Tryon Institute was instrumental in having the school expanded from one to two rooms, and we provided desks, installed chemical toilets, purchased a piano, cupboards, maps, books, playground equipment, and all the other needs for a rural school. Our Institute also hired Professor William Jones to instruct the pupils in music.

We continue to support community children in their academic, music, and sporting events. We also support the South Shore Arena, the 4-H, the Red Cross swimming program, and Englewood and Bluefield Schools. We host community showers, canvass for charities, and organize the annual Roadside Cleanup. We maintain the old schoolhouse as a Community Centre, and host annual Christmas Parties and Canada Day Celebrations.

In 1977 we received three Rural Beautification awards for our community improvements. These awards provided seed funding for the community history, *Remember Yesterday 1769-1992*. This two volume work not only covers community history but also provides genealogical information, and over 500 photographs on the families that lived in the community between 1769 and 1992.

Four members of the North Tryon Women's Institute have served on the executive of the Federated Women's Institutes of PEI – Adelaide Wood, Convener of Education from 1941-1945; Hazel Robinson, Convener of Agriculture and Chairperson of "From Farm to Table" from 1989-1991; Thelma Inman, Convener of Canadian Industry and Safety from 1995-1997 and Convener of Agriculture and Forestry from 1997-1999; and Margaret Scott, Radio Convener for the Federated Women's Institute of PEI from 1989-1990.

North Tryon WI received the Elaine Burke Award in 1998. This is a national award given to a volunteer group in each province, as recognition for planting trees in the community. We established Memorial Park around Lord's Pond, and installed a walking trail through the park and a footbridge across the stream. We planted many trees in the park as well as at our Community Center.

We celebrated the 70th anniversary of our WI on December 9, 1997. We currently have nineteen members, and meet on the first Monday of each month. Our officers are Heather Dixon, President;

Hazel Robinson, Vice-President; Thelma Inman, Secretary; Loraine MacDonald, Treasurer.

North Wiltshire
Irene Godfrey

On October 16th, 1933, a group of dedicated ladies met in North Wiltshire Hall and organized a WI. Our first President was Mrs. Sadie (Bruce) Deacon.

A brief look at the past 63 years shows a variety of activities in the community, such as the upkeep of North Wiltshire School and the Community Hall. We have given sewing classes, provided treats for school children and shut-ins, and sponsored swimming lessons and other projects.

In 1939 when the dark clouds of war threatened all that we hold dear, the rural women of North Wiltshire were organized and ready to help and did their part with Red Cross Projects. They knitted many pairs of socks and mittens, quilted, and made bandages. Now we hold card parties each week and the proceeds go towards maintaining the Hall and other charitable purposes. We have also held "Meet Your Neighbour" nights, and donated the money toward the purchase of the new Mammography machine for the QEH.

Women's Institutes have helped to make our communities a better place to live, and may we as Women's Institute members continue to put our better impulses into action, straightforward and unafraid.

North Winsloe

North Winsloe WI first organized in 1939. The first officers were Mrs. Stanley Younker, President; Mrs. Ray Ford, Vice-President; Mrs. Ray Ford, Secretary.

From 1939 to 1972 this WI branch was active in meeting the needs of their community. They were particularly interested in working with the Red Cross and the Unitarian Service Committee. They also provided a piano and a music teacher for their school.

The North Winsloe WI disbanded in 1972, then re-organized from 1974 to 1979. In 1979 they disbanded again, and have not re-organized since.

O'Brien Road

Also known as Elmsdale West, O'Brien Road WI organized in May of 1932. Their first President was Mrs. Austin O'Brien, Vice-President Mrs. Charles Dunn, and the Secretary-Treasurer Mrs. A. D. O'Brien.

O'Brien Road WI remained active for over thirty years before disbanding.

O'Leary

Excerpted from **Threads of the Past,** *published by the O'Leary Women's Institute in 1993.*

O'Leary Institute first organized in 1928, but disbanded. On September 11, 1947, Mary MacDonald reorganized the WI in this community. The officers were Mrs. James MacWilliams, President; Mrs. B.S. Dumville, Vice-President; Mrs. E.W. Turner, Secretary-Treasurer.

O'Leary WI sponsored Cub and Scout troops for many years. Most of their efforts center on their school and their community. They hired a music teacher, and donated items such as blackboards, playground equipment, and the school's new electric bell. O'Leary WI also contributed to the Red Cross, March of Dimes, Cancer Society, Salvation Army, and the Tuberculosis League. In order to support their activities and donations, O'Leary WI holds bake sales, afternoon teas, bazaars, suppers, auctions, and they occasionally cater to special functions.

O'Leary WI is still active in their community today.

Orwell

Mrs. Ross McKenna

The Women's Institute in Orwell first organized in 1929. Mrs. James Hughes served as first President, and Florence MacDonald, the schoolteacher, was the first Secretary. Other charter members were Maimie Morrissey, Mrs. Laura MacLeod, Mrs. Margaret MacLeod, Mrs. Lea MacDonald, Mrs. Mary MacInnis, Mrs. William Greenwood and Mrs. Laurenne MacLeod.

In 1931 our WI assumed the responsibilities of the Community Hall, and we maintained it until it burned down in 1956. During the war years our members spent many hours knitting and making quilts to be sent overseas. The orphanages were also a priority, and they gave generously. They kept the school clean and comfortable.

From 1950 forward Orwell WI focussed on the school. We bought window blinds, painted, put linoleum on the floor, bought an oil stove to replace the pot bellied coal stove, and provided books, cod liver oil capsules, soups for lunch, and many other things. In 1965 when our members saw that Orwell school would soon be closing, we organized a celebration in honour of the 70th anniversary of the school. Approximately forty former teachers were present, along with the first teacher Ella MacKenzie, a resident of Orwell. Janice McKenna, the youngest girl attending Orwell School at that time, presented Mrs. MacKenzie with a bouquet of flowers.

After the school closed in 1967, we found a broader community for whom to work. We supported 4H, donated to the first kindergarten organized in Vernon River School and continue to do so, sponsored an adopted child from a Third World Country since the early 1970s (the present child is from Haiti), give gifts to newcomers to the district and new babies and newlyweds, give gifts to the White Cross at Christmas time, and sponsor the Terry Fox Run since 1981.

We donated to a Mammography machine in 1976, the Catscan in 1980's, and $500 towards to the purchase of a Stereotactic Mammography machine by the Queen Elizabeth Hospital in 1996. We donated money towards the building of Pownal Rink, and in the 1970s we took turns working in the canteen with our neighbouring Institutes. Our branch has donated clothing to USC, layettes to the Red Cross in the 1980s, and Orwell WI members are Upper Room Angels.

To improve our community, we install flower boxes at each end of the district on the Trans Canada, purchased a Santa Claus suit for concerts at Orwell Corner, presented $1,000 to Vernon River School in 1992, and gave a large donation to the Orwell Corner Museum.

Our membership has always remained quite strong, with an average of eighteen to twenty members since 1979. Eight of those members have their Life Memberships. We have enjoyed twinning with neighbouring Institutes. Orwell WI has had three members on the Provincial Board.

Our WI won the Lord Tweedsmuir Competition in June of 1985 for our history of Orwell. We nominated Mrs. Enid Ross, an Institute member, for Woman of the Year; she was runner-up.

Orwell WI members are grateful to have the use of Orwell Corner Hall, as we use the Hall for fundraising by catering to canteens for special events and the October Fest Supper.

Oyster Bed Bridge

Oyster Bed Bridge WI organized in 1925. The first officers were Mrs. Solomon McKenna, President; Mrs. Raymond Ling, Secretary; Elsie Brown, Treasurer.

Our Institute has always been busy working "For Home and Country."

We fundraise by making quilts and rugs, delivering lunches for special occasions, and holding dinners and coffee parties. We donate to various worthy causes, such as the Catscan and Stereotactic Mammography units at the QEH, and the Women's Auxiliary "Buckle Up Baby" fund.

We have entered our handicraft work in a number of competitions. In 1961, our branch won first prize for hooked chair seats at the FWIC convention in Vancouver. We have also been recognized at the Tweedsmuir competition for our Afghans and hooked rugs. Our wall hanging design won first prize in the PEIWI's 75th anniversary competition.

At Oyster Bed Bridge WI we enjoy many celebrations and outings. We hold a "Family Night" at the Wheatley River Hall and a "Meet Your Neighbour Day" at the Lions Hall in South Rustico. We celebrated our 60th, 65th, and 70th anniversaries, and had twinning parties with the North Granville, New Haven, Dunstaffnage, Breadalbane, Fredericton/Hazel Grove and Greenvale Women's Institutes. We viewed an antique quilt display at the Confederation Centre and a Victorian flower display at Beaconsfield, went to see the play "Anne of Green Gables", and toured The Barachois Inn and the Catholic Church in South Rustico. We have honoured seven of our members with Life Memberships.

Panmure Island

Panmure Island WI first organized in October of 1937. Their first President was Mrs. Mathias Condon. As part of a very small community, this branch struggled for a number of years with low membership. Still the members made their contribution to the area, and particularly to their school. The Panmure Island WI remained active for more than forty years before disbanding.

Parkdale

For almost fifty years Parkdale WI found creative ways to contribute to their community and the province of PEI. First organized in 1937, the first officers were Mrs. Edwin Cook, President; Mrs. Wesley Dennis, Vice-President; Mrs. Olive MacMillan, Secretary; Mrs. Hilbert Frizzell, Treasurer.

Parkdale WI contributed to their school, and participated in Red Cross war work during the Second World War. This branch was largely responsible for the addition of a second wing to the Provincial Sanatorium in 1945. They built their own community hall and maintained it. Parkdale WI won a number of prizes for their work in the arts and in community safety.

This branch disbanded in the early 1980s.

Parkside

Parkside WI organized in 1958, as a branch-off of the Avonlea Institute. This branch was active for more than ten years before disbanding.

Pembroke

Pembroke WI first organized in 1926. This branch was active in their community for more than forty years before disbanding.

Peter's Road

Ione Kelly

On the 15th day of August 1925, eight women of the small community of Peter's Road (Alma) met to organize a Women's Institute. The organization proved invaluable in bringing these women together in fellowship and for projects to raise funds, used primarily to support the one room school and the needs of the community. During the war years the branch worked hard to aid in the war effort.

Although times have changed and our interests have broadened, WI remains a vital part of our community. Through monies raised we meet the needs of the community and support PEIWI projects, the hospitals, and other areas of need.

Peter's Road (Alma) WI now counts ten members, including five Life Members. The monthly meetings continue to bring women together as friends with common goals.

Pisquid East

Pisquid East WI came together for the first time on November 5, 1928. This branch was active for more than forty years before disbanding.

Pleasant Circle

Jane MacKenzie first organized Pleasant Circle WI on October 20, 1926. Mrs. Ewen Cameron served as their first President.

This branch was active for almost fifty years. Their chief interest was in their school, and they sponsored sewing clubs, food clubs and calf clubs.

The Pleasant Circle WI disbanded in 1972.

Pleasant Court

From: "A History of Pleasant Court Institute," Mrs. James MacLeod, held at Provincial Office, PEIWI

"After I came to Kensington in 1965, I rejoined Long River Institute. Bertha MacLeod used to go with me to the meetings. One night when we were coming home, Bertha said, "Wouldn't it be nice to have an Institute in Kensington?" I said I didn't think we could as I thought they were for Rural Districts, but I would find out.

So the next day I called Mrs. Leslie Ramsay and asked her about it. She said, "Yes. Of course they are trying to get Institutes started in Towns." She volunteered to get in contact with them in Charlottetown, and she would let us know when they would come to organize one.

On February 19, 1969, Mrs. Grimmett, Home Economist, came from Charlottetown. Mrs. Louise Marchbank and Mrs. Roma Campbell, PEIWI Vice President and Past President respectively, were also present. The meeting took place in Pleasant Court C Building at 2 o'clock. Ten joined that day. The slate of officers was: myself as President, Ethel Champion as Vice-President, Bertha MacLeod as Secretary, Mrs. Fred Nash as Treasurer, and Alma Paynter as Red Cross Convener. It was decided to name the Institute "Pleasant Court Institute" after the Senior Citizens' Complex in Kensington, and to meet the first Tuesday of each month at 2 p.m.

The ten who joined were: Lina MacLeod, Ethel Champion, Bertha MacLeod, Ann Nash, Alma Paynter, Lily Profitt, Katie Champion, Lizzie Roach, Leona Blackmore, and Emily Mill.

At the next meeting three more joined – Ola Warren, Madge Cotton, and Beatrice Hamilton. And at the next meeting four more joined – Mrs. Hartwell Condon, Margaret Campbell, Miss Hattie Clark, and Mrs. Hilda Duggan.

At the next meeting we were visited by Premier Campbell, Max Thompson (MLA), and Frank Jardine (MLA). We were honored and surprised, as we did not expect them.

I was President from February 19, 1969 until September 14, 1971. Margaret Campbell was made President at that time. She held the office until September 1973. I was put back in again until September 1975. Mrs. Florence Curley was President from then until our annual meeting in September 1977, when Mrs. Ella Wall was elected President.

We did a lot of knitting and sewing for the Red Cross back over the years. Now it is no longer needed. We have made a great many quilts too. The first few years we gave them to the Red Cross to give away. However lately we have been selling them. We made a lot of things for the UNICEF."

The Pleasant Court WI is no longer active.

Pleasant Valley

Louise Weeks

On November 1, 1923, fourteen women met in the Pleasant Valley School, and from that meeting Pleasant Valley Women's Institute formed. Eight charter members enrolled at the first regular meeting on November 12. Before the first year ended, the number of members increased to twenty-four.The first officers were Mrs. Hugh F MacKay, President; Mrs. J. B. MacDowell, Vice-President; Miss. Marion Andrews, Secretary-Treasurer.

Our branch initially focussed on improving the school by supplying needed equipment for the teacher and students, such as maps, globes, a bookcase, books, cleaning supplies, painting the interior and exterior, and adding a sign board and a flag. The next priority was the community. Members called on residents in times of sickness, death, or disasters (fires), and any time help was needed the WI members answered.

In the 1960s we introduced program booklets, hired a music teacher, gave prize money to the regional high school, supported the Swimming Rock Project, and purchased supplies for the new district school built in 1964. We canvassed the district for the fire department, Red Cross, and later for the United Way and Cancer Society.

In 1972, after much protest about the school closure from parents, residents, and WI members, the school closed and children were bused to Hunter River. Following this disappointment, our WI worked together with the community and purchased the school building, debt included, as a Community Centre. We presented each school child with a 1972 silver dollar.

In recent years our membership has declined, but a few faithful members carry on WI work. Many things have changed since the school closed, but we now focus on supporting the needs of our Community Centre and the regional schools that our children attend.

We now cater to various banquets at the Community Centre, and organize the annual community variety concert. Our WI's annual financial reports show an income of over $2,000. We use the money to support the Community Centre and community needs such as treats to the sick, gifts to new comers, and baby gifts. We also support the Bluefield High School prize list, the WI prizes at the exhibition, Queen Elizabeth Hospital, IWK Hospital, our local 4-H club, and the Music Festival.

In 1993 we celebrated our 75th anniversary. It was a night of banquet, entertainment and reminiscing. Former and present members were present, many wearing costumes of the early 1900's.

Our present membership stands at eleven, six of whom are Life Members. Although we are fewer than in 1923, we are still proud to carry on the work that was started here many years ago. Things change but some things remain the same. Our work is still "For Home and Country."

Piusville

Piusville WI organized on May 7, 1930. Their first President was Mrs. John F. Gallant, and their Secretary-Treasurer Mrs. William Gallant.

This branch was active for more than thirty years before disbanding.

Pont Prim – Mount Buchanan

We at Point Prim-Mount Buchanan WI have always been active. Some members have retired, and many have passed on, leaving us with many precious memories. We hold our meetings in our homes on the second Tuesday of each month. At present, we have approximately twenty-two members, many of whom are young women, very active and full of ambition. We work together to make things click.

We are fortunate to have the oldest lighthouse in Canada in our district. With funding from the Belfast CIC, we maintain the grounds and supply picnic tables and swings for the children. In July and August we hire three students through the Department of Industry to give tours and information to the visitors at the lighthouse. This year we had 3,600 visitors sign the guest book.

In 1995 we celebrated the 150th Anniversary of the Point Prim lighthouse. With the help of the Coop we planned a program of speakers, music by the Belfast Pipe Band, violin music by local players, and singing. We supplied an anniversary cake baked by a member. All present enjoyed the event. It was a gala occasion with young and old dressed in period costumes.

Our main means of fundraising are annual fashion shows, bake sales, and selling tickets on craft items made by our members.

We support our local school by contributing to sports and playground equipment, the library and computer programs, and the summer swimming program. We also support the Kindergarten and the Belfast Pipe Band and Highland Dancers. At Christmas, we give treats to all shut-ins and seniors, and food boxes to needy families. We organize showers for all newly-weds in our community, and all new babies get a special gift. We present a Women's Institute cookbook to all new residents, and support the Queen Elizabeth Hospital, the IWK Grace, and many other charities.

Our members all enjoy the social part of our club, especially our annual Christmas party, where we discover the identity of our secret pal. Our summer picnic is also a very special day, and meeting with our twin WI is both interesting and enjoyable. Over the past years we have presented many members with Life Memberships.

In all, we support our motto "For Home and Country".

Poplar Grove – MacNeill's Mills
Verna Barlow

On November 24, 1924 Poplar Grove Women's Institute organized with the guidance of E. Windsor, Director of the Women's Institute. Nineteen members paid the twenty-five cent membership fee at the first regular meeting.

In the early 1970s MacNeill's Mills WI's membership declined. Some were unable to attend due to ill health, some were just getting older, but the outcome was that they were unable to maintain their own branch. The remaining members joined Poplar Grove WI. Although MacNeill's Mills had been part of the Poplar Grove WI for more than ten years by that time, the official amalgamation was in September 1985.

Institute night in the early days was a big night for the men as well as the women. In horse and buggy days, and even in many of the years following the arrival of cars, men-folk provided the transportation. There was great attendance at the meetings and sometimes after the meeting! Members served lunch, and if there was a violin around and someone to play it, they rolled back the carpets and everyone enjoyed a reel or two.

To look back over the years, many pictures pass before our minds – pictures of good times, hard times, happy days, sad days, war times, and peace times. Through all of these years, the women of our group have worked tirelessly filling each year with a record of deeds done "For Home and Country".

During the war our members were busy giving both their time and money to the Red Cross, and packing parcels for the many from our communities who served overseas. When peace returned, our branch undertook other tasks. We collected for worthy societies, visited the sick and shut-ins, brought comfort to the bereaved, support to the needy, and always looked to the needs of our school and its teachers. We welcomed newcomers to the district, gave community brides a wedding gift, and in later years, packed boxes of goodies for the aged in the community at Christmas.

We fundraise in various ways. We hold Ice Cream Socials, concerts, dances, bazaars, suppers, pantry sales, plays, and we cater to banquets. A travelling apron also makes its rounds each year and realizes a tidy bit of money.

We have celebrated several special anniversaries over the years with a special meal. The first was our 34th in 1958, then there was the 50th, the 60th, and our latest was our 70th anniversary on October 27, 1994. We have given fifteen Life Memberships, and seven of these members are still active.

Poplar Grove – MacNeill's Mills WI members have worked together, and our co-operation and fellowship has added a great deal to each one of our lives and has made us better citizens in serving "Home and Country".

Our WI has stood the test of time well. But what of today? What does the future hold for us as a small group in this uncertainty and change? Does our Creed not say, "Let us take time for all things"? One evening each month spent with neighbours and friends can prove to be a rich and rewarding experience. With the wisdom of the last on which to build our future, let us go on confident of our success. At present we have fifteen active members. We are very proud of our organization, knowing we have kept it together all those years, and we feel that with the continued co-operation of everyone, we have a bright and prosperous future.

Port Hill

Miss Matheson first organized Port Hill WI on November 6, 1923, with Mary Adams as President and Jennie Jardine their Secretary-Treasurer.

The school has always been our main concern, but we are also very active in other aspects of our community. As an example of our early contributions to the school, in 1924 we assisted in moving and renovating it. We continued to look after its upkeep by cleaning, painting and donations for a new floor, blackboard, maps, stove, desks and wiring. Our branch raised money by holding dances, ice-cream socials, plays, concerts, bean suppers, card parties and making and selling tickets on an autograph quilt.

During the war we sent boxes to our soldiers overseas, and on their return we held a welcome home party and presented them with gifts. We place a wreath at the Cenotaph each Remembrance Day.

When the Stewart Memorial Health Centre opened in 1951, we gave donations of money, blankets, pillows, knitting goods, toys and clothing for patients. We continue to help with suppers and teas to raise money.

In 1953 WI District #3 was host to a delegation of the Associated Country Women of the World. Tyne Valley served dinner, and we had the pleasure of hosting some of the delegates in Port Hill overnight.

At our District Convention in 1973 we put on a fashion show with clothes from the past 100 years. We were invited to our Annual Island Convention in Charlottetown to portray the styles and way of life on PEI sixty years ago, and to present our fashion show at the Lobster Carnival in Summerside on WI night. In August of the same year His Excellency Roland Michener officially opened the Green Park Shipbuilding Site. Birch Hill, Arlington and our WI had the pleasure of serving tea at the Yeo House to Their Excellencies and 500 other guests.

We raise money for our rink by helping with the Oyster Festival. We contribute to the maintenance of King George Hall by cleaning and donating to funds for wiring, an oil stove, silverware and dishes. We also help with the Blueberry Festival at the Yeo House, Green Park.

Our WI was instrumental in having a light placed at Port Hill Corner. We give a blanket to each fire victim in our WI district, and sponsor a shower for each lady or gent when married. In the last ten years, we have presented plaques to four of our members who celebrated their ninetieth birthdays.

Pownal

Francis Jones

In February of 1937 a group of women from the communities of Alexandra and Pownal met at the home of Mrs. Walter Ings in Pownal. These women organized a Women's Institute branch, and within two years the branch had grown to the point where they deemed it necessary to separate and have a WI in each community.

Our Pownal branch carried on as a very active organization. Improving and supplying needs for the one room school was the main concern in the early years, as was assisting in the war effort. For many years we organized and provided leadership to Girls and Boys Clubs (4H). We supported all provincial projects, such as music, drama, Red Cross, swimming lessons. Two of our members served on the PEIWI Provincial Board.

On our 50th anniversary, five of our charter members received Life Memberships – Hazel Smith, Florence Smith, Florence MacMillan, Margaret Jenkins, and Winnie Herman. Four additional members received Life Memberships at our 55th anniversary – Francis Jones, Bertha Brown, Doris Worth, and Ruth Judson.

Priest Pond

Priest Pond WI organized in May of 1922. Their first officers were Mrs. Leith Cowan, President; Mrs. D.A. Horton, Vice-President; Mrs. George Beck, Secretary-Treasurer. This branch was active for over forty years before disbanding.

Queen Mary

Queen Mary WI first organized in 1919. This branch operated in Murray Harbour. Their first President was Mrs. Freeman Reynolds, and their first Vice-President was Mrs. Wallace White. The Queen Mary branch originally encompassed White Sands, Beach Point, and Guernsey Cove, but the former two eventually formed their own branches. The women of White Sands named their WI branch "Royal Oak."

Queen Mary WI was very active in their community for over sixty years. They purchased the old one-room school when it closed and converted it into a community centre. This branch was also highly involved with the Unitarian Service Committee and the Red Cross.

The Queen Mary WI disbanded in the 1980s.

Ray of Hope
Zelda MacNevin

Eighty-two years represents three or four generations in the life of a community. In Murray River, it represents the many contributions of the Ray of Hope WI to Murray River and to the wider community.

On October 13, 1914, nine women met with Miss Dunbrack to form an organization that "would give them a forum for the discussion of rural problems, and enable them to acquire information regarding their responsibilities as homemakers and as citizens." The charter members of the organization were Mrs. L. Brehaut, Mrs. A. Hardy, Mrs. W. Kearney, Mrs. R. Keenan, Mrs. P. Lowe, Mrs. A. MacKenzie, Mrs. M. MacLeod, Miss. S. MacLeod (Mrs. A. Bell), and Mrs. M. MacLure. The events of world history altered their agenda by adding many responsibilities.

In 1914 Murray River WI amalgamated with the Women's Patriotic Association, and as "The Ray of Hope" (hence the origin of the current name) began their work. During World War 1 they raised over $1,000, knitted 500 pairs of socks, many pairs of mittens, shirts, pajamas, and made two quilts – one for France in 1916, and one for a Canadian hospital in England in 1917. They supported the Red Cross, the Halifax Relief Fund, and the Belgian Relief Fund. Each month they sent boxes to soldiers from the district who were serving overseas. In 1919 they held a welcome home reception, and each soldier received an engraved signet ring. They accomplished all of these things in their first four years!

During the 1920s and the 1930s new issues in education, health, and society arose and became the focus for Ray of Hope's ingenuity and industry. Members carried out school inspections and purchased much-needed articles for the classrooms, they built new sidewalks (and later were instrumental in installing the first streetlights) and they supported the Protestant Orphanage. They contributed to the Provincial Sanatorium and a dental clinic. These demanding years saw membership increase – the records from 1925-1926 show a membership of forty members.

During World War 2 our branch actively supported the war effort by sending care packages and knitting for the Red Cross. At the same time, the members continued their active participation in school and community affairs.

Ray of Hope members gave their full support to the Murray River Library. We have provided financial support since the Library opened, and in 1953 we made a donation to the new Library site. This financial help continued until the Library became the responsibility of the Murray River Council.

Ray of Hope WI has responded to appeals from the Prince Edward Island Hospital, the Montague Hospital, the King's County Memorial Hospital, and the Queen Elizabeth Hospital. We contributed to hospital equipment funds, such as the Mammography machine for QEH and a monitor for KCMH.

PEIWI programs have always been central to the development of the Ray of Hope Branch. Our members served as members of the Provincial Board, and we attended the Provincial and District Conventions and workshops. We give financial support to the Helen Herring Scholarship Fund, Pennies for Friendship, Bob the Beaver, and the Red Cross Swim Program.

Our capacity for friendship has also been a major contributing factor to our growth and success. The recent addition of five new members proves the relevance and vitality of the Ray of Hope Branch.

Red Point

Bessie Ching

Ida Ching brought the Women's Institute to Red Point PEI on July 5, 1915 by holding the first meeting at her home. Most of the discussion at that meeting focussed on the call for help from the Red Cross as World War 1 was underway.

In 1917 members collected $3.90, which paid off the debt remaining on the Red Point School. In March 1931, fifteen members and three visitors decided to pay the 50-cent rent on the Baltic Hall. They also voted to donate $5 to each orphanage.

We did more for our local school in the earlier days. Two members visited the school each month to find out what the teacher and children needed. We supplied bedding for the Provincial Sanatorium, repaired the school pump, and purchased a water bucket and dipper. We collected cream from farmers and made homemade ice cream to sell at special occasions such as the field day our farmers held each year. At our annual school fair we gave five dollars in prizes for the children.

We still do pretty much the same work as we always did, such as working for the Red Cross and catering to youth groups from Charlottetown when Allan Andrews was here. We help with swimming lessons held at Red Point, and provide beds for the instructors. We knit and crochet for the Red Cross, send boxes to the Lions Club for needy children, give gifts to the local manor residents at Christmas, give gifts to the White Cross, and make ornaments for patients' trays at Souris Hospital for Christmas. We pay into a scholarship fund for prizes in grades 9, 10, and 11 at Souris Regional High School. We have a birthday party for the manor once a year, with cake, ice cream, and music. We take July and August off from meetings and go to a local restaurant for a meal. In September, we have a potluck supper at a member's home to begin a new year. We make quilts and everyone helps to quilt them. Then we sell tickets on it and the money helps us to help others. We always send two members to attend the WI convention in Charlottetown.

Our Secretary celebrated her 93rd birthday in August 1999. We told her if she stayed until the year 2000, we would try to get someone to take her place. It's later than you think and we don't see anyone looking for her job!

On looking over the membership list from back in the thirties, we had a very large membership. In 1933-34 we had thirty members. Just two of the original members are still active in WI. Many things have changed, but our WI remains with eight members attending monthly meetings. We hope we will all be active, willing, and ready for the year 2000, and hope the Y2K bug will not put us out of order.

Rennie's Road

The Rennie's Road WI first organized on March 2, 1952. This branch remained active for more than twenty-five years before disbanding.

Rice Point

Mary Lou MacLaine

Rice Point WI has struggled through some stormy seas. The group disbanded in 1964 because of low membership, but then reorganized in 1966. In 1970, membership rose to ten, with the following members: Mrs. Louis Burdett, Mrs. Allan MacDonald, Mrs. Mack MacDonald, Mrs. William MacEachern, Mrs. Walter Lepage, Mrs. L.T. Lowther, Mrs. Neil MacEachern, Mrs. Winston Taylor, Mrs. Reginald Taylor, and Mrs. Donald MacLaine.

In 1977 Rice Point again decided to sever ties with organized WI and became a community social club. Seven charter members revived the WI in Rice Point three years later. The 1980 charter members were Christine Taylor, Jean Lepage, Maisie MacLaine, Mary Lou MacLaine, Connie Crosby, Valerie Desroches, and Margie MacKenzie.

Until 1973, the Rice Point School was the focal point of members, with fundraising activities such as socials and pantry sales. In 1967 we purchased an organ for the school, and for some years our WI hired and paid the salary for a music teacher for the children. We sponsored swimming lessons at the Rice Point shore from 1969 to 1973, and each year members volunteered to board the swimming instructor and to pay his salary.

In 1983 Rice Point members made a lovely wool yarn wall hanging bearing our Lady Slipper emblem, which we sent to an FWIC convention in British Columbia to be sold. In 1989, members made an original design quilt under the guidance of member Cynthia Gallant Simpson. The sale of this quilt realized funds of $495, which we distributed to various organizations such as the new Afton Commmunity Centre, Mann House, Anderson House, Red Cross Water Safety, the QEH Cat-Scan fund, and the Sudan project.

For many years Allan and Mary MacDonald treated us to a June meeting lobster supper at their home. Mary received her Life Membership in 1998.

At the beginning of 2000 we have nine members in Rice Point WI. The President is Jane Hall, the Secretary is Ruth Acorn, Nora

MacLaine is the Treasurer, and the following women serve as conveners: Mary MacDonald, Brenda Connolly, Sheila MacMicken, Sharon Connolly, Brenda Brown, and Mary Lou MacLaine.

Riverdale-Churchill

Wanda Corney

Riverdale-Churchill WI first formed on March 18th, 1942. Our Institute is still active after almost sixty years.

We celebrated our 50th anniversary on June 16, 1992. Ten members were present for dinner at the Blue Goose Restaurant. We had three charter members attend, and one of these members is still active. These members were each presented with a corsage for the occasion. The same evening, Betty Watts from the Provincial Board presented Alice MacFadyen with her twenty-year Life Membership pin.

Our WI still works "For Home and Country". We donate to the QEH, White Cross, Anderson House, Bluefield Scholarship Fund, and the IWK. This spring we expect to erect our new district signs for Riverdale-Churchill.

Rollo Bay

Rollo Bay WI organized in 1936, and remained active in their community for over thirty years, but later disbanded.

Rollo Bay West

Rollo Bay West WI first organized in 1928. Their charter officers were Mrs. George Wood, President; Mary Etta McRae, Secretary-Treasurer. This branch was very active in their community. They supported their local school, held community social events, and participated in wartime work for the Red Cross. The Rollo Bay West WI was active for more than forty years, before disbanding in 1973.

Rosebank

The Rosebank WI first organized in 1929. Their first President was Mrs. MacLeod Horne, Vice-President Mrs. Burton Stewart, and their Secretary Treasurer was Mrs. Laughlan Horne.

Rosebank WI remained active for over thirty years before disbanding.

Roseneath

This Women's Institute branch first organized on December 4, 1946. Roseneath WI is still active in their community today.

Rose Valley

Rose Valley WI organized on April 26, 1932. They were active for more than thirty years before disbanding.

Royal Oak

The year was 1939, and Canada was at war. Young men and women answered the call to serve their country both here at home and overseas. The ladies in the community of White Sands met to see if they could do anything to help. This group of ladies formed a Women's Institute branch. Meanwhile, the world mourned the loss of the British battleship Royal Oak, torpedoed while at anchor in Scapa Bay of the Orkney Islands in Scotland. The ladies of White Sands chose to honour the memory of the 833 men who lost their lives by naming their WI branch "Royal Oak".

Royal Oak WI met monthly in members' homes, where they prepared care packages for the soldiers overseas throughout the war. Old meeting minutes tell us that these ladies were tireless in their efforts to raise funds for their chosen projects. Bake sales, craft sales, hooked rugs, hand made quilts and chicken dinners were but a few of the means used by these enterprising ladies. Many in the community were the recipients of their benevolence, and especially the schoolchildren. The local school was one of their special and ongoing projects. Much effort went into providing the essentials for the school such as a new stove, and they also gave the little extras.

In the early 1960s, women from Guernsey Cove decided to join Royal Oak WI. The names and faces have changed since the early years, but our purpose remains the same. We still meet monthly in members' homes to plan strategies that enable us to raise funds and support projects in our local community. Our community is no longer just White Sands and Guernsey Cove. We have contributed to projects such as "Buckle Up Baby", Red Cross Day Camps, Northumberland Arena, Kings County Memorial Hospital, Queen Elizabeth Hospital, IWK Hospital, Anderson House, treats for seniors, and many other local projects.

One of our founding members, Helen Nicolle, was honoured as PEIWI's Woman of the Year in 1976. Helen served this branch for more than twenty years as Secretary and for many more years kept all of us on track with WI business first. We, the members of the Royal Oak WI, honour Helen's memory each year by presenting a gift to the student in the grade 8 class of Southern Kings Consolidated School showing the greatest progress. This is a project that would be near and dear to Helen's heart.

Sixty good years of meeting together are behind us, and we look forward to the future with optimism. Friendships formed in the Women's Institute meetings span the generations and last a lifetime.

Saint Catherine's

Saint Catherine's WI first organized in July of 1924. The first officers were Mrs. W.R. Shaw, President; Mrs. William Morrow, Secretary-Treasurer.

Saint Catherine's WI has been busy in their community, both in supporting the schools and in community activities. They are still active today.

Saint Eleanor's

Lillian Maxfield

Mrs. Myrtle Callbeck organized St. Eleanor's Women's Institute in 1946, and she served as the first President. The first Secretary was Mrs. Rowena Cannon, and the first Treasurer Mrs. Gladys Bernard. As we look over our WI minute books and scrapbooks, we see a group of caring women working together, "For Home and Country."

We have donated to many worthwhile projects and organizations, such as The Kidney Foundation, Cancer Society, Prince County Hospital and school prizes. We have canvassed door to door many times for a number of charitable organizations. For many years St. Eleanor's WI took complete charge of the handicraft booth at the Summerside Lobster Carnival. From 1991-1994 we joined forces with the Summerside WI to manage this booth. We are also responsible for our community history, **Sketches of Old St. Eleanor's (1773-1973).**

In 1996, we honoured our one Charter Member of 50 years, Mrs. Vera Arsenault. We currently have an enrollment of twenty members, nine of whom are Life Members.

We would like to note that the St. Eleanor's WI members attended all meetings regarding amalgamation with Summerside. We were very much opposed to the idea, and we represented 98% of the residents of St. Eleanor's. Nevertheless, the Liberal Government of the day under Catherine Callbeck passed legislation that took the community of St. Eleanor's off the provincial map.

Saint Ignatius

Inez Doiron, Yvonne Gallant

St. Ignatius first organized on December 15, 1936 under the supervision of Louise Haszard. Eight ladies were present for the meeting at the schoolhouse. The first officers were Mrs. Earl Gallant, President; Mrs. Alphonse Doiron, Vice-President; Mrs. Jerimiah Peters, Secretary-Treasurer. Of the eight founding members, Mrs. Bertha Arsenault remains an active member of St. Ignatius WI

Saint Ignatius WI initially focussed on the welfare of the schoolchildren, and worked to improve their learning environment. For example, in 1952 our WI made a sizable monetary contribution to the cost of constructing a new school. Another great concern for these members was for the needy of other countries. Our branch provided layettes and used clothing through UNESCO and the Red Cross. We have donated to many community projects and organizations. Our records show that over the years we have contributed to over thirty five different causes.

We have also supported all PEIWI projects. We have twinned with North River, Victoria, Pleasant Valley and Ebenezer branches, and enjoyed an evening of fellowship and fun at each event.

We raised funds to support the school and various WI and community projects through card parties, lotteries, auction sales, Bingo, candy, and bake sales, dances and ice cream socials.

Our members have received recognition for their efforts. In 1973, PEI's Centennial year, Irene Gallant compiled the "St. Ignatius: Save Your History Project", which received honourable mention. On four different occasions, a member of our organization received a nomination for the Woman of the Year Award, and two of our members have received nominations for the Adelaide Hoodless Award of Honour. In 1974, Inez Doiron was elected to the Board of Directors of the provincial organization. From 1974-1977 she served as Safety Convener and Chairman of the annual Roadside Cleanup. In 1991, Lobelia Gallant was elected to the Board of Directors, and served as Convener of International Affairs.

We have celebrated our WI's various anniversaries. On our 30th anniversary in 1966, Mrs. Philip Matheson, President of FWIC, presented Life Memberships to three of our members. On our 40th anniversary in 1976, Provincial President Mrs. Mary MacLean presented five Life Memberships. Seven members received Life Memberships at our 50th anniversary, and three received Life Memberships at our 60th anniversary.

In 1991 we held an appreciation night, in co-operation with a neighbouring Institute, to honour the MacDonald Family, whose grocery store business closed down after serving our communities for approximately 50 years. In 1992 we celebrated with neighbouring communities at a block party on the occasion of Canada's 125 birthday.

In June of 1997, St. Ignatius WI spearheaded the celebration of the 100th anniversary of the naming of our community, Mayfield. More than 250 residents and former residents attended this very memorable event.

We were again honoured in 1998 when Irene Gallant received the Golden Book of Recognition Award for Queens County for outstanding contributions to her WI branch. Irene and the late Bertha Arsenault also received "Certificates of Appreciation" for 50 or more continuous years in Women's Institute at this occasion.

After 63 years our organization, with a membership of twelve, continues to work "For Home and Country" under the leadership of our present executive – Barbara Lawrence, President; Sandi Cole, Vice-President; Carol Hill, Secretary; Marina Doiron, Treasurer.

Saint Lawrence

Saint Lawrence WI first organized in November of 1930. The first officers were Mrs. Chester Costain, President; Miss Eileen Handrahan, Secretary-Treasurer. They disbanded in 1938. The same group formed a Red Cross Society in 1941 and did war-work until 1945. Saint Lawrence reorganized as a Women's Institute in 1951, with Mrs. Robert MacInnis as President and Mrs. Stanley Costain as Secretary. This branch remained active in their community for more than thirty years before disbanding.

Saint Margaret's

Saint Margaret's WI organized in December of 1950. This branch was active through the 1960s, but later disbanded.

Saint Peter's Lake

Saint Peter's Lake WI first organized in November of 1931. Their first officers were: Mrs. Vernon Anderson, President; Lily MacDonald, Vice-President; Lottie Rossiter, Secretary-Treasurer. This Women's Institute branch was active in their community for over forty years before disbanding.

Saint Theresa's

Saint Theresa's WI organized in November of 1948. Mrs. Thomas Evans served as their first President. This branch remained active for over twenty years before disbanding.

Searletown (Willing Workers)

Miss Bessie Carruthers, Assistant Supervisor of Women's Institutes, organized the Searletown WI November 25, 1921. Members called it the "Willing Workers Institute". Their first officers were Mrs. Hugh MacLean, President; Mrs. L. W. Trueman, Vice-President; Mrs. Percy Allen, Secretary-Treasurer.

The school was the first interest of this Institute. They provided new blackboards, maps, desks, and flag, and erected a fence around the playground. This Institute organized a Junior Red Cross in their school in 1922. The highlight of their war work was an autograph quilt, which they donated to a Canadian Military Hospital in England.

They sponsored a 4H Garment Club in the community, and paid for a music teacher in the school. Willing Workers WI erected community signs at each end of the district, and contributed to all worthy causes.

Willing Workers WI remains active in their community.

Sea View

Sea View is well named. Our Hall stands at the intersection of five roads, with a panorama of productive fields rolling down to the Gulf shore. In the Gulf grow the lobsters, in the fields grow the crops, and since the 1930s tourists have been coming here to enjoy both land and sea.

Fifteen members enrolled at the organizing meeting for Sea View WI 1917. Numbers climbed rapidly and remained high until a decline in the early 1980s, but today we are back to sixteen. Throughout our eighty-three years, generations of women have served their community through the WI, educating themselves, dealing with the crises of two world wars, supporting the two-roomed school until 1972, and maintaining the Hall since the 1940s. Today's President fishes lobster and mussels with her husband. It is hardly surprising that this Institute branch has been less active at the Provincial level, since our energy and fundraising efforts are centered on Sea View Hall and the enjoyment of it through community gatherings.

If only we could share the excitement of some earlier activities – masquerades, suppers, pie socials, plays, lectures, auctions and quilting parties were a big part of pre-television society. Still, today's concerts, crokinole, flea markets, jamborees, ceilidhs, anniversaries, and reunions still make the rafters ring as the century closes. And yes, we still have some quilting bees!

Excellent minutes survived from the 25th anniversary in 1942. Several papers were read, one on the Club Creed, another on the ideal member. Members sang the Institute Rally Song (which we intend to revive in 2000), and served "a bountiful luncheon, well within the restrictions of War Time Rations." Could this be the same group who held a contest to see who could thread a needle while sitting on a round bottle?

The publication of *From the Ponds to Sea View* in 1987 led to renewed interest in the past and a remarkable celebration at the Hall for Canada's 125th birthday, "Come Home to Sea View", followed by our WI's 75th birthday and the Provincial Anniversary.

We have ended our first century with a major project. In 1995, we raised the Hall onto a new wooden foundation and enlarged it with a new entrance hall and washroom. New curtains for the stage came next. Even with infrastructure funding and donations of floor coverings, this was a formidable undertaking for WI in a community of only forty households. The little white building at Sea View crossroads is a visible symbol of our desire for WI to serve and revitalize rural society.

Selkirk

Teresa McLeod first organized the Selkirk WI on May 16, 1962 with eleven members. Their first President was Mrs. Wilfred MacPhee, their Vice-President Mrs. MacKinnon, and the Secretary-Treasurer was Mrs. Daniel McInnis.

In the early years, our one room school was very important, and we continue to support our consolidated school. We raised funds by holding card games, dances, lotteries, strawberry socials, and other activities. We made layettes for the USC, and knitted and sewed for the Red Cross. We sponsored Defensive Driving Courses and First Aid Courses. We purchased our one-room school, repaired it, and we now use it for meetings, fundraising, and share it with an AA Group. We remember our seniors with cards, visits and treats, and donate to the local hospital, water safety, Salvation Army, Easter Seals, Scholarship funds and prizes for local schools and many more organizations

At present we have ten members and continue to be active in helping improve our community and Island. Our current President is Edith MacKinnon, our Secretary-Treasurer is Hazel McInnis.

Sherbrooke
Peggy Kilbride, Mary Laughlin, Isabel Dekker

Helen McKenna organized Sherbrooke WI on March 17, 1921. The first officers were Mrs. L.B. Linkletter, President; Mrs. Varish Milligan, Vice-President; Mrs. M. N. Woodside, Secretary-Treasurer.

We have averaged fifteen members for the last twenty years, and we meet the first Thursday of each month from September to June. The usual collection is $1.00. We like to open and close our meetings with songs or poems pertaining to that month. We also use the Mary Stewart Collect, O' Canada, God Save the Queen, and the new WI mission statement. We hold most of our meetings at the Sherbrooke Community Centre, with an occasional special meeting at a member's home. Sometimes we go to senior citizens' homes where some non-active Life Members now live.

There is a 25-cent fine for any member who does not participate by answering roll call. We have had various roll call topics, such as jokes or funny stories, famous Canadian women, New Year's resolutions, your favourite season, flower, or gift and why, a foreign word and its meaning, or fund raising and program ideas. We also have donation roll calls, such as eyeglasses for Third World countries, basic items for women's shelters, books or magazines for local waiting rooms, items for the Kinsmen Christmas Appeal, food for the Salvation Army, Pennies for Friendship, and plays, poems and stories for submission to the provincial Wit and Wisdom book. In September we pay our annual WI dues for roll call. In December we try to guess who our WI Secret Pal has been all year. In March we wear something green to commemorate Saint Patrick's Day, and in May we bring bulbs, plants and seeds to exchange with each other.

We try to keep our meetings interesting and informative. Our various conveners educate and entertain us with videos on literacy, PEI National Parks, PEI fisheries and aquaculture, the Farm to Table project, Red Cross services, the Adelaide Hoodless Homestead, and the International Peace Gardens. We have also had numerous speakers on topics such as the importance of donor cards, tips on medications and drugs, the Confederation Bridge, PEI transition housing for abused women, safety in our homes, wills, Alzheimer's disease, the history and care of flags, and the 1998 ACWW conference in Pretoria, South Africa. Sometimes we like to get out for our programs. We have taken the St. John Ambulance course, tours of Eptek and Confederation Centre art galleries, made potpourri hearts and knitted lap blankets for Manor residents, took a health walk tour at a local grocery store, held a 3-Rs auction and information on recycling, a maple syrup company tour, an Easter bonnet parade, line dancing, a Halloween fashion show, and an annual exchange of gifts and cards with a secret pal.

The school and hall were our early members' main concerns, and they donated money for interior and exterior decorating, cleaning, and equipment. We donated 108 quilts during the war, sent numerous boxes to soldiers from the district, and did a great deal of sewing and knitting. Our branch sponsored home nursing and first aid classes, a girl's sewing club, and 4H clubs.

We are still active in our community. We take turns being on the Sick Committee that sends a Carnation Bowl to any hospitalized member, the newspaper correspondent who writes the notes of our meetings for our community's newspapers, and the lunch committee, which provides sandwiches, sweets, juice and tea for everyone. Sometimes each member brings food and we all share. We give special gifts to members celebrating landmark wedding anniversaries, organize shower and anniversary parties, and send cards to residents at occasions of sympathy, get well, anniversaries and births.

One of our special events is organizing the annual community Roadside Cleanup day. We invite everyone, including 4H. We host a get-together with lunch after the work finishes. We have organized Red Cross swimming lessons, distributed cod liver oil pills, been a pilot for the waste-watch system, organized a meet-your-neighbour Halloween afternoon, decorated the Centre for special holidays, and bought supplies for the Centre. We have sponsored a community swim and bowling afternoon, participated in the PEI Community

Promise of Inclusion, made slippers for the children's ward and Christmas tray decorations for the Prince County Hospital, make up and distribute Christmas treat trays to seniors and shut-ins and take part in Remembrance Day services, sometimes speaking and always placing a wreath.

We keep photo albums of newspaper clippings and photos of WI and community activities. 1999 was the official Year of the Elderly, so we held a fall tea and gift-giving afternoon at a local Manor. We also organized a Bingo with prizes at another Manor. We also worked with the community council repair a storage building adjoining the Community Centre property, and to have the flag flown at half-mast when there is a death in the community. We are registering some of our activities with the federal government as special Millennium projects.

We like to fundraise in innovative ways, for instance by selling spice racks and WI cookbooks, having pantry sales, ticket raffles, white elephant sales, blind auctions, Valentine's tea, strawberry socials, and community dinners and parties. We received payment for organizing the domestic science competition at the Summerside Fall Fair and Livestock Exhibition, and we receive rebates for returning grocery store tapes.

We donate to many local initiatives, such as to the schools for graduation prizes, Safe Grad, and libraries. We also donate to the Prince County Music Festival, the Prince County Hospital, the Queen Elizabeth Hospital equipment fund, St. Eleanor's Lioness' Walk for Sight, Notre Dame Housing for the Disabled, Meals on Wheels, Rotary Friendship Park (rose bushes), Girl Guides' participation in an international Guiding event, a teenager with Leukemia, the upkeep of the local war memorial grounds, needy families, a new wheelchair, and a blanket or $25.00 to any newlywed couples in the community.

On a wider scale we donate to the Northern Ireland Children's Event, the CNIB, Children's Wish Foundation, Big Brothers and Sisters, United Way, Cancer, Heart and Stroke Foundation, Red Cross, UNICEF, Arthritis, Alzheimer's, stamps for Oxfam, and incubator blankets for the IWK. Depending on the amount of cash we have on hand and organization, the amount given varies from $5.00 to $75.00

We are also politically involved. We lobbied governments to keep the Summerside Addiction Centre open, to maintain financial support for the dead stock removal company, to install a left hand turning lane at a dangerous highway area, and the hard but futile fight to save half of our community from amalgamation with the city of Summerside. Our WI supported Bill S-13, an anti-smoking legislation, but we spoke out against Bovine Growth Hormone use in Canadian milk products, video lottery terminals, adult movie rental stores and pornography in general, genetically altered foods, vital information missing from Canadian food labels, alcohol, violence, tobacco and other drugs, and separatism.

Many of our ladies have received their Life Membership pins. One Life/charter Member, Mamie Laughlin, won the Adelaide Hoodless Award of Honour, and was Representative Mother of the Year for Remembrance Day. Mamie spearheaded a project to obtain the names of all persons from Sherbrooke who served in World Wars I and II. We printed the names printed on a scroll, framed it, and placed it as a memorial in our Community Centre.

We have celebrated both our sixtieth and our seventy-fifth anniversaries, in 1980 and 1995 respectively. We also organized a district celebration of the FWIC 100th anniversary in 1997. At this event, one of our Life/charter Members, Alma Milligan, was honoured for being a WI member since 1922. Seventy-five years of membership is the longest record in PEI and several other provinces also. Four Life Members – Minnie Harris, Alma Milligan, Margaret Madsen, and Annie Dekker – recently received membership certificates from the PEIWI to commemorate their fifty years and more of WI membership.

As a Canada 125 project we organized a framed membership roll of Sherbrooke WI members from 1921 to 1992, which we display in the Community Centre.

Our national WI twin for many years has been Jonestown, Ontario. Although they have now disbanded, we maintain correspondence with one of the former members. She and her daughter visited us on PEI. We have truly made special friends in Margaret Sayeau and her family. We have also had a number of fun twinning celebrations back and forth with other PEIWIs such as Tyne Valley, Northam, Springfield, McNeill's Mills –Poplar Grove, and Southwest Lot 16.

We always attend the various district and provincial workshops and conventions. We have safely stored our old minute books at the archives in Charlottetown.

Onward into the year 2000 we go, working "For Home and Country", all the while having fun and never failing to enjoy each other's company.

South Bedeque
Katie Affleck

What has South Bedeque WI accomplished since 1922? We are very proud of two Provincial Presidents who served from our district, Hazel Leard and Hazel MacFarlane. Leadership continued to develop when Anne MacFarlane served on the Provincial Board for four years.

During the war years, our branch adopted a WI in England. Many boxes of essential items went overseas. A box of 10 lbs of tea went for $1.50 postage. We sent tea, sugar, pudding powders, raisins, lump sugar, and cans of meat and fish. In 1947 members sacrificed to bake and send a wedding cake to an English war bride. The post-war years saw us support Milk for Britain, the Refugee Children's Fund, Children's War Service Fund, and the many needs resulting from the aftermath of war.

Putting the war behind us, our members joined forces to put together two prize-winning kits, one on quilting, another on snowmobile safety. In 1981 our member, Marjorie Gay, won the Senator Corrine Wilson Award for her poem of a humorous pioneer incident, "The School That Vanished". Another of our members, Isabel Campbell, received the Agricultural Woman of the Year award for PEI in 1988.

We re-learned an old craft by hooking a rug together of an Island scene which we designed ourselves. We re-discovered our skills by piecing a quilt and knitting an Afghan for the Red Cross. When the schools consolidated, our six-year olds had to climb onboard a bus and be away all day. It was obvious to our WI that we needed a pre-school program of some kind to ease the transition from home to school. We organized a pre-school program for sixteen children from April until June with a volunteer teacher, each WI member taking a turn to help. Now local moms have taken over directorship of a year-round kindergarten with a hired teacher who is qualified in Early Childhood Education and assisted by a government helper for two special education students, and an extra play group for four year olds.

We lobbied the Provincial Department of Health to recognize the need for better dental hygiene and care. They acknowledged our resolution, and put a plan into action for fluoride and dental maintenance. Today children ages five to sixteen can have good dental service for a minimal fee of $10 per year.

We are proud of the South Bedeque women who have learned to recognize a real need in their community and organize to respond to it.

South Lake

The South Lake WI first organized in 1953, with Mrs. George Cheverie serving as their first President. This branch remained active in their community for almost thirty years, before disbanding in 1981.

South Milton

South Milton Women's Institute first organized in 1936. We currently have sixteen members. Since 1979 we have recognized fifteen Life Members. Vera Willis is the only remaining charter member, and she celebrates 63 years of dedicated service to date. Alice Curtis has had perfect attendance for 52 years, missing only one meeting due to illness.

Over the years, we have donated to many organizations and charity funds, and we are very active in our community. We contribute annually to the Upper Room Angels, make craft articles and knitted goods for the Red Cross, raise funds for the Milton Community Hall, and donate to the QEH Christmas stockings. We send cards to the elderly and the sick, both in the community and in the nursing homes, and make financial contributions to local schools for their various activities and scholarships (Central Queens Elementary School, East Wiltshire Junior High School, Bluefield Senior High School). We volunteer at the Exhibition during Old Home Week, and participate in Roadside Cleanup. We hold auction sales and invite other WI branches. We plant a flowerbed at the community sign in South Milton. We hold our Christmas party with our invited husbands, guests, and Santa Claus!

We have completed a number of special projects as a WI branch, such as contributing stainless steel jugs to the Milton-Vale Community Hall. We also hosted a very successful "Taste of the Harvest" fundraiser for the Hall in conjunction with the North Milton WI and the community. We donated to the Queen Elizabeth Hospital towards the purchase of a Catscan and Mammogram machine, and donated flannelette baby blankets. We made four quilts for the Unitarian service, and bibs for the Beach Grove Nursing Home. We recognize members who have been married for 50 years and 60 years.

Our WI has received recognition both for branch and individual accomplishments. From 1979-85, Joyce Andrew served as a Provincial Board member. She was also Chairperson at the Provincial Exhibition during that period, attended a Mini-Conference in Memramcook, NB, and worked on publicity for the WI Board. In 1984 Phyllis MacLean received the WI's "Woman of the Year". In 1985 our branch made a historical district quilt, and we won second prize at Old Home Week for our efforts. In 1991 we erected district signs and won second prize for our environmental jingle.

In 1986 South Milton WI celebrated our 50th anniversary at a party, with husbands and former members present for the occasion. Over the years we held many interesting programs with special speakers. We have taken many tours and outings, including tours of the Government House, a boat cruise, a tour of the cheese plant, a visit to Malpeque Gardens, and a tour of the Kensington Water Tower and Gardens.

With thanks, we acknowledge the late Alice Stewart, Edna Poole, Joyce Blackett, Koli Hoogenveen, and Shirlee Curtis.

South Pinette – Flat River

On July 31, 1945 about a dozen ladies organized South Pinette Women's Institute under the leadership of Mary G. MacDonald, the Supervisor at that time. The first officers were Mrs. Alex Campbell, President; Mrs. Neil Morrison, Vice-President; Isabel Morrison, Secretary-Treasurer. By 1981 our membership, which included several ladies from Flat River, had reached seventeen. In 1982 our group became known officially as the South Pinette – Flat River WI. Isabel Morrison MacDonald, an active member today, is a charter member of the original South Pinette WI. Our group has been a strong voice and support in all aspects of community life.

Until our schools consolidated in 1968, we kept the one-room school equipped and improved. Since then we have enriched Belfast Consolidated School with numerous donations for library and classroom books, shrubs, playground equipment, and hands-on assistance with fundraisers. In 1990, as part of a WI community enhancement program, we erected a school sign and started a flowerbed. We give high school graduates a $35 award, and students participating in national sports competition also receive financial assistance from our branch. We donate to the Belfast Kindergarten as the need arises.

In our community, we remember the sick and bereaved with cards, and take homemade treats to shut-ins at Christmas. We planted a pine tree and gave Christmas lights to the Belfast Fire Hall, where for several years we sponsored Christmas Carol sings. We donate each year to the Belfast Pipe and Drum Band, and place a Remembrance Day wreath at the Belfast Monument every November 11. We give local tragedies and times of joy our immediate attention.

In 1990, with the assistance of Canada Employment, we hired two students to work on several areas. In addition to work at the school already listed, they planted flower beds at the Pinette Raceway, painted the Belfast Fire Hall, made a legend map of Belfast for the assistance of tourists, and painted the Pinette wharf, the Eldon Legion, and the Polly Cemetery. We also erected a Heritage sign at Jack's Rd. In the past three summers, we have employed three people under a similar program who perform mosquito-black fly control and work at the Pinette Raceway, the school grounds, and for seniors in the area. Committees from the Women's Institute organize and supervise all these projects.

Both the Kings County Memorial Hospital and the QEH have benefited by our financial support, and in recent years we have made an annual donation to the QEH equipment fund. We petition our local MLAs on various issues such as a proposed sub-division, rural mail delivery, video gambling, and the Northumberland Ferries service.

We support the Salvation Army, Anderson House, the IWK and Mann House, in addition to PEIWI projects such as the Roadside Cleanup, Music Festival, Pennies for Friendship, and Bob the Beaver. In the past, we gave to the Support-a-Child and Women Feed the World Projects. At Christmas we provide treats for the QEH and gifts for the White Cross appeal.

We raise funds with luncheons, quilt raffles, suppers, and card parties, as well as collections, grab bags, auctions, and a birthday bank at our monthly meetings. For our 50th anniversary we enjoyed a supper and tour of Beaconsfield, and had the pleasure of hearing a former member tell of her experiences in coming to PEI as a war bride in 1945. We treat ourselves to special outings, particularly enjoying tours of MacPhail House and the QEH.

Our membership in 1999 is sixteen. One of our members, Evelyn Clow, has been a tireless worker on the Provincial Board for ten years. Another one of our members, Helen MacDonald, has also worked on the Provincial Board.

We have just completed a major part of our community improvement plan, "Welcome to our Community" signs at the beginning of our South Pinette and Flat River districts. We are now working on replacing and/or refinishing signs at the Pinette raceway and Belfast Consolidated School, adding to the upkeep and enhancement of our community.

We strive to assist educational programs, focus on community pride, and promote Women's Institute goals "For Home and Country". We also like to have fun and enjoy each other's company.

South West Lot 16

South West Lot 16 WI first organized in 1932, with Mrs. R.F. MacLean serving as their first President. This branch is still active today.

South Winsloe

South Winsloe WI organized in October of 1937. The first officers were: Mrs. Hope Myers, President; Mrs. Esther Campbell, Secretary-Treasurer. This branch was active for more than thirty years, but disbanded in 1972.

Southport

Southport WI first organized on December 16, 1942. Before that time, members participated in the MacDonald WI. Mrs. John MacKay held the first regular meeting at her home.

Mrs. John MacKay was Southport's first President; at that time twenty-five members enrolled. They became involved with the Music Festivals, Girl Guides, and Brownies. Maylea Manning and Mrs. Neil Matheson organized the first 4H Food Club on the Island. In 1962 Mrs. Margaret Wood reorganized the 4H Club and operated it from her home in Kinlock for a short time.

For a number of years our Institute sponsored Beavers, Cubs, Scouts, Guides and Brownies, and provided a banquet at the end of their year. All of our members have participated in the Roadside Cleanup. We made traffic lights at the Southport intersection a reality by lobbying with the PEI government. We also obtained a flashing light for use at our old school when it was in use. We were, with the RCMP, able to have the speed limit reduced through our village.

One of our recent projects was a fish-rearing project for the Pondside Park pond, where we employed a student for the summer. Southport WI also compiled and published a book, *The History of Southport*, which proved to be a very popular publication.

In 1978 we were honoured to have one of our Life Members, the late Florence Livingstone, chosen as Women's Institute "Woman of the Year". Over the years we have had twenty-five Life Members.

Our enrollment is 23 members at present. We enjoy a monthly meeting at the Stratford Senior Citizens Center. Our members participate in many activities within the community, such as catering to the New Year's Levee, Winter Carnival, Meals on Wheels, and the Community School.

Southport WI ladies have a lot of fun times, such as our annual yard sale, auction sales, our pot-luck supper at Christmas with Santa and elves, and our closing dinner at a favourite restaurant. We donate money to many organizations within the province, and sponsor a child through the International Child Fund. We remember the sick and shut-ins and residents at our group home both throughout the year and at Christmas.

Continued support and encouragement have made these years a memorable and rewarding experience for we the ladies of Southport Women's Institute.

Spring Brook

Miss Hazard and Miss. MacDonald, Supervisor and Assistant Supervisor of PEIWI organized the Spring Brook WI on September 28, 1939. Our first officers were Mrs. Kenneth MacLeod, President; Mrs. Dan MacKay, Vice-President; Mrs. Hillard Meek, Secretary-Treasurer. Except for special events, we have always held our meetings at members' homes.

In the early years members directed much of their attention to the war effort. We knitted for relief work, and sent boxes to the soldiers from our district. When they came home at war's end, we welcomed them with parties. We also supported most of the needs of our local school. Our branch installed a new floor, and supplied bookcases, hot lunches, a teacher's desk and chair, a piano and a music teacher's salary piano, and prizes for worthy students. When the schools consolidated we continued our support by donating prizes and volunteering with the school lunch program.

We are still active in our community. We remember the sick, shut-ins and seniors with treats or flowers, and give memorials for deceased members. We support the local Fire Department by holding fundraisers to purchase equipment, collecting district dues, and supporting their annual variety concert. Our members volunteer at Community Gardens Rink and support the Kensington and Area Harvest Festival. For several years we sponsored a contestant in the Miss Community Gardens Pageant, and we have entered a WI float in the Festival Parade. We support the 4H Club by donating prizes, and we assist them with other expenses. We also organize and take part in the Roadside Cleanup.

We sponsor Red Cross first-aid courses for our residents. In 1960 as a follow up to one course, we entered a First Aid competition over CJRW and won first prize. We have also faithfully supported the Red Cross Water Safety Program, both financially and by volunteering as beach supervisors and bus monitors. Our branch received two citations from the Red Cross Society in recognition of support given to their programs. Members also volunteer at Blood Donor Clinics and the used Clothing Depot. We have erected attractive community signs at the three entrances to our community.

Through the years we have donated or canvassed the district for all worthy causes. We have donated to many special appeals from our hospitals.

Each year since 1977 we have hosted a community picnic for residents of our district and those who have cottages or summer homes. Within our branch we have a Secret Pal program and we participate in the WI twinning program. Once a year (usually at Christmas) we invite husbands or a friend for a smorgasbord supper and social time. In summer members, husbands, friends and guests tour an historic site or attraction.

We fundraise by holding ice cream socials, concerts, plays, card parties, a travelling apron, birthday boxes, valentine socials, suppers, bake sales, sales of garden bulbs, and catering. We also collect at meetings, canvass for donations, and have collecting roll calls such as sing-say-or-pay, or we pay an amount for our shoe sizes, the letters of our names, or our ages.

We observe the anniversaries of our branch, the Provincial WI and FWIC with special events. We hold showers for brides and newlyweds, and anniversary celebrations for those married 25 or 50 years. Eleven of our members have received their Life Memberships in recognition of their years of outstanding and dedicated service. We were saddened in June 1996 by the death of our last charter member- Annie Jollimore Parsons, who was a dedicated WI member as long as her health permitted. She received her Life Membership in 1972.

On September 28, 1999 members, former members, husbands and friends met to celebrate the 60th anniversary of Spring Brook WI. Special guests were Betty Millar, President of the PEIWI, and Enid MacKay, President of Area 6B.Betty Millar presented Certificates of Appreciation for over 50 years of service to Roma Campbell and Doris Paynter. Birthday cake and punch were served to end a most enjoyable evening.

Our branch supports all WI projects – provincial, national, and international. We plan our programs for the year with our objectives in mind, and we have at least one study each year relating to the convenerships. We use kits from the WI office, guest speakers, tapes and videos, demonstrations, and material gathered by the members. Each member is encouraged to take part in programs, and each one has served in the offices and convenerships. One member, Mrs. Arthur Campbell, served as area President and later spent twelve years on the Provincial Board, some of this time as President of the PEIWI.

Our membership has been between ten and twenty members, and we presently have twelve.

We feel the identity of our rural communities will be maintained as long as there is a WI in the community. Our programs and projects may change but we feel our aims and objectives will remain the same as we go forward to meet the many challenges in our work "For Home and Country."

Springfield

Grace Hickox

Springfield WI is one of the oldest in PEI, organized in April 1913 by Katie James of Charlottetown.

During the two World Wars our members turned their attention to raising money for Belgian Relief, Canadian War Services, Milk for

Britain, Salvation Army, and other organizations. Working in conjunction with the Red Cross Society, Springfield members sent many hospital supplies, knitted socks, quilts for refugees, and parcels for soldiers overseas. When the Second World War ended we adopted an English Institute, and we still exchange cards, letters, and gifts.

We also support many worthy causes at home. We donated a television to the Rehabilitation Centre in Charlottetown, a chair and blankets to the Day Training Centre in Kensington, give Christmas gifts to the Red Cross children each year, infant layettes to the USC and local hospitals, and regional school prizes.

In 1953 we celebrated the 125th anniversary of the coming of the first settlers to Springfield. On that occasion Springfield Women's Institute compiled a short history to honour those pioneers, who through strenuous endeavour, left us such a goodly heritage. In 1985 we organized the Springfield History Committee to revise and update this history for the benefit of posterity. We have sold 500 copies to date.

We also compiled and published a brochure, "Lucy Maud Montgomery: The Island's Lady of Stories," under the leadership of Mrs. Reginald Haslam. This has been very popular – we have printed 90,000 copies, some of which are now in libraries as far away as Vancouver, BC; Washington, DC; London, England and Japan.

In 1973, when Mrs. John Haslam was our President and Mrs. John Hagen our Secretary, we celebrated our 60th anniversary. At that time we were pleased to welcome our first President, Mrs. Peter Sinclair and our first Secretary, Mrs. Robert E. Howard.

In 1979 Mrs. Crawford Sinclair won first prize of $25 in the PEIWI Creative Writing Competition with her skit, "Let Age Be No Barrier". In 1983, Mrs. Keith Mayne and Mrs. John Hickox wrote another original skit honouring the 70th anniversary of the Women's Institutes in PEI, and dramatized their skit at the Annual Convention.

On April 8, 1983, a birthday cake, baked and decorated for the occasion by Mrs. Allan Hagen, centered the table of the "Pine Room" of the Linkletter Motel. Members met to celebrate the 70th anniversary of our branch and to honour one of our charter members, Muriel Haslam, an active member for all of those years. The PEIWI recognized our branch as one of the first thirteen organized on the Island, and presented us with a gavel.

In 1988, we celebrated the 75th anniversary of Springfield WI at the home of Crawford and Ethel Sinclair. We reenacted one of the first WI meetings, in costume, and Ann Thurlow Emceed this televised event.

In 1992, through the efforts of Mrs. Clare Haslam, we obtained safety signs from the Department of Highways for our community. In that same year Mrs. Harry Joostema's daughter, Irene, who had attended the Nova Scotia Agricultural College at Truro, spoke at one of our meetings. Part of her assignment was to gather and label 80 families of larvae, which she displayed for us. She belongs to the PEI Institute of Agrology, which helps to protect the public from fraudulent practices.

Another faithful member, Mrs. Gerrit Loo, visited her daughter Margie in Guatemala in 1995. Margie has been working with street children there for a number of years. Joyce returned to PEI with both happy and sad memories that she related at a WI meeting.

It is worthy of note, that one of our charter members, Mrs. William Haslam, who turned 98 years old in January of 1998, still takes an interest in WI work. She recently crocheted a lap robe, which she donated to the Prince County Hospital.

Springton

Springton WI first organized in 1934. The first officers were Mrs. Ewen Lamont, President; Mrs. Cyrus Martin, Vice-President; Miss Dorothy MacKenzie, Secretary-Treasurer.

Springton WI's main efforts focussed on their local school. They moved the school to a new location, landscaped the grounds, erected a fence, and provided furniture and teachers' needs. The Springton branch also erected a tablet in their community to commemorate the men and women who served in the Second World War.

Active for more than thirty years, Springton WI has disbanded.

Springvale

Vera Coles Sicy

On July 30, 1996 Springvale WI celebrated our 50th anniversary. Fourteen members attended, and three of these were charter members and still very active. In September of that year we hosted a social evening where we extended a warm welcome to former members.

Our branch remains very active in the usual community affairs. We remember the sick and shut-ins, and contribute to many worthy causes including the annual QEH equipment drive. We donate to high school graduating students, and in 1988 we gave a substantial donation to the Catscan fund. Each spring finds our members involved in Roadside Cleanup, and in late August we host a "Community Get Together".

We have participated in many handicraft activities over the years. For instance, we made and sold a quilt to raise funds towards the purchase of display racks for the Institute rooms at the Provincial Exhibition. In 1985 Edith MacLeod entered the Tweedsmuir Competition with a history of her 118 year-old home. Our members compiled a scrapbook for a Provincial Competition, and received honorable mention recognition for their efforts. One of our members, Viola Sentner, submitted a quilt block with Maple Leaf applique for the 125th Anniversary Quilt, "A View Through Canada's Windows". Women's Institute members in Ontario completed this quilt, which was on display at Eaton's in Charlottetown as part of its tour across Canada.

In 1989 we were honoured to have one of our members, Kaye Crabbe, elected Provincial President of the Federated Women's Institute of PEI. In 1993 Edith Crabbe, Provincial Environment Convener, received the Environmental Individual Citizen award. The Honourable Barry Hicken, Environmental Resources Minister at the time, presented the plaque to Edith.

We continue to be actively involved locally, nationally and internationally.

Spring Valley

Virjene Cole

Spring Valley Women's Institute first organized in 1935. Eleven members attended the first meeting, and twenty-two more women joined that first year. Our membership has fluctuated over the years, but we still have seventeen members.

In the early years our activities focused on supporting the local school by purchasing needed articles. During the war years we knitted and sent boxes to the soldiers overseas. We have always collected for various organizations such as the United Way.

We always welcomed people in our community by having showers, anniversaries and housewarmings. Since the 1950s our WI has been involved with the larger local community. In 1957 we erected the Black Horse sign at the site of the Institute-established picnic area. In 1959 we built an addition onto the Community Hall, providing kitchen space and cupboards.

Over the years we have raised money for our activities by catering to suppers, hosting card parties, making quilts to sell, and sponsoring concerts and through collections and donations.

In 1995 we celebrated our 60th anniversary. Individual members have received recognition, with the Carson Wilson Award in 1991, the "stuffed toy" award in 1994, and participation since 1991 of one member on the Provincial Board. We have presented several Life Memberships over the years as well.

We feel we have and are still upholding our motto, "For Home and Country."

Stanchel

Stanchel WI organized in April of 1960. Mrs. William Campbell served as their first President. This branch remained active in their community for over thirty years before disbanding in 1994.

Stanhope

Stanhope WI first organized in October of 1928. The first officers were Mrs. Rupert Ross, President; Mrs. Aeneas MacDonald, Vice-President; Miss Dora Doyle, Secretary.

This branch was active in all aspects of school and community life, and won a number of prizes for their work in community safety, history, and the arts. Active for over sixty years, Stanhope WI disbanded in 1993.

Sterling

Marion Reid

Sterling Women's Institute formed on June 19, 1913 at Stanley Bridge Hall. The rural landscape has changed so much since then – school consolidation, expanded farming operations, and the exodus of many senior citizens to towns have resulted in a demographic change. The demands of family and careers have left women with less time to pursue social lives and active membership in community organizations.

The members of our Institute are, like so many, older and fewer in number. Yet our Institute continues to play a meaningful role in all community endeavours. We continue to maintain our Hall, a very historic building and the gathering place for community activities. We have had the Institute Hall painted and reshingled, and had a wheelchair ramp installed. We also maintain the grounds. We own the Swimming Rock property on New London Bay, where all are welcome for a refreshing swim. With a declining membership, supporting the Women's Institute Hall and the Swimming Rock properties has been a challenge, but it is a challenge that we still meet.

We raise money for these projects in many ways. Our annual tradition of a variety concert continues to be a financial success, as are donations by individuals who appreciate the work of the WI members. Our successful campaign for the stereotactic Mammography machine realized $1000.

As WI members we work closely with the Provincial Board and support their programs. We participate in the annual Roadside

Cleanup, scholarships, Provincial Exhibition awards, scholarships for students, treats and visits for the elderly, and gifts for new babies. Sterling WI is also responsible for the erection of attractive district signs with the WI logo.

Over the years our members have received several awards. Alma Fleming, Annie Douglas, Hilda Fyfe and Helen MacEwen merited the twenty-five year Red Cross Service Medal. Hilda Fyfe and Marion Reid both received the 125 Confederation Medal. Our Secretary, the Honourable Marion Reid, is a former Lieutenant Governor, a former Member of the PEI Legislative Assembly, and a recipient of the Order of Canada, the PEI Medal of Merit, and an Honourary Doctorate of Laws from UPEI. Since 1979 nine members have received the honour of Life Memberships.

In 1997 Sterling Women's Institute celebrated 84 years of Women's Institute involvement for "Home and Country". One of our greatest challenges for the future will be the conservation and protection of the resources of our planet. The forests are the lungs of the planet, our soil is our greatest resource, and our existence depends on pure water. We must not compromise our co-existence with nature; to do so is to risk the health and quality of life for future generations and ourselves.

By making responsible decisions, we will be acting in the best interests of "Home and Country".

Summerville

Summerville WI organized in October of 1948. The branch remained active for over twenty years before disbanding.

Ten Mile House

Ten Mile House WI first organized in March of 1950. Their first President was Mrs. William O'Connell. This branch remained active for more than twenty years before disbanding.

Tryon

Mary MacDonald, Supervisor of WIs, organized Tryon Women's Institute on December 3, 1945. Our first officers were Mrs. Walton Toombs, President; Mrs. Howard Callbeck, Vice-President; Mrs. Robert Crawford, Secretary. In 1945 our membership was twenty-seven, and fifty years later we still have fourteen members enrolled.

Our district is very spread out, and through the WI we have made lasting friendships with members throughout the community.

Our branch has always shown a great interest in the school and community. Members were always willing to provide necessities for the school and assisted in various community projects. We successfully raised money with crokinole parties, ice-cream socials, bean suppers, lobster suppers, plays, auctions, festival concerts, pantry sales, and afternoon teas. We supported projects such as installing electricity in the school, and purchasing desks, chairs, blinds, floor covering, oil stoves, blackboards, books, piano, and many other items.

Through the efforts of William (Bill) Jones and Women's Institute members of the surrounding communities, the South Shore Music Festival Association became a reality. The annual Music Festival takes place in Summerside. Students from the surrounding communities participate in this competition, and residents enjoy a concert in the local hall.

We have always contributed to various worthwhile causes, such as treats at Christmas for school children, swimming lessons, cod-liver capsules, girl's sewing club, Red Cross quilts and knitted articles, orphanage, cancer campaign, dental clinics, TB League, Salvation Army, Blue Cross, hospitals, the Crapaud Exhibition and the Provincial Exhibition, Englewood and Bluefield Schools, South Shore Sportsmen's Dinner, Fire Department, figure skating, and fire victims, to name a few. Our most recent major fundraising event was the drive to support the Queen Elizabeth Hospital's purchase of a stereotactic Mammography machine.

We welcome newcomers to our community. At Christmas we send baskets of food and fruit to shut-ins. We try to remember the sick and bereaved as well as former members and friends.

In 1989, Dorothy Taylor, Marion Howatt, Annie Howatt and Clara Davol received their Tryon WI Life Memberships. On November 17th, 1995 we celebrated our 50th anniversary at the Lotus Garden Restaurant in Kensington. Dorothy Wood, a charter member, was a welcome guest. We also held surprise parties for Dorothy and Ernest White and Marion and Sheldon Howatt, both celebrating their fiftieth wedding anniversaries.

Since the Tryon Consolidated School closed, our students attend Englewood School in Crapaud. On July 26th, 1974 Tryon WI purchased the old school. Our members actively care for the interior and exterior, and Tryon Consolidated School proudly stands as an historic site in our community.

For over fifty years our members have worked harmoniously and contributed to many worthy endeavours. The Mary Stewart Collect states it well, as we strive to become better citizens "For Home and Country".

Tyne Valley
Muriel MacDougall

Our Institute first organized on August 27, 1927. Now we have only twelve members, and all are senior citizens. The younger ones do not join, as they are involved in so many other organizations. Our last charter member passed away in October 1992 at the age of 99 years.

Tyne Valley Institute has been the owner of Britannia Hall for many years. We have overseen many renovations, and are responsible for all expenses including heating, electricity, taxes, and insurance. We moved the hall to a new location on the same road in 1995, and added a beautiful restaurant. Our Hall is now the home of a dinner theatre project and regular restaurant activities. Following the relocation of Britannia Hall, the community completely renovated the building and readied it for theatre activities. Our Institute contributed by donating a new furnace and some theatre seats. We are very grateful to the Tyne Valley players who put on plays each year. Some from outside our district also take part, and they all really enjoy doing it.

On one occasion, a swarm of bees formed in a wall of Britannia Hall. We tried everything to get rid of them, as the bees were flying around both inside and outside the hall, and stung several people during entertainment! Finally we had a carpenter tear out the walls, and an exterminator came and pulled out the cones and bees. The honey just kept dripping, and the bees were placed in wire boxes. We haven't had bees since!

Our branch is very active in the community. For example, we catered a banquet in honour of the performers of the Colours of Canada Games Concert 1990. During the Oyster Festival in Tyne Valley we sponsor a contestant for the Oyster Pearl Pageant, and donate toward prizes. We help bake and serve public suppers in aid of the community rink. We also help to trim a float for the parade. When Stewart Memorial added an addition to the hospital, many local artists presented their work. We donated so that all items could be framed. We also hold wedding and baby showers for community residents.

To raise money for these activities, we hold bake sales, rent the Hall, cater to weddings and anniversaries, and sell fudge at Hall plays. In addition to our community support, we are staunch supporters of our local hospital and Prince County Hospital and Queen Elizabeth Hospital, and when the Queen Elizabeth Lodge opened, we were able to make a donation towards that as well. We support our hospital auxiliary with their Easter and Christmas teas, Valentine Ball, and all other needs.

We donate to the Salvation Army, Flowers of Hope, Cancer Fund, Heart Fund, Tyne Valley Play School, wreaths for Remembrance Day, swimming classes, minor hockey, Ellerslie School for prizes in June, food to the Peace Bus celebration on Lennox Island, the Figure Skating program, and many other worthwhile causes.

We participate in many WI activities. For instance, we sponsored a member who went to Charlottetown to walk a mile for hip and knee replacements. In 1980 we brought the ACWW flag to Ellerslie Consolidated School for all Institutes to see. We presented Pennies for Friendship at this celebration. We have used kits from the PEI Women's Institute at several of our meetings, and often have guest speakers on topics of interest. Our members knit squares to send to the Institute headquarters in Charlottetown, and each spring we hold a lobster supper for our members. At one of our meetings in the early 1980's, Dr. G.E. Robinson showed us slides of the Adelaide Hoodless homestead. Other members have given us talks on their visits to England and Scotland.

Uigg-Kinross-Grandview

Uigg-Kinross Women's Institute organized in 1923, and we celebrated 65th anniversary in 1988. Initially two districts comprised the local branch, Uigg and Kinross, but about twenty years ago Grandview joined. Our accomplishments over the years include sponsoring the movement to erect a provincial Sanatorium, promoting the initiative to build a women's residence for students in Charlottetown (Montgomery Hall) and sponsoring the annual Music and Drama festivals. The promotion of improved educational, social and economic conditions was always foremost in our thinking and planning.

Uigg-Kinross-Grandview WI branch continues to be very active. We meet monthly, and average fifteen to twenty members.

When our rural schools consolidated in 1973, the Institute bought the Uigg School. We have maintained it as a Community Centre ever since, with the help of a Centennial grant. The Centre is a focal place in our community, where all residents can meet for various activities such as "meet-your-neighbour" nights and community showers. The Centre is also available for 4H meetings, WI meetings and area WI conventions, and a few rental activities. In 1979 we planned and co-hosted a community celebration with the local 4H Club, commemorating the 150th anniversary of the settlement of Uigg.

Although there have been many changes over the years, we strive to preserve the spirit of neighborliness, kinship and hospitality that was such a valuable tradition in the past. We feel that our branch still makes a valuable and inspiring contribution to our Island way of life.

Unionvale

Unionvale WI organized on May 17, 1950. The first officers were Mrs. Errol Stetson, President, and Mrs. Gerald Gamble, Secretary-Treasurer. This, however, was not the first Institute in the district, as a group organized in 1926, with Mrs. Percy Ramsey as President and Miss Ruth Allen Secretary-Treasurer.

The second Unionvale WI was active in their community for twenty-six years before disbanding in 1976. Unable to encourage new members, the woman who signed the last annual report for Unionvale WI wrote, "I feel I've lost a good friend."

Union Road

Union Road Women's Institute first organized in November of 1939. This branch remained active for over twenty years before disbanding.

Upton

Upton Women's Institute first organized in November of 1929, with Mrs. George Beaton serving as their first President. This branch was active in their community for over thirty years before disbanding.

Valleyfield – Upper Montague

On the first Friday of November 1930, Valleyfield's first Women's Institute meeting took place at the home of Mrs. Florence MacLeod, with about fifteen members from Valleyfield East and West districts attending. They continued to hold their meetings on the first Friday of the month, at a different home each month.

Valleyfield WI held concerts, ice cream socials, and bake sales in order to fundraise for the schools. We provided books for a library and hot school lunches at noon, since in those days the children had to walk sometimes two miles to school. A cup of hot soup was always welcome. Our branch helped the school to buy maps and a world globe, and a teacher's desk. There were also two members appointed to call on the sick and bring them a treat to their home. This went on for many years.

In the early 1940s the Upper Montague WI formed, and had about fifteen members. They were also very active in their district, helping their school hold picnics, concerts, and ice cream festivals as fundraisers. This went on until the late 1960's, when Upper Montague's membership was decreasing. They joined the Valleyfield group, Valleyfield-Upper Montague has been very active ever since.

We donate to many different organizations such as the IWK Hospital, our Island hospitals, the Music Festival, and many more. Now, with a membership of about fifteen people, we are very interested in the area and try to donate to our hospitals, as we feel that health care and education should be "number one" on our agenda today.

Vernon

Vernon WI first organized in October of 1927. This branch remained active for almost fifty years before disbanding in 1975.

Vernon River

Vernon River WI organized in March of 1942. They disbanded in 1980.

Victoria

Miss Carruthers, Assistant Supervisor of Women's Institutes, organized Victoria WI on March 16, 1921. Twenty-two women enrolled.

One of the main objectives in the early years was to pay off the Community Hall debt, as the Hall was the focal point for many activities in the village. In 1924 came the Memorial Honour Roll for First World War volunteers. It seems that we barely got over the first war when the Second World War broke out. During these worrisome years the Red Cross was practically merged with the Institute, and the whole community helped with sewing, knitting, and monetary contributions.

In 1926 our WI purchased a piano for the Hall. The two-room schoolhouse was well taken care of, as was the local rink. Victoria WI also organized a sewing club, which proved very beneficial for the young girls. Our branch contributed to many organizations, both local and beyond our community.

Victoria is girded by the sea, and after two accidents our branch launched a Safety Program in 1966 that enveloped the whole community. Mrs. Evelyn Cudmore urged this committee, convened by Mrs. Kay Wood, to record their achievements. The result was that Victoria won first prize in the Safety in PEI competition, and went on to come second in Canada. Mrs. Louise E. Cannon played a major part in this award with her act of heroism, saving the life of five year old Julianna Boulter who fell over the Victoria wharf on a cold December morning. Mrs. Cannon received the Carnegie Hero Commission Bronze Medal Award. In May 1966, Kay Wood, Louise Cannon and Katherine Boulter were invited to the historic Chateau Frontenac Hotel in Quebec City, where they accepted their safety award.

In 1971 we remembered four charter members with gifts of china and WI pins. They have since departed this life and have gone on to higher service. We now have a new cast of enthusiastic members who follow the Golden Rule set by our predecessors. We celebrate anniversaries, have yearly outings, attend and participate in area and provincial Conventions, and give to many worthy organizations. We continue a long tradition of packing Christmas boxes, welcome new residents and new babies, and we always remember the sick and bereaved.

Kay Wood, our long time Secretary, received first prize in the PEIWI competition on her Log of "Dunrovin". She was also presented to the Queen and Prince Philip for her 1964 Centennial involvement. Kay and Jean Howatt received the Commemorative Medal in 1995.

On May 7th, 1996, at the home of President Margaret McLure, eight long time members received Life Membership pins and citations. These members were Jean Howatt, Katherine Boulter, Ella Boulter, Kay Wood, Annie Craig, Lucilla MacDonald, Doris Thompson and Dorothy Howatt.

May we, the present members of Victoria WI, emulate the high ideals set by our predecessors as we continue to work in unity "For Home and Country."

Victoria West

Victoria West WI organized on November 25, 1924. Their first President was Mrs. Daniel MacLeod, Vice-President Mrs. John Moore, and their Secretary-Treasurer Miss Marjorie Moore.

The following excerpt from Victoria West's contribution to *Through the Years Part I: The Women's Institutes of Prince Edward Island*, describes their experience thusly. "Our Institute's achievements for the past thirty-six years probably would not appear very outstanding. But we are thankful that we were able to meet together each month as a non-partisan organization striving to touch and know the great human heart common to us all. We do hope that our brief meetings together, exchanging ideas and the carrying out of any line of work that has for its object the betterment of the home, school, and conditions of surrounding community life, have fulfilled our Institute motto 'For Home and Country'."

Victoria West WI remained active in their community for almost fifty years before disbanding in 1973.

Village Green
Betty Wickers

Village Green WI organized in October of 1981. There were fourteen original members. We hold our meetings on the first Tuesday of the month at members' homes, and the hostess takes care of a light lunch after the meeting. We have a newspaper reporter, a scrapbook person and a hospitality committee. In November of 1981 Lovelyn Allen received a WI pin for her role in starting the Village Green WI.

Our annual community projects include organizing the Roadside Cleanup and serving hotdogs and snacks to participants, and hosting a Canada Day celebration for the community. Since we do not have a community hall, it is hard for us to host any indoor get-togethers.

Our fundraisers usually consist of bake and craft sales or silent auctions. We have published two cookbooks, the first in 1995 and the second in 1998, and we are still selling these.

Since February 1993 we have made quarterly donations to the Red Cross for children in need all over the world.

In 1992, we started the tradition of having an annual potluck supper for our December meeting, and we started exchanging small homemade gifts. In 1994 we started having a yearly outing during our summer recess. We go out for dinner at a different restaurant every year.

We now have ten members.

Wellington Centre

Wellington Centre WI organized in 1929. Their first officers were Mrs. Joseph McNeill, President; Mrs. J. D. Leckie, Vice-President; Mrs. Emmett MacNeill, Secretary.

This Institute worked to improve their school. They raised the building, provided equipment, painted the interior and exterior, and erected a fence. They sent boxes to the sick and treats to school children. Wellington Centre WI contributed to all charitable causes, including the Provincial Sanatorium and Prince County Hospital. This branch was active for more than thirty years before disbanding.

Westmoreland

Westmoreland WI first organized in September of 1937. Mrs. Vernon Moore served as their first President. Westmoreland WI was active for almost sixty years before disbanding in 1994.

West Cape

West Cape WI first organized in 1930. Mrs. Ed MacWilliams served as their first President, Mrs. Ralph MacLennan their Treasurer. Over the forty years of their activity, West Cape WI was very active in supporting their school and their community. They painted the exterior and interior of the building, and supplied "necessities" such as a globe, dictionary, maps, and a fountain. All brides in their community received a new quilt. They assisted fire victims, and donated articles and money to USC, March of Dimes, and other worthy causes.

West Cape WI disbanded in 1973.

West Covehead

West Covehead WI first organized in November of 1945. The first officers were Mrs. Ramsay Auld, President, and Mrs. Lorne MacMillan, Secretary-Treasurer.

This WI branch was active in many community affairs. They provided for their school, welcomed new citizens and held farewell parties, sponsored collections for charitable causes, and paid the salary for a music teacher at their school.

West Covehead WI was active for more than twenty years, but later disbanded.

West Devon

West Devon WI organized in 1932, and has been a going concern in their community ever since! This branch is still active today.

West Point

West Point WI first organized in the fall of 1927. Their first President was Mrs. Jago Sabine, Vice-President Mrs. John A. Stewart, and their Secretary was Miss Eva Sabine. Almost every woman in the district enrolled as a member when this Institute first organized. The meetings moved from house to house in the winter, and took place in the school in the summer.

West Point WI's main concern was for the school and the community. They provided all manner of equipment and supplies for their one-room school. During the war years, West Point WI set to work making quilts for the Red Cross, knitting, and packing boxes for overseas soldiers. They collected scrap, took part in several concerts, made articles for bazaars, held pantry sales and ice cream socials, and gave the proceeds either to the school or community projects. West Point WI sponsored swimming classes, sewing classes, attended

Blood Donor Clinics, gave gifts to new brides in the community, and contributed to many charities.

West Point WI remained active for more than forty years before disbanding.

West Royalty

Miss MacPhail, Supervisor of Women's Institutes, organized West Royalty WI on May 1, 1930. The first officers were Mrs. Fred Gates, President; Mrs. Gordon Stetson, Vice-President; Mrs. Cyrus Pickard, Secretary-Treasurer.

This branch worked for many years to create a "community spirit". They looked after the needs of the schoolchildren, the sick, and assisted in collecting for health and welfare organizations. They sent monthly letters and packages to soldiers during the war, and sponsored 4H clubs, Brownies, Cubs, and swimming lessons. They also maintained their community hall.

Active for forty-five years, West Royalty WI disbanded in 1975.

Wheatley River

In November of 1926, members of Cymbria WI met at the home of Mrs. Gertie Wares. The members decided to invite Miss McKenna, Supervisor of Women's Institutes, to the December meeting so that she could help organize a separate Institute for Wheatley River. On December 14, 1926 the late Mrs. Norman Ling hosted the organizational meeting at her home. Twelve ladies joined at the first meeting, and by the end of the year twenty-one ladies were members. Today we have seven members.

Our branch has always been very active, and we continue that tradition today. We fundraise with such activities as sales, collections, catering to banquets and weddings, and everyone enjoys our ice-cream festivals and suppers.

Our list of beneficiaries is quite long. For instance, we have collected for the Cancer fund, the Salvation Army, the Kidney Foundation, Heart fund, the Music Festival, Home Economics Scholarship, Transition House, Pennies For Friendship, Queen

Elizabeth Hospital, and some charity benefits, and other worthy causes. In our own community, we give treats to the sick and gifts to new babies, memorial gifts to a worthy organization in memory of departed loved ones and gifts of money to newly weds. We have helped the New Glasgow Fire Department purchase fire truck equipment, supported the local rink, and the food bank.

We continue our commitment to our Hall by raising funds for general upkeep and maintenance and supplying small furnishings. The hall serves as a focal point for many activities (including our meetings!) and for 4H meetings and achievement days. In recent years we added curtains and table covers. We currently have an ongoing project to raise funds for a new carpet for the Hall. Our Hall has won first and second prize in the Rural Beautification Competition.

Every year our WI sponsors various fun activities for the community. We hold "meet-your-neighbour" nights with a pot luck meal, a children's Christmas program, and spring concerts. We have also celebrated 50th and 25th wedding anniversaries for several couples in the community.

Within our branch, we remember our secret pals with cards and gifts, especially at Christmas time. We have been twinned with several different groups over the years, and always enjoy their company. Some members toured Government House in 1994, and we hold farewell parties for members and their families who move from the community. We commemorate our branch and provincial WI anniversaries with special guests and activities.

At the Wheatley River WI, we are always working "For Home and Country."

Whim Road

Whim Road WI first organized on September 29th, 1933, in the Whim Road Hall. From the beginning our Institute has concentrated on improving conditions in the home, the school, the community and the province.

We raised money to carry out our work by donations from members, penny sales, and auctions at the monthly meetings. Residents contributed at events such as card plays, dances, ice cream and cake sales, fudge sales, and ticket sales on items such as a box of groceries, a 98 lb. bag of flour, a hooked rug, or a side of pork to name just a few.

Money raised by our Institute went back into the community in the form of supplies for the school and the hall, school treats for students and pre-schoolers, gifts for new babies, showers for newlyweds, recognition for a new family in the community and always some form of contribution when a community member passed away. For 63 years the WI has always visited and given treats to the sick and shut-ins of the community.

Many worthwhile organizations have benefited from donations made by Whim Road WI. In the early years, it was the orphanage, King's County Hospital, the polio relief fund and the sanatorium. In later years many groups and organizations looked to the Institute for help. Often Institute members canvassed the district for funds for charities.

When Whim Road WI was still in its growing stages the Second World War broke out. These war years seemed to bring our members closer as they struggled to keep home, community and country together. They devoted many hours to sewing and knitting for the Red Cross, packing boxes for the soldiers and assisting each other in the community.

The monthly Institute meeting has always been an important event for members of Whim Road WI. The meetings continue to provide educational and leadership opportunities through activities and programs. Socially, meetings provide members with a chance to share their joys and their sorrows, and through the spirit of friendliness and good fellowship, they help each of us to cope with our ever-changing world.

Wilmot

Marjorie Cairns

Our community worked together for the Red Cross during World War 2. As a result, in 1945 the Silver Birch WI, Read's Corner was organized with Miss Mary MacDonald as supervisor. The following seventeen members joined:

Linnie Beaton, Rhetta Baglole, Helen Cairns, Dorothy MacQuarrie, Prille MacQuarrie, Olive Crozier, Marjorie Cairns, Bertha Yeo, Helen MacArthur, Marion Beairsto, Flossie Condon, Bessie MacQuarrie, Wanda Matheson, Lillian Waugh, Helen Clark, Iva Heckbert, Ernestine Scott.

When Wilmot became a village in 1965, our Institute was known as Wilmot WI. Since there was no school in our village, our interest in the community took many different facets.

In the community we remember the sick, the shut-ins and the bereaved. We chaired a radio appeal that raised the money to buy a van for a young paraplegic. We bought a motorized wagon for a little boy with spina-bifida. We also gave a Braille watch to a blind lady, a donation to Friendship Park in our area and one to the children from Ireland. In 1985 and in 1992 we compiled cookbooks of our favourite recipes. They were popular and sold well.

When a Community Centre was built our Institute was given a meeting room, which we furnished. We also bought a piano for the Centre and a stove, fridge, and dishes for the kitchen.

We now raise funds by holding Spring Luncheons and sponsoring card parties during the fall and winter months. Each year we give to the Prince County Hospital, the Salvation Army, the CNIB, Safe Grad, and supply prizes for Three Oaks High School. We also place a wreath at the War Memorial on Remembrance Day. This year we gave to the Stereotactic Mammography machine in the Queen Elizabeth Hospital.

As our members are getting older and fewer, we do very little catering, but for special anniversaries we make an exception.

Wilmot Valley

Wilmot Valley WI has been a busy club over the years. We have raised money in numerous ways, for instance by making and selling Afghans and quilts. We collect the fire dues for the whole community, and hold an auction sale every December. We have also held a couple of yard sales, and looked after the Institute booth at Lobster Carnival.

Some of our members volunteer to work at the gift shop at the Prince County Hospital, or work at the used clothing depot in Kensington (now closed). We hold a skate for the whole community each year, and lay a wreath at the cenotaph in Traveller's Rest.

We have donated to many different organizations. Each Christmas we adopt a family and make sure that their Christmas is a little brighter. We also pack baskets at Christmas for the elderly and shut-ins. Throughout the year we help anyone in our community who needs it.

We compiled a history of our community, and one of our members has served on the provincial board. Ten of our members have received Life Memberships.

Woodstock

Woodstock WI organized in 1953, with Mrs. Roy Arbing serving as their first President. Active through the 1960s, Woodstock WI later disbanded.

Wood Islands

Alice Margaret MacMillan

Wood Islands WI organized in 1943, and nineteen members joined at that time. Over the years we raised funds for WI and community projects with bake and craft sales, card games, and homemade quilts and hooked rug raffles. In 1969 our branch purchased the Wood Islands West Schoolhouse, and in 1980 and 1981 we restored the building and added a kitchen, washroom and furnace. We invited former pupils, schoolteachers and friends to the open house that followed the restoration. We have commemorated Canada Day at the Women's Institute Hall every year since 1985.

In 1983 we celebrated our 40th anniversary, and invited sister Belfast Institutes to join in the program. We celebrated our 50th anniversary with a dinner, a speaker from the provincial board, a reading of the first 1943 minutes, and entertainment.

We honoured three members in 1997, Elizabeth Brown, Pearl Stewart and Margaret (Bunny) MacMillan, for their active role in the Women's Institute for 50 years.

York Point

York Point WI first organized in 1913 as Cornwall, Meadowbank and York Point. In 1955 York Point separated and carried as a branch of our own.

In the early years, we mainly supported the small community school. When the schools consolidated in 1972, we purchased our school and converted it into a Community Centre. For Canada's 125th birthday, we held a community celebration where two community residents, Willard MacPhail and Donald MacEwen, received the 125 Medal Award.

One of our Life Members, Marion MacEwen, was on the Provincial Board for a number of years.

We still support the four consolidated schools in our area.

Notes

Chapter One

1. Excerpted from original constitution of Stoney Creek Women's Institute, 1897, copy held by PEIWI provincial office, Charlottetown, PEI.

2. Joseph Devereux, *Looking Backwards,* s.n., s.l., circa 1920, held by Robertson Library PEI Collection, University of Prince Edward Island, p. 47.

3. Catherine C. Cole and Judy Larmour, *Many and Remarkable: The Story of the Alberta Women's Institutes* (Edmonton: Alberta Women's Institutes) 1997, p. 5.

4. W.J. Reid, "Resume of Agricultural Instruction Work in PEI, 1913-1922," *Agricultural Gazette of Canada*, Vol. 9, No. 1-6 (January-December 1922), p. 497.

5. Excerpted from Script No. 4 of "A Century of Miracles," originally broadcast on February 7, 1963 on CJRW radio, transcript provided by Prince Edward Island Public Records and Archives.

Chapter Two

1. W.J.P. MacMillan, letter to the Honourable Charles Dalton, Lieutenant Governor of PEI , Dec. 31, 1931. Letter provided by Prince Edward Island Public Records and Archives.

Chapter Three

1. Mrs. Colin Donald, "What Institutes Mean to Our Communities," *Institute News*, Vol. 3. No.1 (January 1931), p. 3.

2. Agnes McGuigan, Convener of Legislation, *Institute News,* Vol. 6, No. 3, (July 1934), p.5.

A Note on Sources

Most of the material for Part One of this book came from a few worthy sources. The Prince Edward Island Women's Institute maintains a substantial collection of archives that include original documents, photographs, articles and histories on the WI written by members and the media, and other primary information. Many early records were lost by fire in the 1950s, but they still have a number of "gems", from the researcher's perspective. The Provincial Records and Archives office in Charlottetown has also become a repository for Women's Institute information - a number of branches have donated their old records to the collection, as have individual members. In addition, the Records and Archives office has a full collection of Journals of the PEI Legislative Assembly. The Women's Institute has been making annual reports to the Minister of Agriculture since 1913, and thus these Journals contain much valuable information.

The PEI Collection at Robertson Library contains some Women's Institute material. The most significant find at Robertson Library that related to the Women's Institute was their copies of the *Agricultural Gazette of Canada.* Women's Institutes across Canada made frequent reports to this federal government publication, which seems to have ceased in the mid-1920s, but is an excellent source of early information.

I would be remiss if I did not mention that a PEIWI member, Mrs. Doreen MacInnis, contributed substantially to the research for this book by allowing me full use of her many scrapbooks, which were chock full of Women's Institute clippings - I went through those scrapbooks more than once! Finally, as mentioned, I also spent a fair amount of time interviewing members. The entire research component of this project took place from May of 1999 until November of 1999, so there was not enough time to interview as many members as I perhaps might have liked, but I did manage to spend time with a number of "Institute women". After discussing the question with my History Committee editors, we decided to leave out names when quoting from the interviews, since many of the experiences that interviewees identified are common to all members.